Yale Studies in Political Science, 6

DAVID HORNE, EDITOR

*Published under the direction of the
Department of Political Science*

The Italian Prefects

A STUDY IN
ADMINISTRATIVE POLITICS

By ROBERT C. FRIED

New Haven and London, Yale University Press, 1963

TO CATHERINE AND MAURA

FOREWORD

PROFESSOR FRIED HERE CONTRIBUTES one of the remarkably few scholarly works in the English language that build toward an understanding of the political and administrative system of Italy. His special concern is the role of the prefects in Italian field administration. Yet, as the reader will quickly discern, that role is bound up with the unstable politics of a nation tormented by fragmentation along class, rural-urban, sectional, religious, and ideological lines of cleavage.

The interplay between administration and its political and social context poses one of the basic theoretical problems of political science. By one interpretation, a strong prefectoral system is usually a specific response to the need for the government to impose stability on an inherently unstable society. By another interpretation, administration is better understood as a mirroring of its social and political environment. The first view is open to attack as a teleological explanation (though this can be escaped by identifying it with systems theory and labeling stability a condition for survival as a political system). The second view is open to attack as a simplistic determinism that denies scope for the exercise of will by the ruling elite or for a bureaucracy's

capacity to resist change. Perhaps administration is neither
an opaque nor a reflecting glass, but partakes of the quality
of a prism that receives and refracts light—and sound and
fury—from the environment and, by redirecting it, alters
the environment itself. Italian field administration affords
a particularly attractive opportunity for examination of
such explanatory hypotheses.

As Mr. Fried indicates, he undertook his inquiry as part
of a more general study of comparative field administration
begun at Yale University with support from the Carnegie
Corporation of New York. The larger study is concerned
with field administration in England, France, Germany,
Italy, and the United States. Mr. Fried's book illustrates
modes of approach to administrative analysis that character-
ize the general project. He assumes that administration does
matter. To be sure, he finds field administration closely
bound up with central administration, and administration
in turn closely related to its political, social, and economic
context. The point is that, having traced this series of links,
he does not then make the common error of assuming that
scholarly attention should be confined to the play of political forces on the assumption that administration automatically falls into place in response to such forces. While
sensitive to the role of theory in guiding scholarly inquiry
and in interpreting its findings, he sets himself the formi-
dable task of amassing and analyzing the relevant data so
that theory spinning may be disciplined by factual evidence.
He knows that human beings matter and yet that institutions and trends must be described in macroscopic terms
that generalize about whole classes of human beings. Perhaps the most obvious characteristic of this book is that it
studies a system over time. It thus avoids the misinterpreta-
tions possible with a contemporaneous, snapshot picture
of a system without discerned past or future. We get instead

a richly informed view of the persistence of system characteristics and, perhaps even more, of the persistence of the
conflict between alternative ways of ordering a field administration system.

Italian experience has both general and specific values
for other countries and for scholars whose interest in Italy
may be incidental to broadly comparative concerns. Two
points will serve to instance the general values. In the second chapter will be found Senator Carlo Cadorna's persua-
sive statement of the case for a strong prefectoral type of
field organization. This classic formulation, though offered
in the Chamber of Deputies in 1866, presents the rationale
and even much of the phrasing that is to be found almost
a century later in France, traditionally the home of the
strong prefect. Nor are Cadorna's arguments and those that
recur throughout Italian history irrelevant to the interests
of Americans and Englishmen. True, their countries lack
the prefectoral system. But the claims and counterclaims
of general field administrators and functional specialists are
reproduced *within* the principal executive agencies of the
United States and Britain. The other illustrative general
value relates to the many newly developing nations that
are choosing to place a single generalist administrator in
charge of each geographic area. For elaboration of this
initial choice the usually available models have been those
of the French prefect and the colonial district commissioner.
As Mr. Fried makes clear, the Italian prefectoral system
offers answers significantly different from those of France
and, of course, different from those of an imperial power
administering a colony. His careful recording and interpreting of the Italian experience consequently expand the
repertory of field systems that developing nations may
consider.

Values of more limited exportability derive from special

Italian circumstances. Southern Italy and the islands have always presented a special, and often acute, problem for Italian field administration. Where poverty is regionally endemic and the gulf between the few well-to-do and the many poor is reproduced in educational opportunity and political power, the field administration system confronts different challenges from those it faces in the rest of the country. Other countries than Italy are characterized by a geographically dualistic society and may benefit from Italy's difficulties in adapting its field system to the problems that result. Too, note should be made of the interposition of a Fascist period between the periods of representative government (albeit varying in monarchical or republican label). A one-party state, such as Mussolini's, encounters novel problems as governmental field administration finds itself paralleled by a geographically organized totalitarian party. Here a comparison may usefully be made with the treatment of the National Socialist period in Herbert Jacob's *German Administration Since Bismarck* (New Haven, Yale University Press, 1963), which is another product of the Yale study. Developing nations that have chosen a one-party political system may benefit from awareness of the confusion in Germany and Italy consequent on competition between party and administrative bureaucracies.

In sum, Mr. Fried has ably served students of Italian government and politics, students of comparative government and field administration, builders of theory about political systems and administrative subsystems, and the leaders and advisers of developing nations who can profit from Western administrative experience only to the extent that that experience is funded and critically appraised.

JAMES W. FESLER

New Haven, Connecticut

ACKNOWLEDGMENTS

IT IS A PLEASURE to express my gratitude to Professor James W. Fesler, Chairman of the Department of Political Science, Yale University, whose constant aid, stimulation, and critical guidance have been of inestimable value to me in writing this book. Professor Fesler is director of the Yale University research project on comparative field administration, financed by the Carnegie Corporation of New York— a project of which this work and its companion piece, Professor Herbert Jacob's *German Administration Since Bismarck*, are products.

I would like to thank also the officials of the Italian Ministry of the Interior, in Rome and in the provinces, who received the inquiries of a foreign scholar with such grace and candor. I am indebted to the Ministry for its generous provision of research facilities, for its introductions to the officials of other Italian ministries, and for its confidence.

I am grateful, as well, to the numerous other Italian public administrators who gave so generously of their time and wisdom. My particular thanks go to the library officials of the Chamber of Deputies, of the Senate, and of the Ministry of the Interior.

May I also thank Giulio Einaudi Editore for permission to quote extensively from Carlo Levi's *L'Orologio* and Giuseppe Laterza e Figli for similar permission with regard to Luigi Einaudi's *Il Buongoverno*.

I would like to thank Marian Neal Ash and Elizabeth F. Hailey of Yale University Press for their editorial assistance and Crimilda Pontes for her design and cartographical contributions.

And finally, for her patient encouragement and inspiring collaboration, I am thankful more than I can say to my wife.

Almost needless to say, for the judgments expressed in this book, I alone am responsible.

ROBERT C. FRIED

Old Saybrook, Connecticut
May 1963

CONTENTS

MAPS AND TABLES

Maps

Tables

INTRODUCTION

A MODERN CENTRAL GOVERNMENT can implement policies throughout its territory by means of three basic types of administrative structure. It can, in the first place, establish specialized networks of field offices throughout its territory, each of which is responsible to a particular functionally specialized unit of the central government and each operating more or less autonomously from the others. This structural pattern, exemplified by the various field services of the American federal government, may be called the functional pattern of field administration because it projects throughout the country the functional division of labor of the central administration.

In the second place, a central government may choose instead to make its decisions effective through a network of general agents (prefects) in the major territorial subdivisions of the state, each of whom is responsible for the execution of all central government programs within his area. This second pattern may be called a prefectoral system of field administration and finds its *locus classicus* in France.

Finally, a central government may decide to utilize the services of legally distinct minor units of government, such as states, provinces, or municipalities, to carry out its policies in what we may call a pattern of decentralization. This pattern may be found in such countries as Great Britain and West Germany.

Of the three patterns, only the first and the last have been intensively studied. Prefectoral systems, with the exception of the French system, have not received much scholarly attention despite the fact that they are to be found in most countries of the world.

Basic questions concerning prefectoral systems remain to be explored:

1. What are the major traits of a prefectoral system?

2. What are the major differences between prefectoral, functional, and decentralized systems with regard to (a) origins, (b) structure, and (c) functions or effects?

3. What are the major types of prefectoral systems and how do these types differ in (a) origins, (b) structure, and (c) functions or effects?

4. What are the major challenges to the stability and survival of prefectoral systems?

5. Is there any necessary relationship between prefectoral systems and stable democracy?

It is hoped that some progress toward answering such questions is made in the following study of the Italian prefectoral system. The study itself deals with the historical dimensions of these questions as they have presented themselves in Italy. The historical approach has been followed for two reasons: first, because the history of Italian public administration has yet to be written and such a history is necessary to the understanding of the contemporary administrative system; and second, because the historical approach is in itself a comparative study of the prefectoral institution under varying social and political conditions, yielding insights which, I trust, are pertinent to the study of contemporary institutions.

This study, then, represents a first attempt to outline the main stages of Italian administrative development, within which I have situated the developing prefectoral system. No histories of Italian administration exist as are available for such countries as the United States, France, Great Britain, or Germany. Any study of Italian public administration is therefore in the nature of pioneering on largely uncharted frontiers. Existing Italian studies, with but few exceptions, have been primarily formalistic treatises on the history of Italian administrative law, offering only occasional glimpses into administrative realities and the relationships between the administrative system and its political, social, and economic environment. Only in a broadly conceived historical context can the contemporary system be understood.

This study also represents perhaps the first attempt to analyze and describe a prefectoral system other than the French. On the basis of this study it should be possible to develop hypothetical propositions about prefectoral systems in general. I have attempted an initial reconnaissance of this territory in the concluding chapter.

Chapter One

THE PIEDMONTESE HERITAGE

THE ROOTS OF ITALIAN administration are Piedmontese: for it was Piedmont that led the process of fusing the seven states of the peninsula into the united kingdom of Italy and that bequeathed to the new nation-state its dynasty, its constitution, and its laws.

THE MEDIEVAL DUKEDOM

Piedmont itself emerged as a political community from the domains of the Counts of Savoy who between the eleventh and fifteenth centuries joined together the lands astride the western Alps from what is now Switzerland to the Mediterranean Sea. Much like the Capetians in neighboring France, the Counts of Savoy aggrandized their holdings through marriage, inheritance, alliance, and conquest. By the early fifteenth century, they had founded a capital in Chambéry and created the instruments for governing what had by then become a dukedom: a council in the capital to administer justice; an itinerant council which followed the peregrinations of the prince to advise him on matters of state; a chamber of accounts to manage finance; and assemblies of estates to vote subsidies. Binding throughout the dukedom were the Statutes of Savoy, a common code of law drafted for the ruling house by Piedmontese and Savoyard jurists to assert the authority of the Duke over feudatories, clerics, and communes.[1]

The Statutes confirmed the thirteenth-century division of the *dominium* into bailiwicks and castellanies—the jurisdictions of the bailiffs and castellans established in all parts of the domain as representatives of the central overlord. As governors of the castles constructed for defense in each castellany (or *mandamentum*), the castellans commanded the local garrison, summoned vassals and commoners to the performance of military and other feudal services, collected domanial revenues, and administered petty justice. Perhaps half a dozen castellanies would be joined together under the authority of a bailiff, the highest regional military officer in times of peace and commander of the troops furnished by the castellans in times of war.[2]

In the bailiffs and castellans, the Duke had revocable officeholders—functionaries remunerated not with grants of land but with stewardships, standing outside of and often opposed to the feudal hierarchy. Rudimentary means were at hand to convert feudal suzerainty into sovereignty.[3]

Savoyard sovereignty, however, depended then and later as much on the interdynastic balance of power as on domestic solidity. A century of domestic turmoil culminated in the absorption of most of the dukedom by France (1536–59).

1. R. Avezou, *Histoire de la Savoie* (Paris, 1949), pp. 28–55.

2. Ibid., p. 55; Mario Chiaudano, *Il Bilancio sabaudo nel secolo XII* (Turin, 1927), pp. 5–21; and Italy, Ministero per la Costituente, Commissione per Studi Attinenti alla Riorganizzazione dello Stato, *Relazione all'Assemblea Costituente* (Rome, 1946), 2, 566–67.

3. Henri Pirenne, *Medieval Cities: Their Origins and the Revival of Trade* (Garden City, Doubleday, 1956), p. 162.

Only upon the restoration of the dynasty by foreign powers could the work of state-building recommence. The French occupation hastened the shift in the center of gravity of the dukedom from Savoy to Piedmont: only across the Alps in Piedmont could a state be built capable of withstanding French pressure. By the end of the sixteenth century, the highest officialdom was being drawn from Piedmont, and the capital, together with the central machinery of government, had been transferred from Chambéry to Turin. The state would be Piedmontese and its leaders oriented toward Italy.[4]

ABSOLUTE MONARCHY

It was Duke Emmanuel Philibert (1553–80) who transformed the medieval parliamentary monarchy into an absolute monarchy, determined and able to affirm its autonomous rule. The creation and maintenance of a powerful military force to protect the existence of the state became then and continued throughout Piedmontese history to be the prime objective of state policy. To sustain and employ a large standing army of mercenaries in an economy of subsistence agriculture required the development of new governmental machinery that could mobilize the meager resources of the realm and plan and control their utilization.[5]

The assemblies of estates that had grown strong in return for the grant of subsidies now grew reluctant to comply with the increased demands of the prince. To this reluc-

4. Avezou, pp. 57–69. For a study of the comparable period in French administrative history, see James W. Fesler, "French Field Administration: The Beginnings," *Comparative Studies in Society and History* 5, (October 1962), 76–111.

5. Antonio Marongiù, *Storia del diritto pubblico: principi e istituti di governo in Italia dalla metà del IX secolo alla metà del XIX secolo* (Milan, 1956), pp. 323–27.

tance Emmanuel Philibert reacted by refusing henceforth to summon them into session and successfully putting forth the right of the sovereign to tax on a continuing basis without consent. So doing, he destroyed the major institutional counterweight to the expansion of his power.

He transformed his council, no longer itinerant, into a personal advisory body and called to it his Grand Chancellor, the Archbishop of Turin, the First Secretary of State, and such others (especially jurists and ambassadors) as he from time to time desired to assist him. He established a chamber of accounts in Turin for his domains "on this side of the mountains." He appointed a single General of Finance with responsibility for the collection of revenues and a single Controller General for the supervision of expenditures, replacing the several existing treasurers and receivers general. He appointed still a third great administrative officer—the Paymaster General (*Contadore Generale*)—to direct the services for supplying and supervising the military.[6]

In an attempt to unify and simplify the welter of laws, usages, and statutes particular to each locality and to bring major disputes into his own courts, he established under himself, his council, and the Grand Chancellor a network of regional and provincial courts which was to continue well into the nineteenth century. At the apex of this new judicial hierarchy stood the prince—the font of all law and justice—and his councils as supreme courts of appeal. Beneath these, he maintained the regional *Parlements* in Chambéry and Turin (and later in Nice) which he renamed

6. S. Vigna and V. Aliberti, *Dizionario di diritto amministrativo* (Turin, 1840–52), 2, 105–10; Romolo Quazza, *Preponderanze straniere* (Milan, 1938), pp. 370–76; and Luigi Cibrario, *Origini e progressi delle istituzioni della monarchia di Savoia sino alla costituzione del Regno d'Italia* (2d ed. Florence, 1869), pp. 218–19, 269–92.

Senates, acknowledging their right to review and register executive decisions and to remonstrate against and temporarily suspend those deemed illegal or injurious to the state.

To extend the reach of his justice, he placed under the Senates a new set of magistrates, called Prefects, and divided his lands into provinces to serve as their territorial jurisdictions. To the Prefects he transferred most of the judicial powers of the old bailiffs and castellans, who found themselves relegated to the lower echelons of the judicial system. So that the Prefects might establish uniformity of justice throughout his realm, they were given original jurisdiction in cases involving the nobility and appellate jurisdiction in all other civil and criminal cases. Local justice continued to be the preserve of a variety of officials, some of them centrally appointed but most named by the local feudatories and communes and only eventually subjected to the confirmation of the Prefects and the Senates. Seigneurial courts, as well as many other feudal institutions, persisted in Piedmont until the end of the eighteenth century.

The police powers of the bailiffs and castellans were likewise transferred to the Military Governors stationed in the provinces. Between them, the Governors and the Prefects ruled the provinces in the name of the Duke, as visible signs and instruments of his political supremacy.[7]

The successors to Emmanuel Philibert continued, as well as they were able, along the path of absolutist centralization. It was only with Victor Amadeus II (1685–1730) that the goal was closely approximated. The determination "to extend to the greatest possible extent the field of action and intervention of the monarchy against any obstacle" led to the further rationalization and development of an im-

7. Giovanni Battista Borelli, *Editti, antichi, e nuovi de' sovrani prencipi della Real Casa di Savoia, delle loro tutrici e de' magistrati di quà da' monti* (Turin, 1681), pp. 482–83; R. Quazza, pp. 370–71; Cibrario, p. 213.

personal bureaucracy: through this bureaucracy, the prince could expand and mobilize the resources of his subjects for the purposes of survival and gain in a competitive system of dynastic states.[8]

Victor Amadeus II, who became King of Sardinia upon acquiring the island in 1720 by virtue of international treaty and whose dominions became known as the Kingdom of Sardinia or the Sardinian States, took on the task of acting as his own prime minister. For almost a century the post of First Secretary of State had been held by members of the same family. A single, not to mention dynastic, first minister detracted too much from the King's own power of decision and represented an overshadowing, if not threatening, alter ego. This, together with the growing press of public business, pointed to a division of responsibility and power. Accordingly, by an edict of February 17, 1717, the office of First Secretary was split into two secretariats, one for internal, the other for foreign affairs. A First Secretary of State for War had been appointed in 1692 to coordinate the various branches of military administration: he was now to constitute the third member of the secretarial triumvirate.[9]

At the same time, the first bourgeois ministers were brought into office—men who owed their careers, fortunes, and power to royal preferment, rather than to birth. Middle-class ministers would not only be more dependable than noblemen, but they could also provide experience in preparing and carrying through mercantilist policies. The

8. Guido Quazza, *Le Riforme in Piemonte nella prima metà del settecento* (Modena, 1957), *1*, 15.

9. Ibid., *1*, 23–24, 56–57. See also Felice Amato Duboin, *Raccolta per ordine di materia delle leggi, editti, manifesti, ecc. pubblicati sino agli 8 dicembre 1798 sotto il felicissimo dominio della Real Casa di Savoia* (Turin, Eredi Bianco, 1818–68), Tome VIII, *10*, 331–48; and Cibrario, pp. 291–92.

nobility were to be confined to the arts of war and diplomacy and ousted from their traditional predominance in the state.[10]

The February edict also reformed the Council of State into what was to be a general policy-making organ as well as a central court of equity. In the former guise, however, it was seldom convened, for an ambitious monarch preferred to deal with his ministers individually rather than create an instrument for collective government.[11]

The greatest weakness of Piedmontese administration by this time had come to lie in the lack of coordinated fiscal policy and administration. There were too many central officials with ill-defined responsibilities involving the collection, custody, and expenditure of state funds, and they lacked a common coordinating point of reference. To remedy this state of affairs, Victor Amadeus II promulgated another edict on April 11, 1717, which reduced their number, clarified their responsibilities, and joined the leading ones into a powerful Council of Finance.

Chaired by the First President of the Chamber of Accounts, the council included the Secretary of War, the Controller General, the General of Finance, and the Paymaster General. To these ex officio members, the King might from time to time add other high officials; in any case, he reserved the right to approve its decisions, change its membership, and summon it into session. He gave the council authority—subject to his assent—over the finances of the state. It determined the budgets of the departments; it made the more important day-to-day operational decisions with financial implications; it examined the accounts of the departments; it appointed all financial officials and

10. G. Quazza, *1*, 23–24.

11. Ibid., *1*, 58–59. See also Domenico Carutti, *Storia del regno di Vittorio Amedeo II* (Turin, 1856), p. 372.

could summon any of them for questioning. It owed such power to the fact that financial questions facing the government had become so involved and technical that they could not be satisfactorily disposed of—as could political matters —in the bilateral relations between the King and the individual department heads.[12]

The April decree also provided for the establishment of four *aziende* or operating bureaus under the authority of the Council of Finance and the secretaries of state. There were to be bureaus for finance, war, artillery, and the royal household. The Bureau of Finance was headed by the General of Finance, who had become a minister of finance in all but rank and title. The Bureau of War was headed by the Paymaster General and it was through his office that the Crown controlled military contracts, personnel, and inspection.[13]

The heads of the bureaus took policy directives from the appropriate First Secretaries of State and financial directives from the Council of Finance, but they were not completely subordinate to either, since they had direct access to the King himself. This central administrative system was based on a separation of the political and the financial aspects of administration, between the ministers on the one hand and the Council of Finance on the other, each having independent but incomplete access to the operations of the bureaus: this provided internal checks on the ministers by creating separate islands of power directly under royal control. Only the bureaus could make disbursements, let contracts, etc., and in these activities they were under the tight control of the Council of Finance. Systematic regularity was achieved at the price of complication and slowness, but

12. G. Quazza, *1*, 62–63; Duboin, Tome VIII, *10*, 331–48, 567–607; Carutti, p. 373.

13. G. Quazza, *1*, 110–11; Cibrario, pp. 292–94.

perhaps these were minor costs in eighteenth-century government.

Mercantilist policies, involving the detailed regulation of the social and economic life of the country, could hardly be carried out by officials residing in Turin, however. Centralizing control of provincial resources into the hands of the central government required the permanent stationing of central government agents in the provinces. Locally based authorities such as the communes, the bishops, and the feudal nobility could hardly be expected to administer policies that often aimed to diminish their power and injure their economic interests. Nor could the courts of law or the Military Governors—although responsible agents of the central government—be expected to administer the complex, largely financial tasks to be performed. A new type of central agent was called for—one with a range and diversity of functions as broad as those involved in mercantilism itself. This was the origin of the Piedmontese Intendants.

The Intendants were initially called Referendaries and placed in each province by an order of January 12, 1624, with responsibility for apportionment and collection of direct taxes; collection of domanial revenues; compulsory delivery of food supplies; inspection of mines, mills, and rice fields; enforcement of regulations on weights, measures, and coinage; maintenance of roads and fortifications; supervision of conscription; and collection of population and production statistics. They were classified as magistrates and ranked in status immediately beneath the Prefects. Since they were given authority to adjudicate cases involving violation of the regulations that they themselves were charged with enforcing, classification among the judiciary was not unreasonable.[14]

14. Borelli, pp. 472–74; Vigna and Aliberti, 2, 589–94, and 3, 343–44.

The chief operating agencies of the central government had long been the municipal (communal) authorities; it was they who assessed and collected direct taxes, repaired roads and dikes, kept the land-register, billeted troops, and carried out conscription on behalf of the Crown. As the demands of the center increased, however, they became unable or unwilling to cope with them. As a result, the central government began through the Referendaries not only to direct and supervise communal performance of functions, such as tax collection, in which it was immediately interested, but to bring all aspects of communal government under its control. Instructions of July 17, 1693, gave the Referendaries power to examine, modify, and approve communal budgets and tax rolls; to inspect the operations of communal justice and finance; and to enforce uniform regulations on such matters as elections, staff appointments, and the organization of communal government. But neither these instructions nor those promulgated in the eighteenth century applied to all the communes of the kingdom: each region, each province, each locality preserved some special corporate privileges, even if substantially deprived of its autonomy.[15]

The Referendaries or, as they were renamed in an edict of May 12, 1696, the Intendants of Justice and Finance became the principal agents of mercantilist centralization. To ensure their responsiveness to central government directives, especially those requiring action against the nobility and the clergy, the government recruited Intendants from among middle-class lawyers, magistrates, and financial officials; preference was given to Piedmontese, even for posts in Savoy, since the Savoyards were suspected of over-

15. R. Quazza, pp. 380–81; Vigna and Aliberti, 2, 52–53, and 3, 343–44; G. Quazza, 1, 68–76; and Duboin, Tome IX, 11, 1–15.

susceptibility to French influences.[16] Once appointed, the Intendants were kept under close surveillance by the King, his ministers, and the General of Finance (to whom they were made specifically responsible). Supervision could be quite close, given the small size of the country as compared to Colbert's France. Inspectors were constantly sent out from Turin to report on their activities and to collect complaints that did not arrive in the capital through other channels. And regulations of increasing detail were promulgated to define their responsibilities and limit their discretion.[17]

By virtue of these regulations, the Intendants acted as the long arms of the central government in most of the matters with which that government was concerned. A list of their powers and duties would have included the following headings: state revenues; municipal administration; charitable institutions and poor relief; public health; agricultural improvement; food prices and supplies; building construction; population and production statistics; mining; coinage and bills; equalization of tax burdens; cadastral survey; internal and external customs; domanial revenues; enfranchisement from feudal services; posts; roads and bridges; river and stream control; woods and forests; hunting and fishing; notarization; conscription and billeting, etc.[18]

Many of these powers were useful to the Intendants in executing the monarchy's policies in favor of the unprivileged classes. They could be used to adjust the incidence of state burdens and to alleviate suffering due to famine, pestilence, war, and the pretensions of the nobility and the clergy. Through their powers over tax assessment and their

16. Vigna and Aliberti, *3*, 342–44; G. Quazza, *1*, 26–51, 92–94.
17. G. Quazza, *1*, 65–73.
18. Duboin, Tome IX, *11*, 1–6.

intervention in conflicts involving feudal services, land tenure, rents, and tithes, the Intendants extended the encroachment of the state on the domain of privileged wealth.

The scope of the Intendant's responsibilities expanded as the state assumed new and formerly private functions, especially those traditionally exercised by the Church, such as education and poor relief. An edict of June 23, 1716, for example, required the Intendants to collect and submit information on existing charitable institutions. On the basis of their reports, a system of public poor relief was gradually organized under the Intendants in the form of communal boards of charity (*congregazioni di carità*). State aid, regulation, and inspection were extended to cover hospitals, orphanages, pawn banks, and granaries, just as they had been extended to the municipal authorities themselves. Despite the lack of funds, the hostility of the clergy, and the resistance of communes and feudatories to state control over charitable institutions, the monarchy was able by midcentury to establish under its own control over six hundred charity boards and through them to rival the Church in the field of assistance.[19]

The same centralizing impulse led to the creation of royal secondary schools, which deprived the religious orders of their monopoly in the field of education. Under the control of a Magistracy for the Reform of Studies, in Turin, the secondary schools, although they could not yet be staffed with lay teachers, provided uniform education throughout the kingdom under firm public direction. Elementary education remained a communal responsibility but under the supervision of a state-appointed (and unpaid) Reformer in every province.[20]

The Intendants were responsible for all royal activities in the provinces except in the field of public order and

19. G. Quazza, 2, 313–18.
20. Ibid., 2, 313–16, 382–408.

police. In these matters, the Military Governors retained their traditional powers as the provincial police authorities. The Governors, in fact, continued throughout the eighteenth century to be considered the highest royal officials in the province and the direct representatives of the King.[21] As military officers and members of the nobility, they had successfully resisted attempts to bring police matters under civilian control. A central police office in civilian hands (the *Sovrintendenza Generale di Politica e di Polizia*) had been set up in Turin as early as 1679 but was unable to wrest control of these matters from the military even in the province of Turin itself, much less in the others.[22]

The continued prevalence of the military in the provinces was related to the general importance of the army and military affairs in Piedmontese life. With a population of 2,500,000, Piedmont managed to maintain a standing army of 57,000 men, spending three-quarters of its annual state revenues to do so.[23] (For just this reason the Secretary of War, but not the Secretaries of Interior and Foreign Affairs, sat in the Council of Finance.) Such a disproportionate military effort, exceeded perhaps only by that of the then much admired Prussia, had become traditional in this small mountainous state, wedged in between France and the dominant powers in Italy, and not without ambitions of its own.

21. Nicomede Bianchi, *Storia della monarchia piemontese dal 1773 sino al 1861* (2d ed. Turin, 1887–89), *1*, 189–92. See also Roberto Bergadani, *Vittorio Amedeo III (1726–1796)* (Turin, 1939), pp. 63–64.

22. G. Quazza, *1*, 77–78; Cibrario, pp. 213–14; and Ministero dell'Interno, Direzione Generale della P. S., Div. Affari Legislativi e Documentazione, "La Polizia Sabauda in Piemonte" (2 vols. mimeographed, 1958).

23. Luigi Mondini "Le Istituzioni militari nel Piemonte nei secoli XVI–XVIII," in Guido Astuti et al., *La Monarchia piemontese nei secoli XVI–XVIII* (Rome, 1951), p. 45. See also S. J. Woolf, "Sviluppo economico e struttura sociale in Piemonte da Emanuele Filiberto a Carlo Emanuele III," *Nuova Rivista Storica, 46* (1962), 1–57.

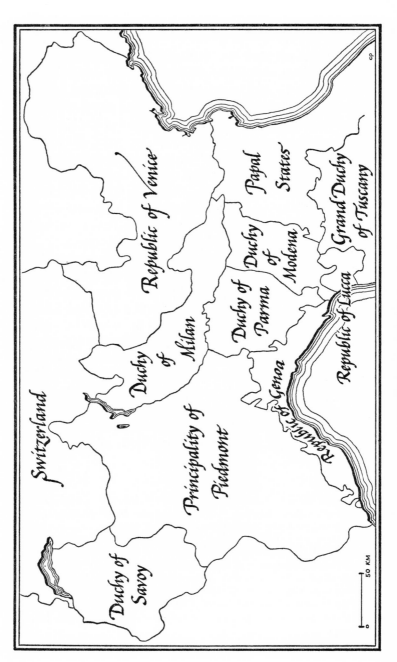

NORTHERN ITALY (1748–97)

PIEDMONT AND NAPOLEON

Militaristic and efficient as it was, Piedmont was nonethe-less only a minor power. In 1792 the armies of the French Republic had little difficulty in conquering the transalpine regions of the kingdom and six years later, the rest of the mainland territories. Savoy became France's Department of Mont Blanc, and Nice, her Department of the Maritime Alps. In April 1801, Piedmont was organized as the Twenty-seventh French Military Division with headquarters in Turin and divided into six subdivisions, each under the military authority of a French brigadier general. The same territorial framework was used for the simultaneous intro-duction of the French prefectoral system: each of the mili-tary subdivisions was to serve also as a department within which the Law of *28 Pluviôse An VIII* (February 17, 1800) would be applied.[24]

Under the terms of this law, the territory of each de-partment was divided into *arrondissements* (in practice, from four to six in number) and the latter, in turn, into communes. Most of the eighteen former provinces of Pied-mont proper became arrondissements, although some were large enough to be divided into two or more of them.[25]

In each area, whether department, arrondissement, or commune, there were placed an executive authority and a council. The executive of the department was, of course, the Prefect. Article Three of the Law of *28 Pluviôse* stated his powers rather succinctly, as follows: "Le Préfet sera chargé seul de l'Administration." The Prefect's role was perhaps more explicitly defined in the French-inspired Law on the Organization of the Administrative Authorities

24. Bianchi, *4*, 2–26. See also the *Bulletin des actes de l'Administration Générale du Piémont* (Turin, n.d.), Nos. 1 and 6.
25. *Bulletin des actes*, No. 6.

promulgated in the neighboring Republic of Italy (which included the former Duchy of Milan and Republic of Venice). The pertinent articles read as follows:[26]

> Art. 7. The Prefect is the immediate organ of the Government in the Department. He dispatches the laws and regulations to all the Communes, publishes them, and has them executed.
> Art. 8. The administration of all the assets and liabilities of the Nation in the Department is exclusively entrusted to him.
> Art. 9. He superintends the police and supervises the preservation of public tranquillity.
> Art. 10. The Prefect prepares each year the budget of national expenditures in his Department for the coming year and transmits it to the respective Ministers within the deadline fixed by the Government.

In each department there was also a general council of sixteen to twenty-four members to represent the common interests of the localities grouped in the department. The council was permitted to meet for two weeks each year in order to apportion state direct taxes among the arrondissements, decide upon the resulting appeals, determine within statutory limits the surtaxes *(centimes additionnels)* to be imposed for departmental expenses, hear the annual report of the Prefect on his employment of the revenue from those surtaxes, and express its opinion on the state and needs of the department.

There were similar councils alongside of the executives of the arrondissements, the Subprefects, and those of the communes, the mayors. A smaller, more specialized prefectoral council was established at the department level

26. *Bollettino delle leggi della Repubblica Italiana* (Milan, n.d.), *1*, Law of July 24, 1802, No. 54.

as an administrative tribunal with authority to decide cases involving the administration, such as public works contracts and taxation.

Napoleon himself as First Consul appointed the Prefects, the Subprefects, the members of the departmental, arrondissement, and prefectoral councils, as well as the mayors of the towns of more than 5,000 inhabitants. The Prefect appointed the municipal councillors and the mayors of the smaller communes. His approval was required for all municipal council decisions. He had general hierarchical powers over both the Subprefects and the mayors, who were considered state officials.

Even after Piedmont was directly annexed to France in September 1802, it was not, in theory at least, governed directly from Paris. The government in Paris "deconcentrated"[27] some of its powers to an Administrator General, later a Governor General, in Turin, who was given charge of nine of the annexed Italian departments, including the Piedmontese. The Governor General was assisted by an intendant of the treasury, a military chief of staff, and a director of police, for financial, military, and police affairs. The Prefects as well as these regional functional directors had the right of direct communication with the ministries in Paris and they made frequent use of these independent channels to settle matters directly with Paris, without the mediation of the Governor General. The tangles that resulted when the Governor General himself attempted to decide matters were in large measure due to his own failure to attend to the less honorific aspects of his post.[28]

27. By "deconcentration" is meant the devolution of authority *within* the hierarchy of the state administration, usually from a central administration to the field. The devolution of authority from the central government to legally distinct minor units of government, such as provinces and communes, will be referred to as "decentralization."

28. Bianchi, *4*, 2–5, 11–12.

For a dozen years, Piedmont was governed under French laws by an administration directed by Frenchmen in Paris, Turin, and the departments. Only one of the Piedmontese appointed as Prefects was still in office by 1805: the rest had been replaced by Frenchmen.[29]

The system of provincial administration that the French introduced to Piedmont was different in several respects from the one it replaced.

The departments were almost three times as large as the former Piedmontese provinces. Their boundaries were drawn primarily to serve the field administration purposes of the central government, whereas the former provinces had been shaped also by an accidental process of assimilating intact newly acquired and feudally denominated territories.[30] Centralization, however, required the establishment of an area (the arrondissement) between the larger department and the localities so as to bring the national official within this area (the Subprefect) as close to the localities as the former Intendant had been. This intermediate area and official had not been necessary within the smaller bounds of the old province.

The larger area of the department meant that the national official in charge, the Prefect, had control over more people and territory than his predecessor, the Intendant, and consequently greater prominence and prestige. An even

29. Ibid., *4*, 22–26.

30. Emmanuel Philibert created seven provinces for the Prefects in 1560. Charles Emmanuel in an edict of October 22, 1622, raised the number of provinces to twelve (in Piedmont); two others (Nice and Aosta) were added in 1624. Regulations of 1723 provide for six provinces in the Duchy of Savoy, eleven in Piedmont, four in the Duchy of Monferrato, and one in the Duchy of Aosta. Two more provinces (Novara and Tortona) were added in 1738 and ten years later, another two, making a total of twenty-six. On this point, see Paolo Bodo, *Le Consuetudini, la legislazione, le istituzioni del vecchio Piemonte* (Turin, 1951), pp. 90–91.

greater source of power and influence derived from the Prefect's status as the direct and political representative of the government. In Piedmont, this representational role had belonged to the Governor, as had control of the police, now under the Prefect's authority. The Piedmontese Secretary of the Interior had worked as much through the Governors as through the Intendants in political matters.[31] The powers of both of these officials (except in strictly military affairs) were now combined over a wider area in a single official, the Prefect.

A similar difference had existed between the Intendants of both countries before the French Revolution: the French Intendants had accumulated vaster powers over much vaster territories. The Piedmontese Intendants were entitled Intendants of Justice and Finance, while their counterparts in France were Intendants of Justice, Finance, and Police. The French Intendants had replaced the provincial governors as police authorities, after the latter had used their prestige and power in the rebellion against royal authority known as the *Fronde*. The Piedmontese Military Governors had perhaps retained their political and police roles and, unlike their counterparts in France, had not been transformed into sinecurists because they had remained on the whole responsive and loyal to the Crown. Moreover, all of the Sardinian States might have been included in only two or three *généralités*—the territorial jurisdictions of the French Intendants: for this reason, the Piedmontese Intendants had no need for subdelegates, the agents of the French Intendant in the localities of his *généralité*.[32]

In many ways, however, the Intendants in both countries were alike. In both, they were the instruments of centraliza-

31. Bianchi, *1*, 189–92.
32. On the French Intendant, see the vast bibliography in Henri Fréville, *L'Intendance de Bretagne (1689–1790)* (Rennes, Plihon, 1953).

tion at the expense of local autonomies—communal, sei-gneurial, and corporate. In both, they were predominantly agents of the fisc and subject to the immediate direction of the equivalent of a minister of finance—in France, the Controller General, in Piedmont, the General of Finance. In both, they were functionaries appointed and dismissed at the Crown's pleasure and, as such, unlike the general run of royal officers whose offices were acquired through purchase or inheritance.

The control of local life by a locally irresponsible agent of the central government was accordingly not a novelty in Piedmont. There, as in France, absolute monarchy had created similar, if not identical, *instrumenti regni*.

The administrative system introduced by the French was at once more centralized and more decentralized than its predecessor. It was more centralized because it subjected all communities to the same penetrating central controls and regulations, whereas Piedmont till then had abounded in a diversity of local privileges. But it was more decentral-ized in that it provided for a measure of local interest rep-resentation in administration above the communal level: there had been no provincial councils in Piedmont since the last of the medieval estates in the sixteenth century. Thus the power to apportion direct taxes among the com-munities had been exercised unilaterally by the Piedmon-tese Intendant while it was now decentralized to locally based, if centrally appointed, councils at the arrondissement and department levels under the French. Even the authori-tarian Napoleonic state was prepared to allow the depart-ment to be used as the framework for a measure, albeit quite limited, of local self-determination.

The impact of the conciliar element, however, was slight as compared to that of the executive agents. The Prefects in particular were active in promoting the social and economic welfare of the populations entrusted to their care. They introduced modern agricultural methods, reformed and encouraged welfare and educational institutions, and undertook broad programs of public works. But they also presided over the exaction of the Imperial tributes in money and men which alienated the Piedmontese from the Napoleonic regime.

PIEDMONT AND THE RESTORATION (1814–48)

For sixteen years the House of Savoy waited out the Napoleonic storm on its island of Sardinia: when the storm had finally passed, its latest head, King Victor Emmanuel I, returned to Turin determined to obliterate the traces of the Napoleonic regime. In a decree of May 1814, he declared that "with no regard to any other law, from the date of the present Edict the Royal Constitutions of 1770, and the other providences issued until June 23, 1800, by our Royal predecessors shall be observed."[33]

At one stroke, all the institutions of the old regime were legislated back into existence. At the same time, the court almanac of 1798 was consulted and all those in service at that date who had refused to serve the French were reinstated in their former positions. Those who had served the French were removed. When the 1798 incumbents were dead, senile, or otherwise unavailable, their sons and nephews were allowed to replace them; when even these were

33. I shall employ the standard Italian form of legal citation, which includes the date of the law or decree and the number assigned to it in the official collection or *Raccolta*. The series begins with the *Raccolta degli atti di governo di S.M. il Re di Sardegna* (Turin, 1842–61) for the period 1814–61; continues with the *Raccolta ufficiale delle leggi e dei decreti del Regno d'Italia* (Turin, Florence, and Rome, 1861–1946), and the present *Raccolta ufficiale delle leggi e dei decreti della Repubblica Italiana* (Rome, 1946–   ). The decree in question is Royal Decree of May 21, 1814, No. 14.

not available, the next in seniority as of 1798 were moved up. Lowly but legitimist employees were sometimes catapulted into leading positions in the army, the judiciary, and the civil administration.[34]

In the army, the Napoleonic veterans could not be dispensed with, but they were demoted to the ranks and placed under incompetent legitimists, some too old and disused to command, some the inexperienced scions of noble houses.[35] The aristocracy was restored to its former privileged status and political predominance in the state. It and the clergy became the bulwarks of the Restoration regime. The nobles were given a de facto monopoly of the leading posts in the army, the civil administration, and (to a lesser extent) the judiciary. The King reserved for noblemen such posts as Governor, Intendant, and mayor of a large city.[36] Reactionary decrees restored the anachronistic guilds and guild regulations; segregated the Jews in the old ghettoes under their former legal disabilities; required attendance of all subjects at Easter mass; and restored the former inequalities between Waldensians, Jews, and Catholics, nobles, clergy, and commoners, men and women.[37] The French judicial codes and organization were abolished in favor of the old ways, with their disproportion-

---

34. Italo Raulich, *Storia del risorgimento politico d'Italia* (Bologna, Zanichelli, 1920), *1*, 5–10. Typical was the case of a minor customs employee who suddenly found himself chief of the Bureau of Customs. He recommended that the great new bridge across the Po River in Turin be destroyed since it had been built by the French. The move was blocked, it appears, only because the new bridge was convenient in reaching the Queen's villa. For this see Alberto Acquarone, "La Politica legislativa della restaurazione nel regno di Sardegna," *Bollettino Storico-Bibliografico Subalpino, 57* (1959), 28–29.

35. Acquarone, pp. 43–44.

36. Louis des Ambrois de Nevache, *Notes et souvenirs inédits du chevalier Louis des Ambrois de Nevache* (Bologna, 1901), p. 54.

37. Acquarone, pp. 25–27.

ate punishments, the payment of magistrates through fees, the multiplicity of special courts for special classes, the confusion of judicial and administrative functions, arbitrary interference of the Crown in private litigation involving aristocrats, and the removability of judges at royal discretion.[38]

Some leading characteristics of the old regime were not resuscitated, such as feudal servitudes, seigneurial courts, the use of torture in criminal procedure, and the sale of public offices. The sale of offices was abolished despite the fact that it had become in the eighteenth century a highly popular form of public debt; the posts offered for sale had provided high social status, good salaries, and opportunities for profit.[39]

Characteristic of the Restoration regime was the establishment of a Ministry of Police (or, as it was euphemistically called, of "Buon Governo") by Royal Patents of October 15, 1816, No. 446. One of the first acts of the restored ruler had been to create an armed police force on the model of the French *gendarmerie,* the Arm of the Carabiniers, as an integral part of the army to be used for internal police duties, including the political surveillance of the public administration.[40] The Ministry of "Good Government" was short-lived, however, being abolished after the otherwise unsuccessful revolt of liberal army officers and nobles in 1821. Control of the police was handed over to the Secretary of the Interior late that year and an extensive network

38. Ibid., pp. 30–32.

39. Luigi Einaudi, *La Finanza sabauda all'aprirsi del secolo XVIII e durante la guerra di successione spagnuola* (Turin, Nazionale, 1908), pp. 245–54. See also G. Felloni, "Le Entrate degli stati sabaudi dal 1825 al 1860," *Archivio Economico dell'Unificazione Italiana, 3–4,* 9.

40. Royal Patents of July 13, 1814, No. 40. See also Archivio di Stato di Torino, *Rubriche della polizia piemontese (1821–1848)* (Rome, 1938), pp. x–xi; Vigna and Aliberti, 2, 123–24.

of spies was developed to keep under surveillance the dissident groups: liberal elements among the gentry; the middle classes in the cities resentful of the loss of civic equality; and Mazzinian democrats in the newly acquired territories of the former Republic of Genoa. Against these groups, the monarchy relied upon the largely legitimist army, nobility, clergy, and peasantry in its resistance to the anticlericalism, constitutionalism, nationalism, and egalitarianism of the opposition.[41]

Victor Emmanuel's attempt to restore the old order was particularly infelicitous in financial matters. The century-old system of public finance was no longer adapted to the pace required by the expanding economy set in motion by Napoleon. Tax collections fell off sharply; irregular financial documents accumulated; the creditors of the state protested—reform was unavoidable.[42] The result of the financial crisis was a basic reorganization of central administration. Patents of March 31, 1817, No. 553, created four regular ministries—Foreign Affairs, War and Navy, Interior, and Finance. (The former General of Finance became the Minister of Finance.) The ministers were given general command power over the heads of the several operating bureaus (*aziende*), which, by 1824, included royal household, foreign affairs, interior, artillery and fortifications, customs and excise, and finance. The individual ministers were given the powers of the Council of Finance, which became a somewhat lifeless body on budgets and contracts whose decisions were reported to the King only via the responsible ministers. The new division of labor between the ministries and the bureaus was expressed in this formula: "Every head of ministry shall be accountable for the orders he shall have given to the bureau head subordinate to him, whereas the

41. Archivio di Stato di Torino, *Rubriche,* pp. xi–xv.
42. Cibrario, pp. 294–95, 303.

latter [the bureau head] shall be accountable for the operations of execution." The bureau heads could no longer
report directly to the King, but they did retain direct and
exclusive authority to prepare the budgets, draw up contracts, issue payment vouchers, keep the accounts, and direct most of the operating tasks of the ministries. Their
transactions were subject to the controls of the Ministry of
Finance and the Controller General. Thus the functional
lines of responsibility were much more clearly delineated
than before, presumably under the influence of French
ministerial structure and the growth of public business.

Domestic affairs were now under the control of the
Ministries of Finance and Interior although the Ministry
of Foreign Affairs controlled the postal service until 1856.
Attached to the Ministry of the Interior was the Bureau of
the Interior which was created in 1816 in charge of bridges,
roads, waters, and forests. At the same time, a separate Corps
of Civil Engineers (*Genio Civile*) was detached from the
Corps of Military Engineers (*Genio Militare*) and became,
together with the Royal Forest Service and the Royal
Mining Corps, both created in 1822, the technical services
operating under the Ministry of the Interior. All three were
apparently inspired by analogous technical services in
France.[43]

Further French influence can be seen in the new administrative map drawn for the mainland regions in an edict of
1818.[44] A set of areas was designed which could be used by
all or most of the state field services. The entire mainland
was divided into 2,727 communes for local government
purposes; these were joined together in *mandamenti*—new
units apparently copied from the French cantons—each

43. Domenico De Simone, "Genio Civile," *Il Nuovo Digesto Italiano, 6,*
218–19.
44. Royal Patents of Nov. 10, 1818, No. 858.

of which was to have a judge, a tax exactor, and its own conscription quota. The 410 *mandamenti* were in turn grouped into forty provinces, each with a Military Commander, a Prefectoral Tribunal, and a Provincial Intendant. The provinces, in turn, were aggregated into still larger units, divisions, eight in number, each with a Military Governor and an Intendant General. The other state services were expected to use some combination of these general areas.

The new division corresponded roughly to the French department in size, but was much more closely attached to tradition. There were only eight divisions where there had been eleven French departments. Piedmont was divided into four divisions, but each of the quasi nationalities (in Genoa, Nice, Savoy, and Aosta) was given a division to itself. Thus four of the divisions corresponded to the Duchies of Genoa, Aosta, and Savoy and the County of Nice. Such areas would emphasize the return to feudalistic relationships between the dynasty and its various territorial groups —in form, if no longer in substance. In the same way, the island of Sardinia (feudally, the Kingdom of Sardinia) retained its separate administrative and legal system.

The Intendants were restored together with the other institutions of the old regime, including the Constitutions of 1770 and the Regulations of 1773 and 1775, the most recent formulations of their powers and duties. They were thus called upon to operate under laws and regulations that the past forty years had to a great extent rendered obsolete. They once again became primarily financial officials. It was the Minister of Finance who issued the Instructions of 1818[45] which attempted to reinterpret their responsibilities in accordance with the evolving requirements of Piedmon-

45. Instructions of Dec. 3, 1818, No. 865.

tese society. In this hundred-page manual it was stated clearly that the Minister of Finance was "the direct superior" of
the Intendants and the source of "the orders and directions
necessary for the discharge of the greater part of their
functions."

The Intendants were instructed, however, to correspond
with and carry out the orders of the Minister of the Interior
for matters concerning "the political administration of all
the communes [*pubblici*] of the royal states of the *terra
firma.*" And in fact they were to report to and perform
duties on behalf of all the ministries and bureaus with
domestic responsibilities.

With the return of the old legislation, the Intendants'
duties with regard to communal administration varied from
region to region, and from commune to commune, as opposed to the uniformity of treatment under the French. As a
general rule, however, the Intendants approved those communal appointments to office and decisions that were not
reserved for the approval of the courts, the central ministries, or the King himself. Communes were generally run
by self-perpetuating oligarchies of nobles and men of substance.

The Instructions of 1818 made no general declaration
of the Intendant's status among the officers of the Crown
in the province. The revival of the old system, however,
involved the restoration of the pre-eminent authority of
the Military Governor and Commanders. The Instructions
urged the Intendant to have "the most intimate relations"
with the Governor and Commanders "for all that concerns
the exactness of the royal service in the provinces . . . the
regular administration of the communes of which they are
composed, and the greater prosperity of their respective
populations." The Intendant was further instructed to conclude "all opportune understandings" with the military

and to recommend to the Ministers of Finance and Interior any measures required in these matters. This implied that the military had retained the general authority in provincial affairs which under the French had been placed in the Prefect.

And in fact the military were given important administrative tasks as the chairmen of provincial health and vaccination boards. The provincial health boards (composed also of the Intendant, the prefectoral magistrate, the mayor of the provincial capital, and a representative of the proto-medical magistracy—a corps of physicians and surgeons working under the medical faculties of the universities to police the medical and allied professions) were responsible for enforcing the public health regulations under the authority of regional health courts *(magistrati di sanità)*. Provincial vaccination juntas, created in 1819, carried out the compulsory vaccination laws and consisted of the Military Commander (chairman), the Intendant, the mayor of the provincial capital, the Reformer of Studies, and the representative of the proto-medical corps. The Governors and Commanders retained control of the police and responsibility for public security even after the transfer of central control to the Ministry of the Interior in 1821.[46]

The Instructions of 1818 demonstrate, however, the great extent to which the Intendants were the major operational or supervisory center of administration in the province. They performed a multitude of functions as the agents of every ministry and bureau with domestic reference. It was largely up to them to take measures for the development of their provinces, to stimulate the construction of public

---

46. *Calendario generale pe' regii stati, I* (1824), 230–34, 417–18, 447–48. This is the first in a series of official yearbooks published continuously from 1824 to 1922.

works, dams, highways, and other measures for civic improvement. The Intendants acted for the central ministries except when the latter had specialized agents, and even then the Intendants were often given supervisory responsibility. The direction of most domestic administration now lay with the Ministers of the Interior and of Finance and both relied on the Intendants to transact the more important and delicate part of their provincial business (except police). The jurisdictional difficulties inherent in a bipartite division of responsibility in domestic affairs were presumably eased by reliance on a joint provincial agent.

The directive role of the Intendants was recognized when new and basically technical field services were created. The Civil Engineers were placed under the Intendants and given the same operational areas. In each province, the Provincial Engineer was charged with the technical aspects of public works administration: drafting projects, supervising construction, inspecting the state of roads and streams, reporting violations of regulations, and proposing works to be undertaken. It was left to the Intendant to consult with local property owners and taxpayers on the engineer's proposals and on the provincial surtaxes to be imposed to pay for them; to submit the projects for central approval; to provide for the execution of approved projects by collecting the revenues, letting the contracts, keeping the accounts, and promulgating the condemnation decrees; and to ensure communal compliance with obligations in the field of public works.[47]

A similar division of labor was arranged between the Intendants and the new forest inspectors. Financial, administrative, political, and regulatory powers, as well as matters involving appointments and the supervision of municipal activities, were lodged directly with the Intendants, while

47. Ibid., p. 305; Vigna and Aliberti, 4, 202–06, 367–71.

technical and police operations were the responsibility of the forest inspectors and their staffs of wardens. Again when the new chambers of commerce were chartered in Turin and Genoa to represent and regulate commerce and industry and to advise the government on measures of promotion in these spheres, the Intendants General of Turin and Genoa were placed at their head.[48]

The Intendants General had little control over the Provincial Intendants: the title of Intendant General indicated a rank, rather than a supervisory function. There had been Intendants General in the eighteenth century but only in some regions (Savoy, Nice, and Sardinia) and this was now generalized throughout the mainland as a means of tightening control over the Provincial Intendants by the interposition of a supervisory echelon. But the Intendant General was given little authority over his nominal subordinates: his duties outside of his own province involved mostly the collection of reports and information. The Provincial Intendants, unlike the French Subprefects, continued to communicate directly with Turin and to exercise authority in their own right.[49] The provinces, averaging about five hundred square miles in area, continued to be the fundamental areas of field administration.[50]

Piedmont made some modest steps out of the past under King Charles Albert (1831–49), who wished as did some other Italian rulers of the time to make concessions to the growing liberal opposition, without affecting his absolute political power. Thus the first genuine legal codes were promulgated; feudalism was abolished (at least on paper) in Sardinia; the guilds, which had so long impeded commercial and industrial development, were dissolved; the

48. Ibid., pp. 241, 312–13.
49. Royal Patents of Aug. 25, 1842, No. 391.
50. Instructions of Dec. 3, 1818, No. 865.

state made loans to industry and undertook directly the construction and operation of the railways and telegraphs; tariffs were reduced; agricultural societies and chambers of commerce were chartered; the state opened and subsidized normal, elementary, and technical schools; state property (especially canals) was developed; greater state supervision was exercised over public and private charities. In permitting such measures, the King had to overcome an obscurantist Establishment which rightly saw in railways and developing trade and communications the channels for the invasion and spread of ideas subversive of traditional religion, morality, and authority.[51]

Much of the work of drafting the new legal codes was carried out by a new Ministry of Ecclesiastical Affairs, Grace, and Justice, created out of the centuries-old Grand Chancery by Patents of July 23, 1831, No. 2409. The new department took over the Interior's duties with regard to religious affairs, the management of vacant benefices, and the direction of the judicial and correctional system. At the same time, Charles Albert converted the Council of State from a court of equity (headed by the Grand Chancellor) into a high-level body of functionaries patterned on the French institution of the same name, with responsibility for the scrutiny of draft budgets, laws and regulations, and of the accounts and contracts of the various ministries and bureaus. The new council absorbed the functions and powers of a host of councils, including the Council of Finance. Liberals, at first pleased by the institution of a body that might act as an independent check on the government, were dismayed when the new council was packed with reactionary friends of the ministers. The Military Governor of Turin (who was also the Marshal of the Royal Armies) be-

51. Des Ambrois de Nevache, p. 18.

came the customary head of the new council and acted to inform the King not only of military affairs and the security of the capital, but also of what transpired in the Council of State. The council, though reactionary, was not uncritical of ministerial operations and its criticisms induced the King to institute weekly "conference councils" of all his ministers as a systematic form of interministerial coordination and royal control.[52]

Most of the internal reforms of the Albertine period were carried out by the Minister of the Interior. When, in 1841, the incumbent fell into disgrace, the less reactionary royal counselors sought to stave off the appointment of a reactionary to the post and devised the expedient of unifying the Ministries of the Interior and Finance under the then Minister of Finance of liberal repute. Unification avoided the clashes between the two ministries that had occurred because of their opposing orientations (the one, Finance, concerned with economy; the other, Interior, with developmental expeditures) and the large area of overlapping jurisdiction in provincial and communal administration.[53] At the same time, however, the King transferred control of the police to the Ministry of War so that control of internal and external security was now completely in military hands at all levels. The Chief of Police, a Carabinieri officer, reported directly to the King, however, and often conflicted with the Minister of War in evaluating dangers to state security. This Police Chief continued to share with the Minister of Interior and Finance the responsibility for the appointment of mayors, in consultation with the bishops and local clergy—then as now highly influential in local affairs.[54]

52. Ibid., pp. 105–09; Cibrario, pp. 299–301.
53. Des Ambrois de Nevache, pp. 92–96.
54. Ibid., pp. 74–76, 133–35.

The combined Ministry of Interior and Finance was not a success: the incumbent was incapable of leaving matters of detail to his subordinates. Faced with an enormous backlog of unsettled business, he was forced to resign in 1844 and to recommend a return to separate ministries.[55] During his term of office, however, he had carried out a significant reform in Piedmontese field administration.

This reform represented a partial return to the Napoleonic prefectoral system. The number of intendancies general and divisions was increased from eight to fourteen and the number of Intendants and provinces reduced from forty to thirty-seven. The areas of the divisions no longer coincided with the major semimilitary areas. The fourteen Intendants General were given most of the powers of the Intendants, who were required to channel their communications to Turin via their Intendant General. Much as the French Subprefects, the Provincial Intendants were reduced to the status of transmission belts between the communes and the Intendant General, with little authority in their own right. This was a step away from provincialism and it also reduced the span of control of the joint Minister of Finance and Interior.

Secondly, the quasi-judicial powers of the Intendants General were conferred upon a collegial organ, the Intendant's council, on the model of the French prefectoral council, thus providing a separation of powers in accordance with liberal theory. Also in accord with liberal propensities was the collegiality of judicial organs. The members of the new council, however, were the bureaucratic subordinates of the Intendant.

Finally, the provinces were given representative councils on the model of arrondissement councils of the Napoleonic

55. Ibid., pp. 92–96.

period. The King selected the members of these councils from lists drafted by the Intendants; the councils met once a year to discuss local public works and to elect their representative to a divisional council (analogous to the French department's *Conseil Général*). The divisional council examined and voted upon the provincial councils' proposals and in turn proposed a budget for divisional public works and assistance projects to the Intendant General; the budgets required the approval of the Council of State. The provincial councils also elected representatives to sit with the Intendant and the bishop on the accounts commission created in 1836 to administer state regulation of charitable institutions. The bishop had been given chairmanship of the commission to allay suspicions that state control might endanger ecclesiastical predominance in charitable activities.[56]

The return to the French system was incomplete, however, for it did not establish the supremacy of the Intendants General over all state officials in their jurisdiction, nor invest them with powers over public security and the police. It did represent a break with the reactionary tendencies till then prevailing in Piedmontese administrative organization in that it provided for a form, if highly attenuated, of outside participation in administration and for a separation of judicial and administrative functions.

CONSTITUTIONAL MONARCHY (1848–59)

The constitutional revolution of 1847–48, provoked by the reforms and constitutions granted by the Pope and the King of Naples and by popular demands for similar concessions in Piedmont, was critical in Piedmontese (and Italian) his-

56. Royal Patents of Aug. 25, 1842, No. 391, and Dec. 31, 1842, No. 399. See also Vigna and Aliberti, 2, 825–32.

tory. With the octroi of the *Statuto* or constitution in March 1848, governmental power ceased to be a monopoly of the Crown and passed into the hands of a Council of Ministers responsible to an elective representative assembly, the Chamber of Deputies. The new constitution was virtually a direct copy of the French Constitution of 1830, which had been chosen as a model by the King and his ministers because it preserved much of the power of the King; because its consequences, as observable for the past eighteen years in France, could be predicted; and because it would be as liberal as those granted by the other rulers of Italy that year.[57] The monarch and the hitherto ruling classes continued to exercise considerable influence through the royally appointed Senate, which was granted an equal share of the legislative power. But the middle classes for the first time acquired national political power through their representatives in the Chamber, elected on the basis of a highly restricted suffrage.

The executive henceforth would have to act within the statutory and financial limitations imposed by a distinct and independent legislature; its actions would be subject to public scrutiny in the legislature and a free press; it would have to respect the civil rights guaranteed by the constitution; and it would have to adapt the actions of its field agents to the reactions of the elected representatives of the provinces in the Chamber.

The principle of ministerial responsibility would tend to bring all executive activity under the control of some particular minister, to promote the clarification of jurisdictions as among the several coordinate ministers, and to make the ministerial division of labor a reflection of the changing policy emphases of the legislative majority. In-

57. Des Ambrois de Nevache, pp. 15–17.

dividual ministerial responsibility, with its tendency to undermine interministerial coordination, would be counteracted by the collective responsibility of the Council of Ministers and its president.

National policy would no longer be made privately by the monarch, balancing the narrow range of conflicting interests represented by his ministers and subject only to the occasional remonstrances and easily suppressed demonstrations of those whose interests were not sufficiently represented, if at all. It would now be the outcome of a public and competitive process, involving numerous participants representing a wider range of interests.

The liberal bourgeois revolution of 1848 could not fail to have important effects upon the pattern of Piedmontese administration. Its impact can be seen in (1) the creation of a Ministry of Public Instruction designed to promote a completely secularized and nationally uniform system of public education to compete with and possibly supplant the institutions of the religious orders;[58] (2) the transfer of responsibility for public security from the War Ministry to the Interior and the passage of a general law of public security, subjecting police operations to restrictions which absolute monarchs had found inconvenient or unwise to impose upon themselves;[59] and (3) the creation of a Ministry of Public Works, Agriculture, and Commerce to sponsor economic development, taking over the responsibilities of the Ministry of the Interior in matters of public works, town planning, forests, mines, weights and measures, industry, commerce, agriculture, railroads, etc.[60]

A separate Ministry of Marine, Agriculture, and Com-

58. Royal Patents of Nov. 30, 1847, No. 652, and Law of Oct. 4, 1848, No. 818.
59. Law of July 11, 1852, No. 937.
60. Royal Decree of Dec. 7, 1847, No. 650.

merce, created in 1850, went down in a wave of economy two years later. Involved with its abolition was a controversy between the government and Parliament concerning the locus of reorganization authority, as well as doctrinal disputes over the role of government in the economy. The ministry in question was abolished by executive fiat and, after some criticism, the government's majority acquiesced to the *fait accompli*. Cavour himself opposed the idea of reorganization by decree and secured statutory approval for the restoration of a separate Ministry of Agriculture, Industry, and Commerce in the Law of July 5, 1860, No. 4150.[61]

It was also Cavour, as Minister of Finance, who sponsored a general reform of Piedmontese central administration, enacted into the Law of March 23, 1853, No. 1483. This act removed the long-standing dualism between the ministries and the bureaus (*aziende*) by abolishing all of the bureaus and transferring their staffs and powers to the ministries. This was an almost inevitable corollary to the principle of ministerial responsibility, for, even after the 1817 reform, the bureaus had remained independent offices with direct control over central administrative finances and operations, thus diffusing responsibility and slowing down operations. Bureau heads had conducted most of their business with the ministries through correspondence; much of the work of the ministries involved examination of bureau recommendations and thus a duplication of bureau activities; friction between bureau heads and ministers had not been unusual. The ministers, on the other hand, had had no direct supervision of budgetary execution; they had no accounts, no records of payments and contracts—these lay in the bureaus. The division of labor between the ministries,

61. Ministero per la Costituente, *Relazione, 1,* 321.

responsible for policy, and the bureaus, responsible for operations, was not in keeping with a parliamentary regime (although this system has nonetheless been preserved in Sweden).

To absorb the bureaus into the ministries, new basic subdivisions were created on the pattern of Belgian central administration. Belgian institutions were viewed with considerable sympathy in Piedmont because Belgium, like Piedmont, was among the few liberal constitutional monarchies on the Continent. A Belgian minister had complete control over both policy and operations. In some Belgian ministries, services that were particularly important in terms of the size of staff and the volume of operations were unified under directors general—officials with the rank of the Piedmontese first officer, the traditional civil servants at the head of Piedmontese ministries. Some of the bureaus, especially those in finance which employed large staffs involved in highly complex operations, were incorporated into the ministries as general directorates, but most of them, as divisions or simply accounting offices. There would no longer be the anomaly of a single bureau serving several ministries.[62]

Under the new system, grades and titles were made uniform throughout the central administration in a rank order that ran as follows:

> Secretary General
> Director General
> Division Chief
> Section Chief
> Secretary (two classes)
> Clerk (four classes)

62. Edoardo Bellono, *Commentario delle leggi, 3* (1853), 137–79.

The central administrative structure was reorganized into four basic units: ministries, general directorates, divisions, and sections. The secretary general, despite his higher rank, was not given charge of the directors general, if any, in his ministry: both worked directly with the minister; the secretary general was put in charge of all divisions and offices, except the minister's private cabinet, which did not come under the authority of some director general. Secretaries and directors general were appointed by the King on the advice of the Council of Ministers; all other state employees were appointed by the King on the advice of the individual ministers.

The change of regime had far-reaching repercussions in Piedmontese field administration and local government. One of the most widely hailed reforms was the transfer of the police from military to civilian control, at first at the provincial level and after the establishment of the first constitutional government at the divisional level as well. The King had resisted this last step.[63] The post of Governor General of the division was abolished and the police powers inherent in the post were transferred to the Intendants General.[64] An Administration of Public Security was created in the Ministry of the Interior to direct the police operations of the Intendants General and Provincial Intendants. The military Governors General and Provincial Commanders had incurred considerable popular hostility by their violent and often arbitrary use of police powers, checked only by networks of secret informers and the King's informants among the nobility. Assignment to territorial police commands was avoided in the army and passed off to the least esteemed senior officers: the better officers could be recruited for such assignments only at the personal be-

63. Des Ambrois de Nevache, p. 11.
64. Royal Decree of Sept. 30, 1848, No. 798.

hest of the King. The military as police officials tended to be ignorant of and indifferent to existing legal protections of civil rights. Military control of the police had become identified with all the vexations of the absolute police state.[65]

To assist the Intendants General in the discharge of their new police responsibilities there was created the post of *Questore,* with the rank of Intendant, to act as full-time head of public security in the division. The *Questori* were initially recruited from among the judiciary, as guarantee of their respect for the law. The Provincial Intendants were given Public Security Delegates as their agents in each *mandamento.* The mayors of communes in which no state police official was stationed became the responsible public security officials in their jurisdictions, subject to the authority of their superiors in the hierarchy of state police officials.[66]

The creation of a National Guard was considered a *sine qua non* of constitutional monarchy, for only the armed citizenry, it was felt, could ensure that the King would maintain his contractual obligations under the *Statuto.* The Law on the National Guard was copied from the French law on the same corps. The guard was recruited primarily from among the middle classes and constituted a middle-class counterpoise to the regular army and the Carabinieri which were royalist and aristocratic. Units of the National Guard were organized by the Intendants to serve as auxiliary and amateur police forces, which elected their own officers.[67]

In 1852 a new police formation was organized, the Corps

65. Archivio di Stato di Torino, *Rubriche,* pp. xviii–xix; Ferdinando A. Pinelli, *Storia militare del Piemonte* (Turin, De Giorgis, 1855), *3,* 142–43.
66. Royal Decree of Sept. 30, 1848, No. 798.
67. Des Ambrois de Nevache, pp. 18–21.

of Public Security Guards, to replace the Carabinieri and the National Guard in the policing of the largest cities. The new corps, like the Carabinieri, was a uniformed professional force, organized in military fashion, but, unlike the Carabinieri, exclusively under the control of the Ministry of the Interior. The Carabinieri in contrast were a branch of the regular army, units of which served in active combat, and subject to the control of the Interior only for domestic and predominantly rural police operations. The National Guard was not considered sufficiently reliable because of its amateur nature nor suited to the performance of the specialized tasks of judicial police. All three formations, it should be noted, were strictly under the control of the central government.[68]

As the divisional chiefs of public security, the Intendants General were authorized to request the intervention of the regular army, organized for this purpose into eight military divisions.[69] The territorial Military Commanders would assume police powers henceforth only upon declaration of a state of siege.

The Military Governors and Commanders also lost their powers as chairmen and members of the provincial health and vaccination boards to the Intendants, who took charge of public health matters as part of their general police powers. The regional health courts (*magistrati di sanità*) with their life and death powers were abolished, together with numerous other special tribunals; their suitably trimmed powers were transferred to the regular courts of law and to administrative boards, such as the provincial health boards. Thus, there was a general separation of military, judicial, and administrative functions and hierarchies, a

68. Ministero dell'Interno, Direzione Generale della P. S., *Le Origini delle Guardie di P.S.* (Rome, 1957), pp. 10–11.
69. Royal Decree of Nov. 18, 1848, No. 850.

separation which more often than not resulted in greater power and responsibility for the Intendants.[70]

The Military Governors had hitherto also acted as the political representatives of the Crown in the provinces. This function, too, was now transferred to the Intendants and it became crucially important under the new representative regime. There was now at the head of the executive a government of ministers which depended for continued tenure of office on maintaining the confidence of a majority in the Chamber; this majority, in turn, was composed of representatives of the localities of the kingdom, and issued from electoral competitions in those localities. The government of the day would henceforth use its control of the administration to maintain its majority in the Chamber and to ensure the return of its supporters at election time. Its representatives in the provinces would play a major role in building and maintaining support in the localities for the government and its supporters. Their performance would be appraised in these terms.

The Intendants were declared to be the "representatives of the Government" in the Local Government Act of 1848 (the Law of October 7, 1848, No. 807). They were expected to follow and report to the Minister of the Interior (who had replaced the Minister of Finance as their particular superior) on all politically relevant events, conditions, and states of opinion; to evaluate the political aspects of claims upon the government and to transmit them accordingly; to work for the successful implementation of government policies and programs; to negotiate on behalf of the government for the support of local *grand'elettori*—all with an eye to shaping the outcome of elections. The localities had won a legal and institutionalized means for influencing

70. Royal Decree of July 24, 1848, No. 754; *Calendario generale del regno pel 1850,* pp. 719–24.

state action in contrast to their previous ability to petition and occasionally to revolt: now their representatives in the Chamber could withdraw their support from the government and perhaps cause its downfall. The fate of the ministers now hung to some extent on the political talents of their official representatives in the localities.

Politicization of the Intendants had an immediate impact on both the personnel of the corps and the stability of their assignments. By 1849, all the intendancies general had changed hands; by 1850, eleven out of fourteen had changed hands once again and by that year, only three of the Intendants General had held that rank before the revolution of 1847–48. Under the absolute monarchy the personnel of the corps and assignments had been very stable, with major shake-ups only at the accession of a new monarch; under the new regime, shake-ups in personnel and assignments became frequent, following the rhythmic alternation of governments in power. There were major movements of personnel at the head of the intendancies in 1848, 1849, and 1850; when Cavour became Prime Minister, in 1852, he changed the incumbents in ten out of fourteen intendancies general. Thus the greater political instability of the new regime was perforce reflected in a greater instability among the government representatives in the field.[71]

The Intendants became the electoral agents of the government. One of them, for example, sent this circular to the "most influential electors" in a certain constituency:[72]

> Alba. December 5, 1849. Confidential. In accordance with the communications and information I have received, I must inform you in all confidence and secrecy that the candidate proposed for the constituency of

71. See the *Calendario generale* for the period 1840–59.
72. *Rivista Amministrativa del Regno, 1* (1851), 169–92.

Casale is Baron Sappa [formerly Intendant General of Sardinia and in 1846 Intendant General of Chambéry], Councillor of State, from whom we can expect effective action to achieve the important objective of the triumph of order and the public weal and the return of the state to that prosperity to which our common desires are directed. Inform all those from whom assistance may be expected about this; exhort them to lend same energetically, and accept, etc. . . .

Intendant General Spinola

In reply to criticism in the Chamber of the Intendant General's behavior, the Minister of the Interior declared that his agent had indeed acted improperly, but only by making secret what he should instead have broadcast, namely, the list of government-approved candidates. Cavour himself approved of this candid declaration of principle (although shortly before he had been defeated by such government pressure) and actively used the Intendants to return his supporters upon becoming Prime Minister, assuming the portfolio of the Interior expressly for this purpose.[73]

That the intervention of the Intendants might be effective was directly related to the narrowness of the franchise. The number of eligible voters per constituency in 1858, for example, was 571. Only 116,536 Piedmontese subjects were eligible to vote out of a total population of over five million. Some constituencies had less than 150 eligible voters.[74]

The Intendants were forced to undergo further electoral trials in the sphere of local government: for the liberal (if not democratic) movement of 1848 had won representative

73. Ibid., 170–74; D. Mack Smith, *Italy: A Modern History* (Ann Arbor, 1959), p. 34, and "Cavour and Parliament," *Cambridge Historical Journal, 13* (1957), 52.

74. *Calendario generale del regno pel 1859, 36* (1859), 123–24.

government at the local, as well as at the national, level. The Local Government Act of 1848 marked an important, if highly cautious, step in the direction of decentralization.

The fourteen divisions were recognized as corporate entities, with the right to own property and to administer divisional interests through a directly elected representative council. The franchise in local elections was extended to almost twice the number of people eligible in national elections.[75] Divisional councils were permitted to vote funds for such matters as roads, bridges, dikes, and public education; to elect representatives to a divisional board which supervised charitable institutions; and to make general recommendations for state action concerning divisional interests. All of these decisions were subject to central government ratification; the council could be dissolved at the central government's discretion (although new elections had to be held within a specified period); and the council had to rely for the preparation and execution of its decisions on a national official, the Intendant General. The latter thus became both a national official and the chief executive of a semiautonomous divisional government, convening the council, preparing and executing its budget and decisions, hiring and firing divisional employees, representing the council in court, etc. The provinces were also given elective councils which had, however, only powers of recommendation.

At the lowest level were the communes, now recognized as corporate bodies. The communes, which together covered all the territory of the kingdom, were now to have elective councils elected by the local government or "administrative" (as opposed to the "political") electorate, instead of by a combination of royal appointment and co-optation as

75. Ibid., p. 142.

hitherto. Under the new law, the mayors were to act as both national field agents and chief executives of the communal governments. As state officials, the mayors performed many tasks in such matters as military conscription, the land-register, and public order which were deconcentrated to them by the ministries in Turin, but under the hierarchical direction of the Intendants, General and Provincial. As national officials, they were covered by the constitutional provision that all national officials were to be appointed by the Crown. A concession was made to the principle of local self-government in that they were to be chosen by the Crown (i.e. the Cabinet) from among the local councillors. They could, however, be suspended by the Intendant General and removed from office at the government's pleasure.

The communes were required to provide certain services: maintenance of the land-register; elementary education; medical care for the poor; upkeep of churches and cemeteries; conduct of the census and maintenance of vital statistics records; maintenance of local roads and streets; protection of rural property and woodlands. They were also required to allocate funds for the housing of various state field offices including the police, tax officials, courts and jails. They were permitted to regulate such matters as the production and sale of foodstuffs, fairs and markets, street cleaning and garbage collection, building construction, and the utilization of local water resources. They were required to let the contract for the office of Communal Tax Exactor, who collected local and national direct taxes in return for a commission on collection and acted as communal treasurer. An executive committee, appointed by the communal council, prepared its budget, electoral lists, tax rolls, and conscription lists, with the assistance of the Communal Secretary, and subject to the council's approval.

Central government sanction was required for the more

important communal decisions, including the budget, all contracts, and all loans, etc., and what escaped the central net fell into the purview of the Intendants, General and Provincial. The central government, however, could no longer arbitrarily determine communal budgets but only require legally obligatory expenditures. The Intendant General had to approve communal tax assessments. Central controls, whether exercised in Turin or in the provincial capitals, still covered local government decisions of any significance; but given the electoral bases of central and local government, these controls would henceforth have to be exercised with an eye to the reactions of the local electorate.

The Local Government Act of 1848 was the first such law to apply equally to the entire kingdom. It treated every commune, whether a Sardinian village or the capital city of Turin itself, substantially the same and under the same leveling concept of civic equality. It abolished the distinctions in the laws and regulations governing local administrations as they applied to the various feudally denominated regions—the Duchies of Savoy, Genoa, and Aosta, the principality of Piedmont, the Kingdom of Sardinia, and the County of Nice. Cities and towns lost their special statutes which had usually been won centuries before from the Crown in return for voluntary submission to its sovereignty. All localities were to be represented in a single national assembly; all were to be equal, like citizens, before the law.

The island of Sardinia, acquired in 1720, finally became an integral part of the kingdom. The separate Ministry for Sardinian Affairs (which had existed in the periods 1759–79, 1796–1815, and 1833–47) in Turin was abolished, as were the royal offices (such as that of Viceroy) peculiar to the island. Sardinia was divided into three divisions, each under an Intendant General and each directly administered by the ministries in the national capital. The legislation and administrative organization of the mainland were gradually extended to the island.[76]

The same march toward national uniformity could be seen in the abolition of the customs barriers among the various regions, the introduction of a standard system of weights and measures, the unification of coinage, the introduction of uniform legal codes, and the transformation of the regional Senates (with their vestiges of political power) into strictly judicial Courts of Appeal under the authority of a single national Court of Cassation in Turin.

The Intendants gained further powers under the Education Act of 1848 (the Law of October 4, 1848, No. 818). In Turin the new Ministry of Public Instruction supervised the state universities directly and through university bodies, it supervised secondary schools, both public and ecclesiastical. Primary education remained a municipal responsibility to be discharged under the supervision of a state educational official in each province, the *Provveditore agli Studi* or Purveyor of Studies (in lieu of the Reformers of Studies, who had usually been clergymen) and also of a provincial school board, chaired by the Intendant. The Education Act of 1857 (the Law of June 22, 1857, No. 2328) transferred authority over secondary education from the universities to the Purveyors of Studies, and authority over primary schools to an Inspector of Primary Schools, both working under the joint supervison of the Ministry and of the provincial board. The board, still presided over by the Intendant, included representatives of the teachers and administrators, of the provincial capital's city council, and of the provincial council; its principal responsibility was the

76. Ibid., Appendix, pp. 103–09. See also Francesco Loddo Canepa, *Inventario delle R. Segreteria di Stato e di Guerra del Regno di Sardegna: 1720–1848* (Rome, 1934), pp. 13–21.

examination and ratification of municipal education activities, notably teacher appointments. The Intendants owed their entry into the field of education to two factors: (1) the political aspects of implementing an essentially anticlerical program of secular education; and (2) their position as the tutelage authorities of the communes, who had received decentralized responsibilities in this field.

The Intendants emerged considerably enhanced in prestige and power from the constitutional revolution of 1848. They were given responsibility for administering vital programs on behalf of all the central ministries. (1) As agents of the Ministry of Public Instruction and heads of the provincial school boards, they were responsible for ensuring municipal compliance with national education standards. (2) As agents of the Interior, they had charge of police, elections, the National Guard, public health, statistics, prisons, public assistance, and local government. (3) For the Ministry of War, the Intendants provided billeting and conveyance for troops in transit and supervised military conscription. (4) As agents of the Ministry of Public Works, they were responsible for condemnation proceedings and for the financial and administrative aspects of state works projects. (5) For the Ministry of Finance, they directed and supervised all treasury operations and the apportionment and collection of direct taxes, issued all payment vouchers, adjudicated claims arising from taxation, verified and rendered executory all tax rolls, verified and settled the accounts of all accountable tax agents, directed the sale and service of state securities, collected the state's share of communal excises, performed all the field operations of the state accounting system, and awarded concessions to utilize water resources and to explore and exploit mineral resources.[77]

77. *Rivista Amministrativa del Regno,* 7 (1856), 81–107.

The effects of the constitutional revolution were to expand the range of Intendant authority from such traditional sectors as finance, local government, public works, and charity to such new and vital sectors as public security, religion, and public health. And this expansion took place just when the traditional ministries, Interior and Finance, were losing power to new and specialized ministries, such as Public Instruction, Public Works and Agriculture, Industry and Commerce. The fragmentation of central administrative power would be offset—at least in the short run—by the continued joint use of the hierarchy of general administrators, the Intendants.

The period 1824–59 was characterized by the creation of new specialized field services and also by the development of the existing ones. Some important services were created during this period: (1) mining inspection (1826), (2) railway construction and operation (1847), (3) telegraph construction and operation (1848), (4) weights and measures inspection (1850), (5) direct taxation (1852), and (6) urban police (1852). But more important was the expansion of the postal, engineering, and financial services, as well as in the number of public educational institutions.[78]

The development of the state field establishment was paralleled by the growth of municipal services. The city of Turin, for example, employed only about thirty people in 1824, but thirty-five years later, its paid staff numbered over 650.[79] Thus the growth of the state field establishment did not by any means supplant or preclude the parallel expansion of decentralized administration; both stemmed from the governmental problems created by the rapid growth of population, trade, commercial agriculture, and manufacturing. Under Cavour's vigorous parliamentary

78. Compare the *Calendario* of 1859 with that for 1824.
79. *Calendario, 1* (1824), 469–75; *36* (1859), 640–43.

leadership, Piedmont in the 1850s recovered from the military defeats and financial exhaustion of the war against Austria in 1848–49 to become a model constitutional state, with a balanced budget (which doubled between 1824 and 1859), and a costly program of public investment in railways and education, a policy of free trade, a reorganized and effective administration—all sustaining a successful attempt to win the credit and sympathy of the powers in Europe and of patriots in the Italian states.[80]

THE OTHER STATES OF ITALY

In 1815 the Congress of Vienna had consigned the Italians to the care of eight mutually independent rulers. To the Bourbons, it had restored the Kingdom of Naples and the Kingdom of Sicily, forming what was diplomatically known as the Kingdom of the Two Sicilies and comprising the island of Sicily and most of the southern half of the peninsular mainland. To the Pope it had restored the temporal power over most of the central portion of the peninsula, from the Roman provinces across the Apennines to the Adriatic Marches and northward to the Legations touching the Po River. To the Emperor of Austria had been given the territories of the former Duchy of Milan and Republic of Venice, henceforth to constitute the Kingdom of Lombardy–Venetia, and an integral part of the Austrian Empire. Between Piedmont (to which it had joined the former Republic of Genoa), the Papal States, and Lombardy–Venetia, it had restored the Duchies of Parma, Modena, and Lucca, as well as the Grand Duchy of Tuscany—all four under Austrian princes.[81]

By midcentury bureaucracies, central and peripheral,

80. Smith, *Italy*, pp. 17–51.
81. Lucca was subsequently absorbed by Tuscany and Parma.

had been developed in all of these states: the process of development and the forms evolved were similar, but conditioned by the particularities of each state.[82]

TABLE 1 Civil Services in the Italian States in 1859

State	Employees	Judicial	Teachers	Subaltern	Total
Piedmont	7,240	1,210	983	1,517	10,950
Two Sicilies	17,123	2,335	1,571	3,941	24,970
Papal States	5,272	498	234	1,561	7,565
Lombardy–Venitia	7,409	996	757	2,237	11,399
Parma	995	128	116	238	1,477
Modena	1,398	78	131	301	1,908
Tuscany	3,149	314	188	866	4,517

Source: Alberto Caracciolo, *Stato e società civile* (Turin, 1960), p. 119.

The Kingdom of Lombardy–Venetia, for example, as a part of the Austrian Empire, was governed to some extent from Vienna itself. In a sense, then, it had no central administration of its own, apart from the ministries in the Imperial capital. There was, to be sure, a Viceroy or (after 1857) a Governor of the kingdom in the person of the Emperor's brother, the Archduke Maximilian (of Mexican notoriety), but policy was determined in the last instance

82. The standard source on the administrative history of the former Italian states is Carlo Schupfer, "I precedenti storici del diritto amministrativo vigente in Italia: Organizzazione amministrativa degli stati italiani avanti l'unificazione legislativa," in V. E. Orlando, ed., *Primo Trattato completo di diritto amministrativo italiano* (Milan, 1897–1920), *1*, 1087–1284. A more recent survey may be found in the *Relazione* of the Ministero per la Costituente cited above in note 2, *2*, 559–99. See also Alberto Caracciolo, *Stato e società civile: problemi dell'unificazione italiana* (Turin, 1960), pp. 19–34.

THE ITALIAN STATES IN 1859

by the Viennese authorities.[83] Moreover, Lombardy and Venetia were administered separately by regional Lieutenants in Milan and Venice who had charge of regional accounting, taxation, education, and police offices acting on behalf of their counterpart home offices in Vienna. There were, however, some offices which had jurisdiction in both parts of the kingdom: the railway, postal, and telegraph directorates.[84]

The administration of the Papal States reflected the fact that, like the administration of Lombardy–Venetia, it was only one ramification of a vast imperial power. Only part of the central administration in Rome was devoted to the purpose of governing the Italian territories subject to the temporal power; the remaining and possibly greater part was occupied with the exercise of ecclesiastical functions abroad. Under pressure from liberals at home and from foreign powers, the Papacy had made efforts to differentiate

TABLE 2 The Population and Territory of the Italian States in 1857

State	Population (1857 est.)	Territory (sq. km.)
Piedmont	4,555,705	64,257
Two Sicilies	9,281,279	104,626
Papal States	3,127,027	41,434
Lombardy–Venetia	5,584,371	45,467
Parma	514,083	6,201
Modena	616,883	6,019
Tuscany	1,794,658	22,082

Source: *Annuario statistico italiano, 1 (1857–58)* (Turin, 1858), 381.

83. Augusto Sandonà, *Il Regno Lombardo–Veneto, 1814–1859: La costituzione e l'amministrazione* (Milan, 1912), p. 119.
84. Ibid., pp. 20–45.

between the temporal and ecclesiastical spheres in its governmental structure. On the eve of unification, however, the temporal government was still in the hands of members of the clergy at both the central and provincial levels.[85]

The various states of Italy differed considerably in the size of their populations and territories, as shown in Table 2.

All of the Italian states, with the prominent exception of Piedmont, were absolute divine right monarchies: administrative agencies were accountable only to the head of state and he, in turn, only to God. Much depended, therefore, on the personal character and opinions of the ruler, on his choice of ministers, on his desire and ability to make his ministers work together, on his willingness to adapt the structure and operations of his administration to the evolving needs and demands of his subjects.

By the late 1850s there had developed in the different states a number of ministries to assist the ruler in the exercise of his theoretically unlimited powers. The number of ministries, and consequently the division of labor among them, varied from state to state, as can be seen in Table 3.

Some form of prefectoral government had developed in all the seven Italian states. The localities were grouped into units equivalent to the Piedmontese divisions and French departments, and in each of these there was a general representative of the central government with duties similar to those of the Piedmontese Intendant General and the French Prefect. Except in the smallest states (Parma and Modena), these administrative areas were divided into subareas corresponding to the Piedmontese provinces and the French arrondissements and to each of these subareas was assigned a subprefectoral agent resembling the Pied-

85. Alfonso Ventrone, *L'Amministrazione dello Stato Pontificio: dal 1814 al 1870* (Rome, 1942), pp. 211–15.

montese Intendant and the French Subprefect. The prefectoral hierarchy was completed in all of the states by the
authorities of the communes, usually including a mayor.

TABLE 3 Ministries in the Various Italian States in 1859

State		*Ministries*
Tuscany	Foreign Affairs	War
	Interior	Ecclesiastical Affairs
	Grace and Justice	Finance, Commerce, and
	Public Instruction	Public Works
Two Sicilies	Foreign Affairs	Presidency of the Council
	Interior	Police
	Grace and Justice	Navy
	War	Public Works
	Finance	Agriculture
	Public Instruction	Sicilian Affairs
	Ecclesiastical Affairs	
Parma	Foreign Affairs	War
	Interior	Finance
	Grace and Justice	Intimate Cabinet
Modena	Foreign Affairs	Finance
	Interior	Ducal Cabinet
	Grace and Justice	Police
	War	
Papal States	Foreign Affairs	Interior, Grace, and Justice
	Arms	Public Works and Commerce
	Finance	Chamberlain's Office
	Congregation of Studies	
Piedmont	Foreign Affairs	Finance
	Interior	Public Instruction
	Grace and Justice	Navy
	War	Public Works

Source: Rodolfo Benini, "La burocrazia di stato in Italia dal 1859
al 1891," *Riforma Sociale, 4* (1895), 254–55.

The hierarchies of areas and officials in each state are listed in Table 4.*

The Napoleonic prefectoral system had been established in all the various Italian states except for the islands of Sicily and Sardinia. Much of the peninsula had for a time been directly annexed to the Napoleonic Empire. The French-inspired and French-dominated regimes in the rest of the peninsula adopted the same machinery of local administration. In all cases, however, the French system represented only a rationalization of the centralizing machinery created by the former absolutist governments. The restoration of the legitimate ruling houses brought much less reaction to the French institutions in most of the Italian states than was the case in Piedmont. Only the Papal States joined Piedmont in a complete reversion to former institutions. Elsewhere, and most notably in the Kingdom of Naples, the form, if not the underlying spirit, of administration remained French.

The prefectoral-type officials at the head of the combined field administration and local government areas were in all cases appointed and removed by the central government at its pleasure. As a rule, they were not local residents and could be freely transferred from one province to another. They were not viceroys or proconsuls or bailiffs exercising

*The Papal States were divided by the *Motu Proprio* of July 6, 1816, into seventeen provinces or delegations, the more important of which, when placed under Cardinal Legates, were called legations. The system was greatly changed by an edict of November 22, 1850, which grouped all the provinces or delegations (except those around Rome itself) into four legations and subordinated all the Delegates to the four Legates placed in charge. The Cardinal Legates after 1850 were no longer merely more important provincial heads, but the directors of groups of provincial heads and thus what we would today call "super-prefects" or regional prefects in charge of groups of prefects. Beneath the Legates and Delegates, in turn, there were Governors equivalent to the subprefectoral officials in the other states. On this, see Ventrone, pp. 39–45.

TABLE 4 Prefectoral-Type Officials in the Italian States in 1859

State	Piedmont	Lombardy–Venetia	Two Sicilies	Tuscany	Parma	Modena
Major areas	Divisions (14)	Provinces (17)	Provinces (22)	Compartments (6)	Provinces (5)	Provinces (6)
Prefects	Intendants General	Delegates	Intendants	Prefects	Governors, Prefects	Delegates
Subareas	Provinces (50)	Districts (102)	Districts (77)	Districts (11)	—	—
Subprefects	Intendants	District Commissioners	Subintendants	Subprefects	—	—
Local areas	Communes (3,099)	Communes (2,921)	Communes (2,120)	Communes (246)	Communes (105)	Communes (70)

Source: *Enciclopedia italiana*, 10 (1938), 413; Ministero per la Costituente, *Relazione*, 2, 559–99; see also the court almanacs of the different states.

all central government powers in the province: a minimum of specialization had produced everywhere separate judicial and military hierarchies directly dependent on the central government: and specialization had in all cases produced several other distinct services subordinate, directly or indirectly, to their functional counterparts in the central government. By midcentury, there had developed alongside the general or prefectoral administration distinct services for such matters as finance, public works, police, public health, forest inspection, and public education. Everywhere, however, the prefectoral officials were superior in rank and prestige to the directors of these specialized services in the province. Everywhere they performed functions on behalf of all central functional units, took orders from them, and reported to them. Everywhere a high degree of centralization had required the use of such generalist agents to replace and to supervise local governments in a range of activities that cut across the jurisdictional lines among the central departments.

There were, however, some differences among the prefectoral officials in the several states. A Cardinal Legate, for example, enjoyed a prominence and independence that his counterparts in the other states could not match: for, as a Cardinal, he enjoyed the same status as his nominal superior, the Cardinal Secretary of State, both being members of the Sacred College, both inferior in standing only to the Pontiff himself.[86]

Prefectoral officials varied not only in their autonomy vis-à-vis the central government, but also in the degree to which they were placed in control of the different field services operating in their provinces. The strongest one

86. Narciso Nada, *Metternich e le riforme nello stato pontificio: La missione Sebregondi a Roma (1832–1836)* (Turin, Deputazione Subalpina di Storia Patria, 1957), pp. 45–66, 212–19.

among them in this respect would appear to have been the Neapolitan Intendant. Unlike his counterpart in Piedmont, the Intendant here was given a sweeping statutory grant of authority. The pertinent articles of the statute concerned, the Law on the Civil Administration (December 12, 1816), read as follows:[87]

> Art. 4. The Intendant is the first authority of the province. He is charged with the administration of the communes, of which he is the immediate tutor, with that of the public establishments, and in general with all internal administration; with financial administration; with the recruitment of our army and with any other military service which is not entrusted to particular authorities and military administrations; with high police, excluding only the province of Naples for so long as there is in that province a prefecture of police. In every other province the attributions of the prefect of police are fused with that of the Intendant: and when under extraordinary circumstances it shall be necessary to appoint a police agent, the latter shall always be under the orders of the Intendant.
>
> Art. 5. The Intendant is under the orders of and in direct correspondence with the Ministry of the Interior for all which relates to internal administration; the Ministry of Finance, for all which concerns public revenues, and the vigilance which he exercises over the same; the Ministry of War, for all that interests recruitment and every other military service; the Ministry of General Police, in all that relates to public security.
>
> The Intendant shall correspond with every other of our Ministries or Secretariats of State, and shall be

87. Kingdom of the Two Sicilies, *Collezione delle leggi e decreti reali del Regno delle Due Sicilie, Anno 1816, Semestre II* (Naples, 1816), pp. 425–508.

subordinate to them in all that they commit to him in their respective departments.

Art. 6. The Intendant watches over the publication of our laws and decrees, and gives the analogous instructions to accelerate and ensure the execution of them. He does the same for ministerial regulations and orders. The acts which are published by the Intendant for such purposes shall have the name of *instructions* or of *ordinances* according to the case . . .

Art. 11. The *gendarmeria,* the Provincial Legion, and the internal police, under any denomination whatsoever, are subordinate to and at the disposition of the Intendant for the service of the administration which is entrusted to him; all remaining, however, for military discipline under the command of their respective superiors.

Art. 12. The Intendant may request in writing from the commander of the province the military force of the troops of our army which are under the latter's orders in the same province, provided that the public service requires it. The commander can in no case refuse it to him . . .

Art. 14. The Intendant as the first authority of the province is the president of every board or council, permanent or temporary, which may be established in the province for any branch of administration, whatever the grade or dignity of the individuals who are members . . .

Art. 18. It is expressly forbidden to the Intendants to establish any taxation for any purpose or apportion any taxation beyond the sums fixed by the law or to make any loans without authorization . . . [!]

Art. 28. The secretariat of every Intendancy shall be divided into offices according to the attributions of the different ministries.

Art. 73. No [municipal council] decision may be executed without the approval of the Intendant, which the mayor must solicit.

The position of the Royal Delegate in the Lombard–Venetian provinces presents something of a contrast. On the one hand, the Delegate was directly in control of some of the major specialist field officials: the Provincial Engineer, the Provincial Medical Officer, the Press Censor were all attached to the delegation itself. But contrariwise, all the financial and allied services of the province were under the authority of a senior official of the financial administration, the Intendant of Finance. And the Intendancy of Finance was constituted as a separate and autonomous office, directly linked to regional financial offices in Milan and Venice. The Intendant was chief of the domain, mortgage, registry, customs, fiscal monopolies, lottery, finance guards, postal, and forestry services in the province. Only direct taxation, handled by the delegation, lay outside his purview.[88]

The independence of the financial services in the Kingdom of Lombardy–Venetia was indicative of the general tendency of financial services toward increasing diversification, complexity, and autonomy in all the states. It is ironic that the administration of finance which in most cases lay at the origin of the modern prefectoral generalists should also prove to be the most resistant to prefectoral integration. Financial services demonstrate the same drive toward in-

88. Antonio Lorenzoni, *Istituzioni del diritto pubblico interno pel Regno Lombardo–Veneto* (Padua, 1835), *1*, 66–67; Ministero per la Costituente, *Relazione, 2*, 588–89.

dependence traditionally shown by the judiciary and the military. The judiciary have been aided by the doctrine of the separation of powers; the military, by the primarily external nature of their functions. The financial services cannot claim autonomy on constitutional grounds, nor on the domestic nature of their functions; they rest their claim instead on a need for expertise, efficiency, discipline, national uniformity, and impartiality—a need allegedly particular to financial administration. These arguments would reappear in the crucial decade following unification when the institutions of the new Italy were being forged.

Chapter Two

THE UNITED KINGDOM OF ITALY (1859-70)

PREPARATION FOR UNITY: 1859

IN THE DECADE after the revolutions of 1848, Piedmont under Cavour assumed the leadership of the movement to create a unified Italy. Nationalists in all parts of the peninsula and islands came to see in the House of Savoy and in Piedmontese arms and diplomacy the only effective instrumentalities of unification. And it was Piedmontese diplomacy that secured the backing of Napoleon III for a war to drive the Austrians from northwestern Italy, and Piedmontese arms that, with considerable French military aid, early in 1859 conquered Lombardy, sparking off revolutions in Parma, Modena, Tuscany, and the Papal Legations. The Austrian princes and Papal Legates were ousted and replaced with provisional governments, as a prelude to outright annexation to Piedmont. This was to be the pattern of unification: Italy was to be formed by the voluntary acceptance of Piedmontese sovereignty as manifested in plebiscites in all the former states. The head of the House of Savoy (the oldest ruling house in Europe) was to be proclaimed King of Italy. The Parliament of the Sardinian States, enlarged to include representatives from the other regions, was to become the Italian national parliament. Turin would be the capital of united Italy.[1]

Late in 1859 the government in Turin hastily drafted and promulgated a series of decree-laws that modified the existing Piedmontese institutions with a view to their immediate extension to Lombardy and eventual extension to such other Italian territories as could be brought within the enlarging kingdom. Among the most important of these was a new organic act on local administration, Royal Decree No. 3702 of October 23, 1859, amending the Local Government Act of 1848.

The new law provided for the division of the national territory into provinces (instead of divisions), *circondari* or "districts" (instead of provinces), *mandamenti,* and communes. The new names for Piedmontese institutions would make them less Piedmontese and therefore more acceptable in the new parts of the kingdom where other names had been in use. At the same time, the administrative maps of the Sardinian States and of Lombardy were redrawn. Seven provinces were created in the Sardinian States where there had formerly been eleven divisions; Lombardy was deprived of two provincial capitals. Merger of the existing areas into larger aggregations was considered necessary for the central control of an expanding kingdom.[2]

A second innovation in the new Provincial and Communal Act was the establishment in each of the new provinces of a Governor and a Vice-Governor. The Piedmontese Intendant General had been until then a high-ranking administrative official, a career functionary completely dependent on the ministry. The new law renamed the Intend-

1. Franco Valsecchi, *Storia del risorgimento* (Turin, 1958), pp. 35–67.
2. *Rivista amministrativa del regno, 11* (1860), 81–85.

ant General, giving him the title of Vice-Governor, and placed above him a political figure—the Governor—who, at least in the major cities, would be a politician sharing the political complexion of the government of the day. The idea of a political Governor was apparently inspired by institutions of the same name in Belgium and Spain. The Governor would perform the more political functions hitherto exercised by the Intendants General. It was felt that career officials might, in the absence of central directives, either act contrary to government policy or not act at all for fear of compromising themselves. Politicians from the government coalition would bring enthusiasm and drive into the state services; they would identify their own fate with that of the government and would stir themselves to greater efforts on its behalf than would career officials. The latter would continue to handle the administrative tasks requiring detailed knowledge of laws, regulations, and standard procedures.

Opponents of the new scheme charged that it was more expensive since it doubled a highly paid post which had been single. They argued further that as politicians, the provincial heads would be turned out and replaced with every change in the government of the day and this instability would have harmful repercussions in administration. Finally, the posts would become a mass of patronage with which the government would attempt to corrupt the legislature.[3]

Such arguments might have carried greater weight in more normal circumstances. Late in 1859, however, considerations of economy, administrative stability, and the independence of the legislature counted for little as compared to the goal of national unification. Provinces hitherto under foreign domination were to be brought into the king-

3. Ibid., pp. 85–87.

dom and the nationalist forces within them strengthened as against the partisans of the former regimes. The tasks of the Governors would be to win and hold the allegiance of the new provinces to a new regime. At times such as these, "prefectoral" appointments are bound to be political, and partisan political at that.

It was in the same 1859 Act that the definition of the Governor's (shortly after the Prefect's) powers appeared which was to become a standard feature of successive provincial and communal acts until the Fascist edition of 1934.

Article Three

The Governor represents the Executive Power throughout the Province.

He maintains the powers of the Administrative Authorities and secures the settlement of conflicts of jurisdiction between them and the judicial authorities by the appropriate arbitrating authority.

He provides for the publication and for the execution of the laws.

He keeps watch over the activities of all the public Administrations, and in case of urgency adopts the measures which he believes indispensable in the different branches of the service.

He superintends public security and has the right to dispose of the public police forces and to request the intervention of the armed forces.

In Provincial and Communal administration, he exercises the powers determined by law.

He is subordinate to the Minister of the Interior, and executes the latter's instructions.

This definition of the Governor's role, since it became the standard and only general statement of prefectoral duties and powers, calls for some comment.

The 1848 Act, it will be remembered, called the Intendant General the "representative of the Government." His successor at the head of the province is now called the representative of the "Executive Power." The change in diction is usually taken as indicating an attempt to make of the Governor or Prefect someone more than the mandatary of a transient government of the day.[4] In practice, however, the change made no difference: the official concerned continued to act as the agent of the current depositories of the executive power—the changing members of the Council of Ministers. The same phrase incidentally was used in the French Law of August 10, 1871: "Le préfet est le représentant du pouvoir éxécutif dans le Département."

Of all the state officials in the province, only the Prefect represented *all* the ministers, and in two particular senses: (1) he performed administrative duties for all of the ministries, not only for the Interior; and (2) he acted as the political agent of all the ministers considered (ideally) as a collective body of politicians with its own political orientation. He also acted for all the ministries constituting the executive branch when he took steps to protect the autonomous power of the executive against judicial encroachment. If a court attempted to decide or review matters reserved by statute to the jurisdiction of the executive or of administrative tribunals, or if administrative officials were brought before courts that lacked jurisdiction, it was (and is) the Prefect's duty to suspend court action by decree and to submit the case to the magistrates authorized to adjudicate such jurisdictional conflicts.[5]

Prefectoral intervention in the affairs of the state services operating in the province might also be justified by the

4. See, for example, Guido Zanobini, *Corso di diritto amministrativo*, (Milan, 1957–58), *3* (6th ed.), 93.

5. Ibid., p. 94.

Prefect's duty to see to the execution of the laws. A less tenuous justification was provided, in the following clause, by his duty to watch over the activities of all public administrative agencies in the province. The rest of Article Three, however, restricted by implication the scope of such intervention. His power to decide matters formally lying within the normal competence of other administrative officials was confined to cases of urgency: in the ordinary course of affairs, only the hierarchical superiors of those officials were to enjoy an unlimited right of intervention. In cases of emergency, there were virtually no legal limits to prefectoral action; but short of such situations, and in the absence of special legislation conferring upon the Prefect the right of hierarchical superiority, the Prefect could not legally attempt to make decisions reserved to the other state officials in the province, could not give them orders or instructions, could not annul or modify their decisions.

The following clause did, in fact, confer upon the Prefect the rights of hierarchical superiority with regard to one particular sector of administration—public security. This clause made the Prefect the chief of all public security or police officials in the province constituting *la forza pubblica* (in contrast to *la forza armata*): the Public Security Guards and the Carabinieri. The Prefect could thus direct these officials in the day-to-day exercise of even those powers directly conferred upon them by laws and regulations (except insofar as they acted under the authority of the courts as agents of the judicial police).

Every state official in the province was linked to his ministry in the capital by a chain of command. Only by special legislation or in emergencies did the Prefect become a superior link in that chain. The Prefect himself was specifically subordinated to the Minister of the Interior; but, as subsequent regulations made clear, only he was subject to the orders and directives of authorities standing outside of his particular chain of command—each minister in the sphere of his particular competence.[6]

Compared to the exalted legal status of the French Prefect or the Neapolitan Intendant, the status of the Piedmontese and Italian Governor-Prefect was modest indeed. The reason for this may well lie in the contrasting political ideologies of those who respectively shaped the prefectoral institutions. The stronger provincial head (one who was made the hierarchical chief of all the state services in the province) was designed to reproduce in the province the absolute and concentrated authority of the head of state. A liberal regime of dispersed powers may be less apt to create a set of provincial monocrats.[7]

This hypothesis is in accord with the decentralizing provisions on local government contained in the 1859 Act. The electorate for provincial and communal council elections (the "administrative" electorate) was expanded from a fixed proportion of taxpayers in each constituency to broader categories of those who paid more than specified amounts of taxes. Most of the powers of the mayor as communal executive were transferred to an executive committee—the *Giunta Municipale*—directly elected by the municipal council; the mayor himself was still, however, to be appointed by the Crown from among council members. Likewise, most of the powers of the Intendant General as chief executive of the province went to a new collegial provincial executive—the *Deputazione Provinciale*—chaired by the Governor but elected by the provincial council (which also gained the right to elect its own presiding officer). The powers of the Crown and of the Intendant General to approve municipal financial and other transactions were

6. Ibid., p. 98.
7. *Rivista amministrativa del regno, 11* (1860), 94–95.

handed over to the new provincial deputation, the Crown retaining the right to approve municipal bylaws on taxation and police and to veto illegal decisions of any sort. Crown authority over charitable institutions was also transferred to the provincial deputation.[8]

There was, however, a provision in the same Act (Article 241) which was distinctly contrary to the above decentralizing provisions: it deprived the provincial council of the right to vote a budget for provincial services, transferring the expenses for them to the state. In effect, the provincial councils were reduced to the function of electing a deputation for the tutelage of municipal and charitable institutions.

The Act of 1859 was extended to the various regions of the country as they were annexed to Piedmont. Application of the act in Lombardy and in the other annexed territories aroused much discontent. Not only did it bring a seldom-welcome change in institutions and names; not only were its provisions (especially those on the provinces) more centralized than those to which some of the regions, like Lombardy and Tuscany, had been accustomed; not only was it a Piedmontese law—but it also wiped out the traces of the former political communities, relegating their capitals to the status of provincial capitals and parceling their territories into units most suitable for government from Turin.[9] To alleviate some of this discontent, the act underwent more or less broad revisions as it was extended to the different regions. Tuscany in fact managed to retain a separate local government act which had been promulgated by its provisional government, after the House of Lorraine had

---

8. The old provincial councils were abolished at this time.

9. Ministero dell'Interno, *Relazione sull'andamento delle amministrazioni dipendenti dal Ministero dell'Interno nell'anno 1866, presentato dal ministro al parlamento il 22 dicembre* (Florence, 1866), p. 5.

been driven out. The provision on provincial budgets (Article 241) was not put into effect outside of Piedmont and Lombardy.[10]

THE DECENTRALIZATION TENDENCY (1860–61)

By the summer of 1860 the problem of organizing a new state in north and north-central Italy had been dramatically transformed into the problem of organizing a state in almost all of the peninsula and the islands.[11] Garibaldi, at the head of his Thousand, had invaded Sicily and ousted the troops of the King of Naples: it was not unlikely that he might be able to conquer the Neapolitan provinces as well. In these changed circumstances, the government in Turin (now back in the hands of Cavour) set to work preparing a new system of local government. It established a consultative committee of members of Parliament and Councillors of State on June 24, 1860, to draft legislation in line with what the government proposed to do.[12]

The government's proposals were outlined in a memorandum to the committee by the Minister of the Interior (Farini). Above the provincial and communal administrations existing under the 1859 Act the government would establish a set of Regional Governors in a system which would, in the Minister's words, "coordinate the strong unity of the State with the speedy development of local

10. Gabriele Amendola, "La Provincia nell'amministrazione dello stato," in Orlando, *Primo Trattato, 3,* Pt. III, 91.

11. On the general history of this period, see D. Mack Smith, *Cavour and Garibaldi, 1860: A Study in Political Conflict* (Cambridge, Eng., Cambridge University Press, 1954).

12. The minutes of this body were published under the title, *Estratti dai verbali delle adunanze della Commissione Temporanea di Legislazione istituita presso il Consiglio di Stato colla legge 24 giugno 1860: amministrazione comunale, provinciale, e regionale.* (No facts of publication are given.)

life, with the solid liberty of the provinces, the communes, and the consortia [or unions of provinces and communes], with the gradual emancipation of education and welfare, and provincial and municipal institutions from the restrictions of the central bureaucracy."[13]

The provinces as areas and corporate institutions would remain much as they then were (with the boundary changes effected by the various provisional governments) since it would be dangerous, the Minister said, to tamper with such natural and historical units. The provinces would, however, be grouped into regions to be headed by Regional Governors, directly responsible to the central government. The government would deconcentrate many of its powers to the Governors, including the appointment of the police and lower civil servants, and control of the "Provincial Intendants" and public security. The regions were not to be local government areas: they would serve only as what we would call field administrative areas. Elective regional authorities, the government feared, might detract from the authority of the national parliament and undermine national unity.[14]

In its first report, dated August 3, 1860, the consultative committee insisted that the regions become not only field administrative areas but also corporate entities with councils elected by the provincial councils to deliberate upon matters of regional interest. It proposed that the Regional Governor as a national official appointed and dismissed by the central government be given ceremonial precedence over all other authorities in the region; that he be the "direct superior of the political, public security, and administrative services" of the Interior; that he carry out tasks for other ministries as required by special laws or delegation;

13. *Estratti*, p. 5.
14. Ibid., pp. 3–14.

that he watch over "in the interest of the public order and security" the activities and discipline of all the state services, without any right to intervene in the affairs of the military or the judiciary; that the chiefs of the different field services be required to inform him of anything affecting public order; that he have the right to investigate and inspect the operations of all the state services; that in cases of emergency he have the authority to suspend state officials and the execution of their orders and issue to them binding orders (immediately notifying the government); that all central dispositions on appointments and dismissals be communicated through his office, subject to his right to suspend their execution pending central action on any observations he cared to make; and, finally, that he be the executive authority for the regional council.[15]

By the following November, Garibaldi had completed the conquest of the Neapolitan provinces and had surrendered them to King Victor Emmanuel II. Farini was sent by the Turin government to govern them as Royal Lieutenant (a similar lieutenancy having been created in Palermo for Sicily) and he was replaced at the Interior by Marco Minghetti, who had been a member of the consultative committee and who was anxious that it complete a draft for submission to the first national parliament. In a note (November 28, 1860) addressed to the committee, Minghetti reaffirmed the government's support for a regional system of government and declared its acceptance of regional councils.[16] The reasons for the regions he summed up as follows:[17]

15. Ibid., pp. 33–65. There is a considerable literature on the regionalist schemes of this period. See, for example, the *Relazione* of the Ministero per la Costituente, 2, 165–299 and the extensive bibliography on pp. 298–99.

16. *Estratti*, pp. 65–77.

17. Ibid., p. 68.

The Italian Province is not vast or populous or rich enough to be able to provide, at least for the present, for all those functions . . . which the Government would be disposed to entrust to the citizens. The Prefects are too many in number for the Government to be able to delegate to them all the powers required by a real decentralization [i.e. deconcentration] without running the risk of variety and excessive discrepancy in the operations of the administration.

It is necessary therefore to form another aggregation, another corporate entity greater than the Provinces, such that the representatives of the Government may therein safely have the powers we have indicated; and the joint association of the Provinces suffice for the desired end. Such would be the Regions . . .

On March 14, 1861, the first national parliament, elected in January, proclaimed the existence of the Kingdom of Italy.[18] Symptomatically, however, King Victor Emmanuel II of Sardinia became King Victor Emmanuel II of Italy and this session of Parliament was officially recorded as the Eighth—so great was the continuity between Piedmontese and Italian institutions. Unification was almost complete: only Venetia and the Roman provinces remained outside the new kingdom.

The first national census of December 31, 1861, showed the population of the kingdom to be 21,777,334, living in 59 provinces, 193 districts, and 7,720 communes.[19]

18. Under the Piedmontese electoral law, little over two per cent of the population of the new kingdom had the right to vote and of these, just over half actually voted in the January 1861 elections. See Lucio Luzzatto, *Elezioni politiche e leggi elettorali in Italia* (Rome, 1958), pp. 70–71.

19. Ministero d'Agricoltura, Industria e Commercio, *Popolazione: censimento generale (31 dicembre 1861)* (Turin, 1864), p. xxi.

The provincial boundaries of the new kingdom in most cases had been taken over intact from those of the former regimes. In the other cases, they were redrawn by the provisional governments before annexation.[20] Drawn at separate times by separate administrative mapmakers, the provincial areas were either subdivisions of the former states or of the regions (such as Emilia) which had been subject to a common provisional government prior to annexation. They were not, consequently, the result of a subdivision of the entire national territory in accordance with a uniform set of criteria. It is not surprising, then, that the provinces varied considerably in area and population. In area, they ranged from the 344 square kilometers of the province of Leghorn and the 906 square kilometers of the province of Naples to the 10,247 square kilometers of Turin province, the 10,595 square kilometers of Sassari province, and the 13,483 square kilometers of the province of Cagliari.[21] The range in population is shown in Table 5.

TABLE 5 The Population of the Italian Provinces in 1861

Number of Provinces	Population
7	over 600,000
6	500,001–600,000
8	400,001–500,000
11	300,001–400,000
19	200,001–300,000
8	100,001–200,000
Total 59	

Source: Ministero d'Agricoltura, Industria e Commercio, *Popolazione: censimento generale (31 dicembre 1861)* Turin, 1864), p. xxii.

20. R. Marchetti, *La Formazione del Regno d'Italia ed il decentramento* (Rome, 1893), pp. 32–46.

21. "Circoscrizione amministrativa," *Il Digesto Italiano* (Turin, 1897–1902), *3*, Pt. II, 56–57.

There was a similar diversity in the size of the districts (*circondari* or subprefectoral areas), many of which were equal or greater in population than a good number of provinces, as is shown in Table 6.

TABLE 6 The Population of the Italian Districts in 1861

Number of districts	Population
16	over 200,000
72	100,001–200,000
82	50,001–100,000
23	less than 50,000
Total 193	

Source: See Table 5.

Municipal boundaries were also inherited from the past regimes, each of which had drawn them with different criteria. The result was that after unification there were marked regional differences in the proportion of the number of communes to area and population. In the country as a whole, the communes varied in the number of their inhabitants as shown in Table 7.

Compared, say, to France, Italy was a country of cities and towns. France, with a population at that time of thirty-six million, had only 1,307 communes of over 2,000 inhabitants: Italy, with only twenty-one million, had 2,914. About half the population of Italy lived in communes of over 5,000 population; in France, only about one-fifth. Italy had seventeen cities with more than 50,000 people and sixty-two more with between twenty and fifty thousand: France, with sixty per cent more area and forty per cent more population had only nineteen cities with above 50,000 inhabitants and fifty towns with between twenty and

fifty thousand. The average Italian commune had a population of 2,821; the average French commune, 978.[22]

TABLE 7 The Population of the Italian Communes in 1861

Number of communes	Population
1,097	less than 500
1,606	500–1,000
2,103	1,001–2,000
1,081	2,001–3,000
606	3,001–4,000
337	4,001–5,000
596	5,001–10,000
215	10,001–20,000
36	20,001–30,000
26	30,001–50,000
9	50,001–100,000
8	above 100,000
Total 7,720	

Source: See Table 5.

Partly in consequence of the former political divisions of
the peninsula, there was no single great metropolis in the
new state such as Paris or London which stood far above
the other cities of the country.[23] The eight communes of
over 100,000 population—Naples, Milan, Palermo, Turin,
Genoa, Florence, Bologna, and Messina—were spread over
the country, and, as the major centers of the former states,
they had begun to centralize in themselves the social and
economic life of the surrounding regions. This dispersal of
urban centers would not be changed, moreover, with the
addition to the great cities of the kingdom of Venice (in

22. Ministero d'Agricoltura, *Censimento generale,* pp. xxii–xxvi.
23. Carlo Rodanò, *Mezzogiorno e sviluppo economico* (Bari, Laterza, 1954).

1866) and Rome (in 1870). Venice would add to the number of peripheral centers of trade, culture, and rich historic tradition. And even Rome with its past glories would be but a modest capital: it would not become the largest Italian city until well into the twentieth century.[24]

THE TRIUMPH OF CENTRALIZATION (1861–65)

The system of regional administration that the government proposed to establish in the bills presented to Parliament on March 13, 1861, represented an attempt to accommodate the administrative structure of the country to the divergent requirements of national unification and respect for regional diversity.[25] In his *Relazione* to the bill on the "Division of the Kingdom and Governmental Authorities," the Minister of the Interior (Minghetti) noted that the provinces had until quite recently been grouped into independent states, each with its own institutions, each with a capital city that had developed as a center of art, wealth, and population. It would be unwise, he thought, to try to cancel out the differences among these former states—at least immediately. Political, financial, military, and legislative unification had, of course, to be both immediate and complete: this was not necessary or expedient as regarded what he called "adminis-

24. According to the census of 1871, after the incorporation of Venetia and Rome, the population of the kingdom was 26,801,154 living in an area of 286,589 square kilometers, divided into 69 provinces, 284 districts, and 8,382 communes. Rome and surrounding delegations had been lumped together into one large province of 11,917 square kilometers, with 836,704 people. The nine Venetian provinces were left as they had been, together with the former districts. See Ministero di Agricoltura, Industria e Commercio, Ufficio Centrale di Statistica, *Popolazione presente ed assente: censimento 31 dicembre 1871* (Rome, 1874), *I*, pp. 3–10.

25. *Atti Parlamentari, Legislatura VIII, Sessione 1861–1862, Camera dei Deputati,* Nos. 7–10.

trative" unification where the transition from diversity in customs and institutions to national uniformity had to be gradual. Such diversity could not be allowed from province to province without administrative anarchy; it could and should be allowed, however, within groups of provinces called regions. The regions would serve as devices for the gradual transitions from diversity to uniformity in administrative structure and in the less essential fields of legislation. (The goal of ultimate uniformity was unquestioned.)

The national territory would be divided into regions, provinces, districts, and communes. The bill itself did not venture to delimit the areas of the regions: this delicate task would be left to the determination of a special parliamentary committee.

This parliamentary committee would also be called upon to modify the provincial boundaries. The provinces, the Minister declared, were in most cases not artificial or accidental areas but the product of history and the foci of "real" interests. There was no reason consequently to redraw the provincial boundaries *ab novo*. Instead the existing ones should be improved. The province should have between 200,000 and 500,000 inhabitants. Adjustments should be made to secure provinces of this size. The Lombard provinces as drawn in 1816 should be restored. Cities like Leghorn which had grown to a certain level of population and wealth should be made provincial capitals. The changes to be expected were, however, minor.

Within each of the regions as eventually delimited there was to be a Governor upon whom the central ministries would devolve many of their powers; the institution of the Governor would not detract therefore from the existing powers of the Prefects. There were interesting differences, however, between the government's bill and the proposal of the consultative committee in the way each defined the

Governor's powers and status. In the government's bill, the Governor no longer was explicitly given ceremonial precedence over the other authorities of the region; he no longer had the power to suspend any state official or the execution of a decision of any such official in cases of emergency; and he was no longer necessarily the exclusive channel for central dispositions on personnel. On the other hand, the powers to be devolved upon him by the Ministry of the Interior were explicitly defined. Within the limits imposed by the laws, regulations, ministerial directives, fixed tables of organization, and the budget, he would have the right to appoint, suspend, and dismiss the employees of the lower grades of services under the Interior. Upon the advice of his council, he would make the final decisions on the appeals of provinces and communes (presumably against prefectoral decisions). He would approve the regulations or bylaws voted by the communes and provinces. He would authorize the establishment of fairs and markets (presumably on behalf of the Minister of Agriculture). He would approve changes in the classification of roads and the introduction of tolls. He would give sanction to the regulations or statutes of charitable institutions and the incorporation of such institutions. He would award government endowments and grants to educational, welfare, and religious institutions. He would appoint the directors of institutions and the members of the health boards whose appointment was then reserved to the government. He would exercise supervisory powers over voluntary and compulsory *consorzi* or unions of provinces and communes. Finally, he would convene the regional commission, prepare its agenda, execute its decisions, and appoint regional employees.

The statement of the Prefect's powers in the bill was identical to that contained in the 1859 Act save for explicit powers to direct the judicial prisons and to supervise charitable institutions and *consorzi*—powers he already enjoyed.[26]

A bill on "regional administration" submitted at the same time would have created within each region a commission of up to twenty members, elected by the provincial councils, to deliberate on matters decentralized by the state in three fields: interprovincial roads, higher education, and hydraulic works. It would vote upon the provincial contributions necessary to finance its budget for these items. It would also have authority (within the limits to be set by national legislation or subject to central government approval) to legislate on matters of reclamation, irrigation, hunting, and fishing. The executive power of the region *qua* decentralized authority would be lodged exclusively with the Governor, although the commission could elect two assessors to assist him. The region would thus become not only a field administrative area but also a corporate entity, what the Minister called a "permanent obligatory *consorzio*" of the constituent provinces. The central government reserved the right to approve the most important decisions of the regional commissions. The national legislature could, moreover, vote the direct construction of works in the various regions by the state; and it could also subsidize the poorer regions.[27]

Further decentralization would result from a third bill, one on "Communal and Provincial Administration." The major beneficiary was to be the province. The Prefect was no longer to be the chief of the provincial executive: the provincial deputation would elect its own president. Consequently, the Interior could deconcentrate its tutelage powers over the province to the Prefect. Secondly, the prov-

26. Ibid., pp. 33–34.
27. Ibid., pp. 59–62.

ince would become responsible for a broad range of regulatory and service activities: many types of public works, including provincial roads and river control; secondary and vocational education; archives and monuments; public health, relief (insofar as not provided privately or by the communes); care for foundlings and the insane; forest conservation; regulation of agrarian usages; and the subsidization of communes.

The elimination of the smaller communes would be encouraged by the linking of municipal autonomy to municipal population: the amount of tutelage would vary inversely to the size of communal population. And the communal council itself, now to be elected by all direct taxpayers, would in turn elect the mayor.[28] (The consultative committee had strongly insisted that all communes have equal autonomy and that the mayor remain an appointee of the state.)[29]

This decentralization, the Minister declared, would transform the Ministry of Public Instruction into a maker of policy and standards and an inspector; the regions would be responsible for higher education, the provinces for secondary and vocational education, and the communes for elementary education. The Ministry of Public Works would retain direct responsibility only in matters of national interest such as railroads, the postal and telegraph services, coastal works, and major port works. The Ministry of Agriculture would lose direct responsibility for woodland conservation, agrarian usages, and statistics. The Interior would no longer have direct functions (or budgetary headings) in the fields of relief, aid to foundlings, insane asylums, and public health; it would, however, continue to

28. Ibid., pp. 37–53.
29. Ibid., p. 37.

direct the Governors, the Prefects, the police, and the prison system. The Ministry of Finance would be unaffected.[30]

The Minister concluded his report, stating, "We, sirs, are all in agreement on two points, which, if I may be permitted to say it, are negative. We do not want French centralization . . . On the other hand, we do not want an administrative independence such as that of the United States of America."[31]

This broad scheme of decentralization, however, failed to attract the lawmakers of the new nation. The committee appointed by the Chamber of Deputies to consider the government's bills reported on June 22, 1861. The twenty-four members of the committee were unanimous in rejecting the region as a decentralized authority; eighteen of the twenty-four voted to reject the Regional Governors as well. The committee feared the region as a danger to the political unity of the country. Unification had not been carried out by the unanimous will of the people: it had been won in spite of strong and widespread resistance and in spite of municipal, provincial, and regional rivalries. To establish the region would provide the opponents of national unity with a framework for agitation; it would help nurture the cult of the past; it would detract from faith in national unity. What was needed was not diversity but unity: a freely elected national assembly would shape nationally uniform institutions in laws which, unlike the fiats of dictators or princes, would be readily accepted.

The committee acknowledged that the 1859 Act had not everywhere been well received but since the attempts to draft a new law on local administration had stirred up such fierce controversy it recommended retention of that act

30. Ibid., pp. 59–60.
31. Ibid., p. 60.

with amendments of detail in the direction of greater decentralization. The provinces, it felt, should be directly
tied to the central government without any regional intermediary authority. As a preliminary to general devolution
of authority the government would be allowed to deconcentrate powers to its representatives in the provinces; to
change the various existing names of these representatives
to that of Prefect, giving each of them the same stipends,
rank, and perquisites so that they could be freely transferred from province to province; and to abolish the post
of Vice-Governor. The committee reported that the Vice-
Governorship arrangement had not worked out well. The
Governors and Vice-Governors had tended to duplicate
each other's activities and to come into conflict with each
other, thereby mutually damaging their prestige. The dualism was consequently a senseless drain on the Treasury.[32]

The outcome of the proposals and public debates on the
region was, then, nothing more than a minor decree of
October 8, 1861, No. 250, which changed to Prefect the
titles of the Governors and Intendants General in the different provinces and to Subprefect that of the Intendants
in the districts. The office of Vice-Governor (and of Secretary General in the Neapolitan provinces) was abolished.

The 1859 Provincial and Communal Act remained in
effect (with its various regional amendments) until 1865
when a general revision could no longer be avoided. To
satisfy anti-Piedmontese sentiment, Rome had been proclaimed the capital of the Kingdom of Italy on March 21,
1861, despite the fact that it still lay under the temporal
power of the Pope and the protection of Napoleon III. But
in September 1864, the Italian government concluded a
convention with the French, agreeing to transfer the capital

32. Ibid., pp. 62–67.

from Turin to Florence as a sign that it had renounced its claim on Rome and had definitively selected Florence as its capital. Turin, in fact, had become eccentric as capital of the new state; it was militarily more vulnerable than more centrally located cities; it lacked the historical and cultural associations of many of the former capitals; and it was the symbol of widely resented Piedmontese hegemony.

Florence had none of these defects but it and the rest of Tuscany still enjoyed a separate provincial and communal law and separate legislation on such matters as public security, public works, and administrative justice—all issued by the provisional government of Tuscany before annexation and still in effect. Before the capital should be moved to Florence, it was felt that all such special arrangements or at least those in essential matters would have to give way to nationally uniform institutions.[33]

The result was the Law on Administrative Unification of March 23, 1865, No. 2248, which contained as appendices a series of nationally uniform laws on provincial and communal administration, public security, public health, the Council of State, administrative justice, and public works. In general, these new laws were only slightly modified versions of the Piedmontese legislation of 1859.

The new Provincial and Communal Act was no exception to this rule.[34] With respect to the 1859 Act, the major innovation was the decentralization to the provinces of responsibilities other than the mere supervision of communal and charitable institutions to which they had been restricted in 1859 under Article 241. The provinces were now required to perform the following services: maintenance of

33. Giuseppe Saredo, *La Nuova Legge sull'amministrazione comunale e provinciale 10 febbraio 1889, no. 5921, commentata con la giurisprudenza* (2d ed. Turin, Unione, 1900–04), *1*, 91.

34. Ibid., pp. 91–95.

the indigent mentally ill; construction and maintenance of public works, such as roads, bridges, dikes, lighthouses, and ports, within the range assigned to the provinces; conservation of woodlands and wildlife; subvention of communal activities; maintenance of monuments and archives; provision of barracks for the Carabinieri and of offices and lodgings for the Prefects and Subprefects; regulation of fairs and markets; establishment and support of charitable institutions and public establishments; and supervision of municipal and charitable institutions. The act also made the provinces responsible for the provision of secondary and vocational education, but this provision was never implemented: education at this level remained either private or state.[35]

The act also authorized the government to modify provincial and district boundaries, but the authorization expired at the end of 1865 without any action having been taken. The government had promised not to use these powers on the eve of general elections.[36]

The formula used in the 1865 Act to define the powers of the Prefect was practically identical to the language of the 1859 Act. The implementing *Regolamento* (approved in Royal Decree of June 3, 1865, No. 2321) did, however, elaborate somewhat on his role. It required him to make an annual report to the Minister of the Interior on the general conditions of the province and its corporate bodies, including the following subjects:

1. financial condition of the communes;
2. regularity of elections and turn-out of voters;

35. Vittorio Alemanni, "Istruzione media," *Il Nuovo Digesto Italiano,* 7 (1938), 333.

36. *Atti Parlamentari, Legislatura IX, Sessione 1865–1866, Senato, Documenti,* No. 14, p. 1.

3. the National Guard and how its service was performed;

4. financial and moral condition of charitable institutions;

5. conditions of public health and cemeteries;

6. public security and mendicity;

7. opening of new roads and upkeep of existing ones;

8. public instruction;

9. industry in general, noting if industrial establishments and factories were increasing or decreasing in number;

10. moral and economic conditions in general of the populations of the cities, towns, and countryside, compared to those of the preceding year, and comparison with the relative ease of exacting taxes;

11. all those other matters which might eventually be indicated by the Minister of the Interior.

It also specified that the result of his vigilance over all the public administrations would normally be a report to the competent minister and, by implication at least, not an attempt to take action directly (short of emergencies). Otherwise, it left the modalities and limits of prefectoral vigilance unspecified and ambiguous, as before.

The Regulations also prescribed the standard internal organization of the prefecture, to be divided into four divisions:

FIRST DIVISION: Secretariat: services for the Prefectoral Council and the Provincial Deputation (in the latter's capacity as tutelage authority over the communes).

SECOND DIVISION: Administration of the "corporate bodies," i.e. of the Province, Communes, and charitable institutions.

THIRD DIVISION: Public security; military service; conscription; public health.

FOURTH DIVISION: State administration, accounting, taxation, and matters not attributed elsewhere.

The fundamental importance of the 1865 Act lay, however, in the fact that it established a highly centralized structure of government in the new kingdom. Within the unitary state, a large share of administrative power and responsibilities was reserved to the central government or its direct agents. The functions decentralized to the provinces and communes were to be exercised under close central supervision and control. Powers of taxation and borrowing were narrowly circumscribed by central laws, regulations, and authorization requirements. The use of local revenues was limited by a lengthy list of compulsory expenditures, many of which had no connection with the institutional objectives of local self-government, such as the provision of office space for national field offices. Autonomy was not proportioned to the population or wealth of the minor units of government: Milan and Naples had to operate within the same limits and under the same controls as tiny Alpine hamlets. The mayors of the communes were appointed by the central government and subject to suspension and dismissal, as well as to hierarchical direction in the exercise of the many powers deconcentrated to them as state officials. The chief of the provincial executive was a central government official. Local councils could be dissolved by the central government "for serious motives of public order."

In several respects, however, there would be less centralization than under the 1859 Act or in neighboring France. Provincial councils enjoyed a wider range of powers and duties than in 1859. The supervision of municipalities was exercised by a locally responsible body, the provincial deputation. The provincial council possessed a standing executive committee (the deputation) to care for provincial interests in the interim between council sessions and to share executive responsibilities with the Prefect. But the system was considerably more centralized than it would have been had the Minghetti bills of 1861 been passed: there were no regional councils exercising powers in such matters as reclamation, irrigation, interprovincial roads and public works, and higher education; mayors were still centrally appointed, rather than elected by the communal councils; communal autonomy was not tied to population; the provinces were not given power in so wide a range of matters (e.g. secondary education, vocational education, and public health).

What then accounts for the choice of a highly centralized form of government for the new nation at the time? The factors are many and varied, though it is impossible to ascertain with precision which elements in the surrounding circumstances were decisive. The less important factors appear to have been the resistance of the central ministries to any loss of power to decentralized agencies (regions, provinces, or communes); a tradition of centralized government in all the former states; insistence upon the equality of provinces and communes and the consequent inability to proportion the devolution of power to population, resources, etc.; the strength of localistic rivalries and the association of *municipalismo* and *campanilismo* (the *campanile* or bell tower is the symbol of local identity and autonomy) with the disunity and political decadence of the past; the ferocity of local political strife and the desire of local minorities for the support and protection of the central government against locally dominant groups; and greater respect for the impartiality, incorruptibility, and competence of national officials than for locally elected officials.[37]

Of greater importance perhaps in the victory of centralization was the conversion of the conservative-liberal ("moderate") cabinets and parliamentary majorities from decentralizing to centralizing ideals during the first years of the decade. The conservative-liberals had long admired the liberal institutions of Great Britain, including the broad devolution of power to locally based (decentralized) authorities. The landowners, professional men, small manufacturers, and artisans—the middle classes that dominated the Parliament—considered themselves the natural rulers of the provinces as well. Power in a decentralized system would, they thought, remain in basically the same hands. The centralized institutions of France were viewed with suspicion as serving the purposes either of Jacobin tyranny or Napoleonic dictatorship. What changed all this was the emergence late in 1860 of what came to be known as the "question of the South."

Unification had been carried out by a middle-class minority; there were strong elements in the country who opposed the new regime or were indifferent to it: the ruling classes of the former states (the legitimists), the clergy (threatened by the extension of Piedmontese conquest of most of the

37. Antonio Troccoli, "L'Amministrazione civile nel pensiero politico italiano," *Amministrazione Civile, 1,* No. 5 (October 1957), 26–29, and No. 7 (December 1957), 21–26.

Papal States), the peasantry (constituting the great bulk of the Italian population), and the dissident Mazzinian democrats and republicans. The liberals feared that the dissident groups would utilize decentralized power to cripple the new political system.

Akin to their fears of legitimist reaction and democratic revolution was a paternalistic distrust (strikingly like that of latter-day colonial powers) of the ability of Italians to govern themselves after centuries of absolutism and foreign domination. Liberals were convinced that the mass of the Italian people required an extensive period of tutelage before qualifying for the exercise of power and responsibility.

All of these fears and suspicions came to a focus with the annexation of the southern regions. Northerners were dismayed with the great disparities between the North and the South in economic conditions, standards of administrative and political conduct, and social structure. In the South, they found no sturdy middle classes such as held sway in the North, but rather an incohesive layer of intermediaries between feudal landlords and an oppressed peasantry. Northern politicians and functionaries became convinced that the depressed conditions of the South were due to centuries of misgovernment; that only vigorous action by a strong central government could rehabilitate the South, develop what they mistakenly considered its natural riches, and stamp out traditions of corruption and laxity in government. They feared to place much power in the hands of the southern middle classes for fear it would be used further to oppress the peasantry. And they realized that this southern middle class was too weak to defend the regime against Bourbon reaction or peasant revolution and required the strong protecting hand of the state. The southern peasants, for their part, had seized the opportunity presented by the collapse of the Bourbon state to destroy land titles and tax records, occupy uncultivated estates, and wreak vengeance on their oppressors. It took almost half of the Italian army five years to repress the civil disorder and brigandage which broke out in the South. The middle classes had won their civil war against the legitimist aristocracies only to find themselves engaged in a second civil war against the peasantry. The centralized state was, thus, in large measure, a response to the threat of social revolution in the South. The French system of centralized administration suddenly found admirers among the conservative-liberals as an instrument for social conservation. Continued toleration of the new state and nonintervention by the major European Powers was conditioned upon the ability of the new state to secure and maintain internal order.

In the face of these imperatives, considerations in favor of decentralization—the desire to have local matters (broadly defined) settled locally by those directly interested and informed; the poor state of communications (there being, at the time of unification, no railways connecting the various former states); the desirability of adjusting policy and administration to the remarkable variety of social structures, types of land tenure, customs, standards of public behavior, levels of wealth and economic development, and systems of legislation and administration through local and regional autonomy—these were relatively impotent. *Gleichschaltung,* the forced creation of unity through administrative pressure as well as through a common parliament became the order of the day.[38]

---

38. Ernesto Ragionieri, "Politica e amministrazione nello stato unitario," *Studi Storici, 1* (1960), 472–512; Caracciolo, pp. 67–100.

THE NATIONAL BUREAUCRACY AND

PREFECTORAL POWER

In a centralized state the organization of the national administration, central and field, is of particular importance; for the burden of government lies not so much on local governments as on the central government and its direct agents in the provinces. Two of the major questions to be settled, then, within the framework of the centralized institutions chosen for the newly unified state, were these: (1) Was the national administration to be relatively deconcentrated? (2) Assuming a minimum degree of deconcentration (i.e. the existence of field services performing some part of national administrative operations), were the various national activities in the provinces to be integrated or coordinated in some fashion within the subdivisions of the national territory?

There would have to be a minimum of deconcentration, if only that minimum involved in the very existence of field services. But beyond this bare existence, how much authority would be devolved upon these services? Some measure of deconcentration would be required to parry the demand for decentralization and to make the unavoidable adaptations of administration to marked variations in local circumstances. Some would be needed to make up for the backward state of communications and for the fact that Italy was now to be governed from one, not seven different capital cities. But conditions were not very propitious for the broad deconcentration of central authority. The new national administration—its organization, staffing, policies, methods—was in a state of ferment. The unsettled conditions of the country and the restlessness of Parliament made ministers hesitant to increase the discretion of field services that had in large part been absorbed from those of the former states and whose reliability was yet to be demonstrated. The prevailing notions and practices were those that had been carried over from the former, much smaller states. And most of the reasons in favor of centralization could be applied with equal force in favor of concentration. The problem might well have appeared to be not how much authority could be deconcentrated without undermining a minimum uniformity in state action in the different provinces, but instead, how little could be deconcentrated without overly exasperating the public and preventing realistic decision-making.

The problem of deconcentration was closely tied to that of areal coordination or integration: both, in fact, involved the role of the Prefect. When measures of deconcentration were discussed in Parliament, they were measures involving the deconcentration of powers to the Prefect. For the Prefect was considered the most reliable state official in the field, an official who could safely be entrusted with the more delicate ministerial powers. And just as the deconcentration of such powers to the Prefect was preferred as an alternative to a regional administrative system and to decentralization, so the Prefect was considered the instrumentality for the areal coordination of national field administration, and the province, its framework. Indeed, only deconcentration to the Prefect (rather than to the various functional service chiefs) would be compatible with the goal of integration.

Probably the first indication of official attention to these problems was contained in the bill to amend the Provincial and Communal Act of 1859 presented by the Minister of the Interior (Peruzzi) to the Chamber of Deputies on April 18, 1864. In redrafting the statement of the Prefect's role, the Minister had inserted the following clause:

He [the Prefect] is subordinate to the Minister of the Interior; but he maintains direct correspondence with all the ministers, and exercises an *assiduous* vigilance over all the public administrations [italics added].

In the accompanying *Relazione,* the Minister declared that the new formation would "open the way towards that aggregation of almost all the public services in the prefectures which the Ministry [Cabinet] intends to carry into effect at an opportune moment."[39]

The Chamber committee which reported June 18, 1864, on this bill noted the new definition as well as the Minister's statement of Cabinet policy and declared itself "unanimous in accepting this concept." It went on to declare that "it would be useful if all the agents of the Government were headed up (*facessero capo*) under a single center fixed in the provinces: nor could this center be created elsewhere than in the Prefect." But, it said, to carry this scheme out, i.e. to concentrate all or almost all the state services in the prefectures, would require sweeping changes in the laws, regulations, and practices that governed the various services—changes it would take some time to prepare. After the appropriate studies had been made, the general reform in the guise of deconcentration of ministerial powers to the Prefects and transfer of services to the prefectures could be actuated. Merely adding a clause to the general statement of prefectoral powers in the Provincial and Communal Act would not mean very much in practice.[40]

39. *Atti Parlamentari, Legislatura VIII, Sessione 1863–1864, Camera, Documenti,* No. 14, p. 1.

40. Ibid., pp. 493–95. The idea was also current in the public writings of the day. See, for example, the work of a retired Inspector General of Finance, Costantino Baer, *Del Riordinamento dello stato in Italia* (Turin, Cerutti, 1865), pp. 60–73. According to Baer, the major defects of Italian

Nothing more appeared about the integration proposal until after the promulgation of the Provincial and Communal Act of 1865. Then, on January 26, 1866, the Minister of the Interior submitted to the Senate a bill that would have abolished the subprefectures, transferred subprefectoral powers to the Prefects, and authorized the government to modify provincial boundaries and to appoint Commissioners in at most thirty subprovincial districts "where and when the topographical conditions, the distance from the [provincial] center, and the state of public security" made some sort of subprefect really necessary.[41] The reporting Senate committee stated as follows in its *Relazione* (February 17, 1866):[42]

---

field administration stemmed from the failure to redraw the provincial boundaries; since these were not usable by many services, those services were resorting to a diversity of intersecting areas, resulting in confusion and conflict among the different branches. Regional offices were inconvenient for the public and they did not permit "daily and easy relations with the Prefects. Our administrative and financial services have been organized in almost complete independence of the Prefects, and this is against the law which established this authority as the *representative* of the executive and as supervisor of the operations of all the public administrations (Article 3, Law of March 30, 1865). If one really wants administrative decentralization, it is necessary to give the Prefect greater authority and means of vigilance over all the financial and administrative services. This increase in power is a necessary guarantee for the central administration which will not have to depend exclusively on its own authorities and employees for information [page 63; italics in the original]." He recommended that the number of provinces be reduced to thirty; that the Prefect be made chairman of all boards and commissions and be given direct authority to approve expenditures from appropriations, to make appointments in the various services, and sign contracts—all on the advice of the field directors; and, finally, that the regional offices be replaced by the prefecture or by provincial offices tied to the Prefect by clearance requirements (pages 64–71).

41. *Atti Parlamentari, Legislatura IX, Sessione 1865–1866, Senato, Documenti*, No. 14, pp. 1–7.

42. Ibid., No. 14–A, p. 2.

> We have reported to the Minister the desire expressed by some committee members to see concentrated in the authority who presides over the province the direction of the various public services, from which by virtue of the present organization he remains totally extraneous. We observed that this concentration will be of absolute necessity once it is desired to put into effect the administrative decentralization so often invoked and promised.

It made no concrete proposal, however, or any appropriate change in the bill. The bill itself did not pass.

When the bill reached the floor of the Senate for debate, Senator Carlo Cadorna rose to make an amendment. Senator Cadorna was a member of the Council of State; he had been Minister of Public Instruction (1848–49) in Piedmont; he had been appointed to the Senate and the Council of State in 1858; in 1864 he had been made Prefect of Turin with the task of pacifying the city after the riots caused by the imminent transfer of the capital to Florence; he had since returned to the Council of State.[43] The amendment he proposed ran as follows:[44]

> Article One. The principal Government services of every kind, except those subject to the authority of the Ministries of Grace and Justice, of War, and of the Navy, are placed in each Province in hierarchical subordination to the Prefects, who shall be subordinate in turn to their respective Ministries.

Since the committee report and previous ministerial declarations had shown support for the idea of placing all the

43. Michele Rosi, *Dizionario del risorgimento nazionale* (Milan, Vallardi, 1930), *1*, 461–62.
44. *Atti Parlamentari, Legislatura IX, Sessione 1865–1866, Senato, Discussioni*, pp. 247–49.

state services in the prefectures and under the Prefect's authority, Cadorna stated, this was the occasion to put the proposal into law. When in the government, he had noted that, in his words,[45]

> each Minister acted absolutely in isolation by himself, independently of any intelligence or accord with the other members of the Cabinet, with the exception of a few matters and special cases . . . Each branch of administration had organized itself with its own employees and offices, from the Minister down to the Mayor, so as to be able always to act in isolation and independently, according to its own desires, principles and intentions.

Thus, there were many different hierarchies under the different ministries, each going its own way and responsive only to its particular hierarchical superiors in the capital. He cited examples in the fields of education, finance, and public works.

Then, he said, there was the Ministry of the Interior, which had the Prefects. "Now the Prefects have everything; that is, they have everything minus all that I have just indicated." What kind of influence or power could the Prefect have, what claim to represent all the ministers, he asked, if three-quarters of the state employees and offices were in independent hands? What kind of prestige could the Prefect enjoy when there were regional authorities in specific fields who could claim superiority on the basis of their vaster territorial jurisdiction?

He proceeded then to show the results of this state of affairs.

The first result was the lack of interministerial coordination. At the capital, the ministries and bureaus did not feel

45. Ibid., p. 247.

the need to collaborate with each other on matters of common interest because each had its own field service to carry out its particular policies. Interministerial coordination could be achieved, however, if[46]

> halfway down the hierarchy there was a ring through which all the administrations had to pass; if in the provincial capital there was an office in which everything was concentrated and which by its very own action had to carry out the ideas, the business, and the orders of all the ministers. Every time that some conflict, some difficulty, some difference in measures arose, this man, in whom would be concentrated the responsibility for all the administrations in the province, would be bound to notify the respective Ministers and to ask for directives; and the Ministers would come to some understanding among themselves.

The second result of what we today might call "disintegration" in the field was[47]

> the immense multiplication of communications and offices . . . Those field directors, independent of the Prefect, and mutually independent, cannot communicate among themselves for all those matters which frequently require their simultaneous concourse, except by means of notes and epistolary correspondence.

This correspondence in turn increased the amount of work to be done and consequently the number of employees. "None of this would happen if those [field offices] were only so many divisions of the same office."

As a third result, "there often occur collisions and conflicts between the various offices, which sometimes rise as

46. Ibid., p. 248.
47. Ibid.

high as the Ministries, and which grow bitter as they rise."
With many independent offices, each with its own director,
"the opportunity for conflict is born at every instant." The
several offices often need to work together: their interde-
pendence opens the way to "disagreements and collisions"
which slow down the handling and settling of matters, weak-
en the Administration, and sometimes paralyze it. If the
various services were all unified under a single authority,
the responsibility for decisions would be his; he would act
upon the advice of the interested services.

In the fourth instance, the existing system was costly because it required a large number of directive officials: these
could be replaced by the Prefect and his staff.

Finally, the system allowed the ministries to act as so
many independent governments; this meant the

> radical permanent weakening of the action of the Gov-
> ernment in the country . . . When the Government
> does not have in the province a strong hand to act with
> vigor, its power is diminished in proportion to the
> weakness of its representative . . . This in the present
> circumstances is really fatal; because if there was ever
> a time in which it was necessary for the Government
> to have force and vigor, energetic and prompt action,
> such is certainly the present.

The solution, then, was clear. It was necessary

> to unify under a single chief all the various adminis-
> trations; to eliminate the heads and the presidents of
> these offices with their staffs; to preserve in each branch
> all those employees who are necessary for the expedi-
> tion of business; and to subject them to the Prefect
> who would be subordinate to the appropriate Ministry
> for each matter. The consequence of this would be

that the appointment of the Prefects would be made by common accord in the Cabinet.

The scheme was not an invention of the speaker, but was to be copied from France. "The organization of the administration in France is a genuine model, and I believe that France owes to the force, vitality and goodness of its administrative organization its having passed unharmed through its hundred revolutions." One had to be cautious, of course, in transplanting institutions, but in this case the institution had proved its worth. Nor was it fitting to object that France was a dictatorship whereas Italy had a constitutional regime: every government required a strong administration. Under a liberal government, the administration would be liberal; under a less liberal government, it would be less liberal.[48]

> What must we do to actuate the system of France? . . . It is necessary to concentrate in the Prefect all the governmental public services in the province . . . Let every Ministry have its employees, but make them subordinate to the Prefect; let every Ministry have separate offices, divisions, or sections, but let them be in the Prefecture and make them subordinate to the Prefect.

The Minister, in reply, declared that the Cabinet agreed in general with the Cadorna proposal although this was not a matter that should be settled in one article of a comparatively minor bill on the subprefectures. In any event, he would have to consult the Ministers of Finance, Public Works, and Public Instruction as directly interested parties.[49] On the following day he announced the Cabinet's

48. Ibid., p. 249.
49. Ibid.

rejection of the Cadorna amendment as such. The amendment, he said, would involve about twenty existing autonomous state services "which naturally want not only to be appreciated, but to be organized in a special way when it is a matter of legislating on this concentration in the Prefectures." These services were under the authority of four different ministers; to reorganize them would involve long study in many areas. One of the major impediments to immediate action, he went on, was that "those who have been occupied with this matter, although persuaded of the utility of concentrating such services in the Prefectures, have posed themselves the very grave question of whether it might be necessary to leave two distinct centers, the administrative center and the financial center." He declined to commit the government on this question. Yet another difficulty lay in the fact that many of these services were not using the province as their administrative area. It would therefore be impossible to accept the amendment without further legislation and regulations for those services. On behalf of the government, however, he accepted a Senate resolution, calling upon the government to prepare the necessary legislation.[50]

With a decree of March 15, 1866, the Minister of the Interior established a commission to prepare a bill providing "for the concentration in the prefectures of public services subordinate to the various ministries."[51] The commission proceeded to conduct a superficial survey of the laws and regulations pertaining to the organization and operations of the Ministries of the Interior, Finance, and Public

50. Ibid., pp. 257, 262.
51. Its report was published as *Notizie raccolte per cura della commissione istituita con decreto del Ministero dell'Interno del 15 marzo 1866 per proporre un progetto di legge pel concentramento nelle prefetture di servizi pubblici dependenti dai vari ministeri* (Florence, 1866).

Works, their field services, and the formal relationships between the various field services and the Prefects. In its published report, the commission made no evaluation of the different services nor of the proposal to concentrate some or all of them in the prefectures, nor did it make any legislative proposals.

The report on the existing legal relationships between the Prefects and the various field services did show clearly, however, that in only one case was the Prefect given relatively effective means of supervising the field service of another ministry—the case of the Ministry of Public Works' civil engineers.[52] In the other cases, with regard to the financial services especially, the Prefect's supervision and influence were remote indeed, given the regional organization of many of the services. The Prefect's authority in public works was probably due to the province's duties in this field and his position as provincial chief executive and to the political character of the field and his position as the "political authority" of the province. Other ministries apparently deconcentrated authority to him (a) when, as in the case of the Ministry of Agriculture, the ministry had no general or special agent of its own to perform the function involved; (b) when the function impinged upon the Prefect's role as chief supervisor of local government, chief of police, and political representative of the government; (c) when a function might be controversial, injure local or private interests and rights, or involve severe penalties; (d) when representatives of local interests were to be appointed to participate in administration and to be guided by a representative of the state; (e) when the success of the program depended on the compliance and cooperation of local governments. In all these cases, the Prefect appeared to be the appropriate agent to use. Otherwise, the ministries preferred to use their own subordinate field officials.

52. Ibid., pp. 350–64.

Prospects for action to promote prefectoral coordination looked bright indeed when Senator Cadorna himself was appointed Minister of the Interior on January 17, 1868. Faithful to his previous commitments, three weeks later on February 8th he presented to the Chamber of Deputies a general bill on the "Reorganization of Central and Provincial Administration."[53]

Presenting the bill, Cadorna declared:[54]

> The administrative power is today represented in the different parts of the territory of the State by a great number of isolated authorities which have no common center or point of contact through which to cooperate toward a single objective. Under each Ministry there are functionaries who are not only independent from each other but obliged to follow directives and criteria which are different, and sometimes opposed. Even the agents and functionaries under the control of a single ministry have no common center from which their action, circumscribed within the territory of the province, can be regulated effectively and with uniformity of outlook.

> To end this state of affairs, it is necessary to constitute in the Prefect a provincial authority who represents all the Government and is vested therefore with broad attributions to watch over the activities of all the administrations of the state.

The Prefects would continue to be appointed by all the ministers sitting as the Council of Ministers. The Prefects would be subordinate to all of the ministers and be bound by ministerial orders within the respective spheres of juris-

53. *Atti Parlamentari, Legislatura X, Sessione 1867–1868, Camera, Documenti,* No. 163.
54. Ibid., p. 7.

diction. Appeals from prefectoral decisions could be lodged with the appropriate minister (although the availability of recourse would have to be limited in the interests of deconcentration). The ministers would deconcentrate broad powers over field operations to the Prefects to the extent compatible with ministerial responsibility for policy and supervision.

Field services were to be reorganized as far as possible into provincial offices; regional offices would be abolished whenever not strictly necessary because they impeded the placing of state services in the prefecture as well as the exercise of prefectoral authority over the services concerned. Some of the regional offices that had been established to ease the transition from several bureaucracies and policies to a single national administration and policy had become little ministries, combining both policy-making and operational power; they had become bottlenecks, remote from the public. In contrast, the prefectures and subprefectures were most accessible to the public. Therefore, the most important regional offices—those in finance—were to be split into offices in the prefectures.

This would increase the pace and simplicity of administration, the ease of communication between the public and provincial offices on the one hand and the ministries on the other, the effectiveness of prefectoral oversight and therefore central control of the field. It would also lead to economies in personnel and office overheads.

The financial offices were to become sections of a financial office in the prefecture. But, said Cadorna,

> one has to distinguish in this matter between the *exercise of authority* and the exercise *of special and responsible functions of administrative management (gestione amministrativa)*.

To the Prefect, representative of the Government in the province, should be attributed in the broadest possible measure the exercise of the authority and the vigilance which belongs to the ministers over the personnel of all the public services, over the way in which they are proceeding . . .

But beyond the exercise of authority and vigilance for which it is desired to confer on the Prefects many important attributions, there is in each province the exercise of *special functions of administrative management* under the authority of the various ministries. And the action of [the Prefect] must, as a rule, stop at that limit, beyond which the freedom and responsibility of the heads of the [field] administrations or directorates which are to be conserved might be damaged . . .

In all this, the criterion must always prevail that the exercise of the authority and vigilance of the Prefects, as representatives of the central administration, with more or less amply delegated powers, shall not at all attenuate the responsibility of the heads of the services themselves, to whom belongs the exercise of administrative management.

An absolute concentration even of this activity in the Prefects has not seemed plausible, at least in the present conditions of the State administration in Italy.[55]

It will be observed how far Cadorna had backed down from his original proposal to place all the services under the general hierarchical control of the Prefects. The exact nature of the relationships between the Prefects and the field directors would be worked out in subsequent regulations.

55. Ibid., p. 10 (italics in the original).

In the case of one field director, the Purveyor of Studies, the Prefect would, however, take over the director's powers; the separate office would be abolished and become a section of the prefecture under complete prefectoral control. For, Cadorna said, the functions of the Prefect and the Purveyor were analogous and, in the course of his normal contacts with local government authorities, the Prefect with his greater power and prestige could better cajole these authorities into fulfilling their educational obligations than could an isolated educational authority.[56]

The Prefect, moreover, would be given the right to appoint, discipline, and dismiss the lower grades of employees in all the state services, i.e. those not normally transferred from province to province, usually upon the advice of the service chief. All field reports on personnel and all central personnel dispositions were required to pass through the prefecture. The Prefect was given "authority" as well as "vigilance" over all the services: he was to keep watch on their activities and address observations and proposals to the competent ministries. Central and regional inspectors were to keep him informed of their plans and reports. He was given authority to order audits and investigations of the operations of all handlers of public funds; to suspend (temporarily) field directors and employees in any state service and take any measures he deemed necessary when such action was justified by "serious reasons"; to keep and transmit with observations the quarterly reports on general operations from the various directors to their ministries.

The bill provided expressly that in the event of conflict

---

56. Here Cadorna was regularizing an already existing situation. By Royal Decree of Oct. 20, 1867, No. 4008, the Prefect was made hierarchical director of state educational officials in the province. The Purveyor's office was located in the prefecture, but the Purveyor was permitted and expected to communicate directly with the Ministry of Public Instruction.

between a Prefect and a central director general, the minister himself was to settle the matter even though it lay formally within the competence of the director general.

The continued existence of regional offices for the customs, postal, telegraph, and lottery services was to be tolerated; all the others were to be abolished and their powers transferred either to the central bureaus or to the new financial office in the prefecture.

The military and the judiciary were specifically exempted from most of the provisions on prefectoral authority.

Two months later, however, on April 18, 1868, the Minister of Finance (Cambray-Digny) submitted to the Chamber of Deputies another bill, allegedly to "complement" the bill of his colleague at the Interior.[57] The new bill concerned the organization of the field services of the Ministry of Finance only. It aimed to unify all the financial field services under a single joint director at the provincial level who was to be, however, not the Prefect but a representative of the Minister of Finance, with the title of Intendant of Finance. (The office, as we have seen, existed in the former Kingdom of Lombardy–Venetia.) The Minister declared his agreement with the principles of the Cadorna bill: the abolition of regional offices in favor of provincial offices under a joint director and the strengthening of the Prefect's power to exercise a "high and effective surveillance" over all public services. But neither his report nor his bill referred to Cadorna's plan to place the financial services in the prefecture. In fact, the Minister declared that the Intendancy of Finance would be second only to the prefecture in prestige and importance among the state offices in the province.[58]

57. *Atti Parlamentari, Legislatura X, Sessione 1867–1868, Camera, Documenti*, No. 186.

58. Ibid., p. 5.

Thus, as the Minister's reply to Cadorna in 1866 might have led one to expect, the major opposition to prefectoral integration had come from the Ministry of Finance.

Since the two bills had much to do with the same thing, the Chamber appointed a single committee to handle them. This committee reported for the first time on July 7, 1868, and presented its own bill which incorporated features of both ministerial proposals.[59] It found, however, in favor of the Intendant of Finance: the financial services were to be integrated, and at the provincial level, but under a senior official of the Ministry of Finance. On the other hand, the Intendant would not be completely independent of the Prefect, for the committee, too, agreed with the idea of a stronger Prefect, declaring,

> We have allowed to the Prefect, with very few changes, the greater attributions proposed by [the Minister of the Interior] and *we would have allowed even more if we had not received the completely contrary replies from the other ministers, expressly interpellated* [italics added].

The committee decided upon a form of dual authority which it expressed in the following formula:

> The Intendants, for all which regards the financial service, rigorously such, take orders from and report to the Minister of Finance and the Director-Generals. But being hierarchically subordinate [in rank] to the Prefect and given the Prefect's right of high vigilance over their offices, it is indispensable, in cases of urgency and when taking decisions of the highest importance,

59. Ibid., Nos. 163–A, 186–A.

that they [the Intendants] refer to the Prefect; and that the Minister and the Director-Generals of the financial services inform him directly of all dispositions which may influence the general economic and political situation of the localities placed under him.

Again, however, the specific nature of the Intendant's relationships with the Prefect would be left to the implementing regulations.[60]

The committee's bill was given considerable attention by the Chamber in debates over a five-month period, from December 1868 to April of the following year.[61] In the end, however, no final legislative action was taken.

On the basis of the support shown for the idea during the debates, however, the Minister of Finance secured Cabinet approval for the creation of the Intendants of Finance by executive decree. In his *Relazione* to the King, requesting promulgation of the decree, the Minister outlined the reasons for their establishment as follows. The existing regional offices in finance were not convenient for the public; they had little control of the operating offices outside of their particular province; they were slow in handling claims; they were located in different cities so that taxpayers of a given province might have to travel to different cities for different matters; they meant that twenty provinces had no financial directive office whatsoever. With the creation of the Intendancies, there would be greater

60. Ibid., p. 4.
61. See the fuller report of the same committee of Dec. 1, 1868, Document No. 163–C, 186–C. Cadorna by this time had resigned, partly because of the refusal of the Cabinet and Parliament to accept his ideas. The debate can be found in the *Atti Parlamentari, Legislatura X, Sessione 1867–1868, Camera, Discussioni*, Dec. 8–12, 14–20 (1868); Jan. 13, 14, 18–20; Feb. 1, 2, 17; March 2–6, 13, 15, 19; April 13 (1869).

discipline and efficiency in the financial services; the four interested bureaus would work through 68 (with Rome, 69) provincial offices rather than through a more costly set of 144 regional offices in the various branches; directive offices would be close to the public and to the various operating offices; and there could now be close coordination with the Prefects, especially in matters of direct taxation.

The Minister omitted an argument that he had used during the debates in the Chamber: the Intendant of Finance was necessary if the Minister was to combat the tendency of the central financial bureaus to become self-sufficient, independent governments within the government.

The Intendant of Finance became, aside from the Prefect, the only example of a general representative of a minister, stationed in the field with direct responsibility for all the services of his ministry. It is of some interest, therefore, to examine exactly the Intendant's initial position vis-à-vis not only the Prefect, but also the services directly under his authority.

The Royal Decrees of September 26 and December 18, 1869, Nos. 5286 and 5397, which established and organized the Intendancies, endowed the Intendant with considerable authority over the operating services in the province—authority that the Prefect himself enjoyed only with respect to the Interior's services in the province. The powers of all the existing field directors in finance, that is, the authority to make the major decisions in each branch (except that of the bureaus themselves) were conferred directly upon the Intendant. All financial offices within the province were explicitly placed under his hierarchical authority. His authority and responsibility were stated as follows: "The direction of [all financial] business is entrusted to the Intendant who is responsible for the performance of all the branches of the administration." The field inspectors for the different branches of the service were placed on his staff and under his authority: through them, he was to exercise direction and supervision of the operating offices in the different branches.

Only two exceptions were made: the directors of the customs and fiscal monopolies (salt and tobacco) offices were maintained, and they were permitted to retain some of their former direct authority; otherwise they lay under the Intendant's general authority. Secondly, the regional inspectors of the cadastral survey, responsible for ensuring uniformity of service within their compartments, were directly subordinated to their bureau (direct taxation) in the ministry: they were located, however, in an Intendancy and depended on an Intendant for auxiliary services. Aside from these particular services—with their peculiar requirements as regards territorial jurisdiction—the Intendant had practically absolute control of the operating offices of all the bureaus of the ministry.

The Intendant himself was, however, subject to a certain amount of prefectoral control. The pertinent provisions of the December Regulations ran as follows:

The Intendant of Finance

(a) must in cases of urgency for matters exceeding his attributions have recourse to the Prefect of the Province and carry out the latter's instructions;

(b) must also address himself to the Prefect in any case which requires the use of the public forces;[62]

62. Between March 1868 and these decrees, there had been nationwide bloodshed, involving over 250 deaths and nearly four thousand arrests, following the adoption and enforcement of the hated grist tax. One of the Prefects' major tasks was to suppress these and subsequent tax riots. On this point, see Emilio Sereni, *Il capitalismo nelle campagne (1860–1900)* (Turin, Einaudi, 1958), pp. 108–12.

(c) transmits through the Prefect his annual report on the state of the services;

(d) notifies the Prefect of the entrance into service of his subordinates and of any change thereof, and gives the Prefect, upon request, the necessary information about them;

(e) informs the Prefect of any matters and warns him of any decisions which may affect public order;

(f) reports to the Prefect on such matters as requested;

(g) defers to the authority of the Prefect in the cases provided for by the laws and regulations and when ordered to do so by the Ministry;

(h) submits to the Prefect's approval the names of the persons outside of the financial administration whom he intends to employ in the service of the Intendancy or its subordinate offices, or to appoint as members of boards;

(i) proposes to the Ministry through the Prefect those persons not his own subordinates for honors;

(j) proposes through the Prefect changes in the locations and territorial jurisdictions of the offices or in the formation of inter-communal consortia; the Prefect transmits these with his observations to the Ministry;

The Prefect may always under his own responsibility suspend the issuance or execution of those orders of the Intendant which he believes may compromise public order, reporting this immediately to the Ministry of Finance.

The formative period in the history of Italian field administration concluded with the creation of the Intendancy of Finance. The basic pattern had been chosen and established. That pattern, like all patterns of field administration, had both functional and areal elements.

It was functional in that ministries and bureaus tended to have their own agents in the field and to have complete authority over them. The lines of command and accountability as well as the lines of communication ran directly between the functional units at the center and their counterparts in the field. The functional offices in the field did not depend on the area generalist, the Prefect, for administrative support: they were not located in the prefecture nor did they use its clerical, fiscal, or custodial personnel. The central functional units supervised their field counterparts directly by means of inspectors often stationed permanently in the field. The functional field offices enjoyed powers that were directly delegated by their central superiors or directly conferred by statute, subject in these matters only to the authority of their central superiors. Ministries and bureaus, moreover, tended to select the administrative areas most convenient for the performance of their particular tasks. Often these areas did not coincide with those used by the Prefects.

Yet the pattern was far from being a purely functional one. For each part of the national territory, there was a general representative of all the ministers who was appointed, assigned, and dismissed by their collective decision. This representative, the Prefect, performed tasks deconcentrated from all the departments, took orders from and reported to all of them. He was among the most senior officials of the state: in rank and prestige, he was rivaled in the field only by the military and the judiciary. He was equal in rank to the directors general, the heads of the major functional subdivisions of the ministries. He was responsible for the general oversight of all the officials of the state who operated within his territorial jurisdiction and could report his observations to their functional superiors. In emergencies, he could supersede the specialist field directors in the exercise of their powers. As the political representative of the government, the chief of police, and the supervisor of local government, he had unique sources of information on provincial conditions and interests and would tend to press for their recognition by the central functional departments; his concerns were general, not specialized; and he provided the minimum conditions of health, safety, and welfare to permit the specialized services to operate.

That there would be some form of prefectoral system was never apparently brought into question. The extent of prefectoral power was, on the contrary, a controversial variable. And out of the controversy emerged a Prefect substantially weaker than the Neapolitan Intendant or the Napoleonic Prefect. The reasons seem to be these:

1. The liberal ideology of the ruling groups was not favorable to the accumulation of power in a single provincial official of the vice-regal or proconsular type. The liberalism that removed executive powers from Prefects and mayors and transferred them to collegial executives carried over into the organization of the state administration, overcoming authoritarian desire for a powerful solitary representative of the state in the province.[63]

2. Cabinet government, with individual as well as collective responsibility to the legislature, and vesting each department head with equal status, encouraged the tendency for each minister to create autonomous, self-sufficient instruments for the discharge of his own particular responsibilities. Individual ministers, supported and perhaps

63. See, e.g., the remarks of Bembo in the above debate, p. 8358.

stimulated by their officials, were reluctant to surrender control of their field services to an agent over whom they had much less immediate and complete control than they had over the ministry's particular agents in the field.[64]

3. A related but distinct factor was the preoccupation to create clear lines and spheres of responsibility and the anticipation of difficulties in arranging such lines and spheres as among the central bureaus, their counterparts in the field, and the Prefect. A system of dual authority would mean blurred responsibility and conflict.[65]

4. It was also felt that the functional field services, such as the financial ones (but not apparently civil engineering), required expert direction and full-time coordination if the technical complexities were to be mastered. The Prefect lacked special training or competence in financial policy and administration; he lacked the expertise of the central bureaus or their representatives. As a nonexpert, therefore, he should not, many felt, be allowed to interfere with the work of those particularly qualified.[66]

5. The Prefect, moreover, was tied to the province as the head of its executive. Some services required operations on an interprovincial scale. If the Prefect was allowed to interfere with the work of regional offices, he would encroach on the domains of his fellow Prefects.[67]

6. The Prefect had many tasks to perform on behalf of his own ministry, the Interior, and would not have time to devote to the affairs of other ministries, certainly not enough to provide the amount of direction required by the

64. See the underlined statement in the committee report, quoted above, p. 110.

65. See the remarks of Bembo, pp. 8358–59; Lampertico, p. 8381; and Piccoli, p. 9154.

66. See the remarks of Bembo and Piccoli, pp. 8358–59 and 9154.

67. See the remarks of the Minister of Public Works, p. 9439.

financial services. He might neglect some of his responsibilities in favor of others.[68]

7. The Prefect was a political official; he was the government's electoral agent. As a political official, he was transferred too often to provide sufficient stability in local administration. And he might well introduce political criteria into administration.[69]

8. The drive for national uniformity was stronger than consideration for the special claims of particular areas. Local customs and interests were to be ignored, to be leveled out. National policies and obligations were to be imposed throughout the new nation over and against local demands for special treatment. If Prefects were given greater authority, policies would vary from province to province with the amount and direction of prefectoral intervention. Prefects would be more susceptible to local pressures than functional specialists; the latter, it was contended, would tend to have a more national, professional outlook.[70]

9. Programs administered in the field by directors with the prestige and authority of heads of independent offices would be more successful than those managed by mere heads of prefectoral divisions. It would be easier to recruit eminent or talented specialists if they could be promised the status of independent office head.[71]

10. There was an alternative method of integration or coordination—full-time coordination by specialists (such as the Intendants of Finance) of groups of closely interrelated services.

11. The relationships between the Prefect and the vari-

68. See the remarks of Pepe, p. 9828, and Piccoli, p. 9154.
69. See the remarks of Bembo, pp. 8358–59, and Alfieri, pp. 8365–66.
70. See the remarks of Bembo, pp. 8358–59.
71. See the remarks of Piccoli, p. 9154.

ous functional services should, it was thought, be regulated from time to time and from case to case rather than in any across-the-board determination once and for all. The extent of prefectoral authority could be adjusted in detail to suit the particular needs of the time and the field service concerned.

Chapter Three

THE LIBERAL REGIME (1870–1922)

THE "PREFECTOCRACY"

THE PREFECTS ASSUMED such an important role in the political system of the new state that that system has been described as being a "prefectocracy."[1]

Under the Piedmontese *Statuto* of 1848, the absolute power of the Crown had been fragmented among various elements: the Crown itself, the Council of Ministers, a royally appointed Senate, and a popularly elected Chamber of Deputies. The King retained considerable constitutional power as chief of the executive and commander-in-chief of the armed forces, with power to appoint and dismiss the ministers, to declare war, to appoint the members of the Senate, and to issue decrees with the force of law. In the first decades after unification, however, he ceased to preside over the Cabinet and most of his executive powers were assumed by the Council of Ministers responsible to Parlia-

1. Gaetano Salvemini, *Il Mondo*, 5, No. 19 (May 11, 1954), 3.

ment. The King held on to much influence in the realms of foreign and defense policy and, given the fluidity of political organization within Parliament, he continued to enjoy great latitude in the selection of Prime Ministers. The Senate was another vehicle of royal power but, although it had legislative powers equal to those of the Chamber of Deputies, it could not compel the resignation of a Cabinet that had lost its confidence. The Cabinet, moreover, could and often did pack the Senate with its supporters, the King invariably consenting to this use of the royal prerogative.

Most constitutional power, then, lay with the Council of Ministers and with the Chamber of Deputies elected by the prosperous literate subjects of the King in about 400–500 constituencies.

The narrowness of the franchise, the Papal prohibition of Catholic political participation at the national level, and the alienation of the partisans of the former dynasties combined to produce an electorate that was in substantial agreement so that, until the emergence of socialism, there were no organized national political parties but only shifting amorphous coalitions of regional, personal, and ideological factions. Under the Electoral Law of March 30, 1865, No. 2248, only about two per cent of the population was given the right to vote in national elections and of this privileged group only about half actually went to the polls. Among the restricted interests represented in the Chamber —largely those of the landowning, commercial, and professional classes—there were no fundamental economic or ideological cleavages to serve as the bases for broad partisan differentiation. The political class of the new Italy was largely united behind policies of economic laissez faire, social conservatism, and anticlericalism.[2]

2. Smith, *Italy*, pp. 61–99; Luzzatto, *Elezioni politiche*, pp. 72–73, 289; and Herman Finer, *Mussolini's Italy* (London, 1935), pp. 81–82.

The absence of organized disciplined parties with fixed programs accounts for the relatively short life of most governments. There were some seventy-six governments in the seventy-four years between 1848 and 1922. Most cabinets rested upon highly volatile alliances of parliamentary factions. A few talented Prime Ministers, however, such as Agostino Depretis (1876–87), Francesco Crispi (1887–96), and Giovanni Giolitti (1901–11), managed to construct fairly stable coalitions and to dominate Italian political life in these periods through the manipulation of elections and the judicious distribution of government patronage. The political struggle, then, became a battle not between national parties with definite programs but between government supporters—the *ministeriali*—and their equally heterogeneous opponents—the *antiministeriali*—in each of the hundreds of election districts.

Almost invariably the Prime Minister assumed also the ministerial portfolio of the Interior, for control of the Prefects was essential to the maintenance of power and too dangerous, therefore, to be left in the hands of another minister.

The Prefects played the leading role in the manufacture of parliamentary majorities. On the eve of elections, they received funds from the ministry and instructions as to which candidates were to be favored and which fought. The Prefects retained the unspent portion of these funds as personal income.[3]

They then proceeded to mobilize the government's standing electoral machine in the constituencies: the Subprefects; other state employees, who could be threatened with transfer or promised promotion; state pensioners, per-

3. Amedeo Nasalli Rocca, *Memorie di un prefetto* (Rome, Mediterraneo, 1946), p. 213.

haps 25 per cent of the electorate, whose pensions might be cut off; mayors, other locally elected authorities, and their allies, who required prefectoral protection or state grants-in-aid; and local notables, susceptible to bribery and other forms of inducement, such as decorations and senatorial appointments. In the existing small constituencies, it was not difficult for the Prefect to strike bargains with the dominant cliques for support of the *ministeriali* in exchange for government favors, such as schools, contracts, and railway concessions.

The *antiministeriali,* on the other hand, could be bribed and intimidated. Opposition mayors could be suspended and their councils dissolved so that the local government patronage could be distributed by the Prefect. Opposition meetings could be banned, their organizations dissolved, their press temporarily muzzled.

The Prefect had to adapt his strategy and tactics to the particular area in which he was stationed. The same procedures could not be used in all parts of the country. In the South and Islands, for example, he could use a varied mixture of bribery, promises, intimidation, and compulsion— sometimes even murder—to achieve his ends. In a generally impoverished region where power was in the hands of small bands of landowners and their dependents, support could be bought rather cheaply. The prevailing standards of public morality, inherited from the Spanish and Bourbon regimes, were not unduly restrictive of the range of permissible behavior. It was the South and Islands, then, which, being relatively more dependent on the favor of Rome, regularly provided a numerous band of "ministerials"— no matter what happened to be the complexion of the government of the day.

In the northern and central regions, the standards of

official behavior were higher. Here the Prefect had, at the very least, to use greater discretion.[4]

The Prefects, however, had to keep the system going between elections as well. This they did by directing and channeling the regular traffic in support and patronage between the government and the deputies upon which the Italian parliamentary system was based. The basic principle of that system was summed up in the following formula: "It is necessary for our ministers to have complaisant Prefects, for complaisant Prefects to have corrupt voters, and corrupt voters to have productive deputies."[5]

Prefects were besieged by demands from government supporters for public works, roads, and other legitimate administrative satisfactions. But they were also required by ministers and deputies to commit and condone illegalities, to discriminate among citizens according to the latter's politics, to enforce the law according to the momentary convenience of the minister and his friends.[6]

The increasing interpenetration of politics and administration, with administrators determining elections and politicians determining minor administrative decisions, led to a widespread condemnation of "parliamentarism." Critics complained that the Prefect was not "a high magistrate, subordinate exclusively to the law, defended against arbitrary ministerial action, and against parliamentary and electoral interference."[7] The demand for "justice in ad-

4. On prefectoral election strategy and tactics, see Nasalli Rocca; Teodosio Marchi, "Gli uffici locali nell amministrazione generale dello stato," in Orlando, *Primo Trattato*, 2 (1907), 212–16; Gaetano Mosca, *Teorica dei governi e governo parlamentare* (2d ed. Milan, 1925), pp. 196–97.

5. It should not be assumed that the Italian political system was at all unique in these respects. Comparable practices could be found in all or most constitutional regimes of the time.

6. Marchi, pp. 212–16, and Smith, *Italy*, pp. 199–200.

7. Marchi, p. 211; see also, *inter alia*, Caracciolo, pp. 101–52.

ministration"[8] was therefore often coupled with a vain demand for prefectoral independence from the government.[9]

But the absolute dependence of the Prefects on the central government was a vital part of the whole system and an essential feature of any prefectoral system that must ensure the representativeness of the government's agents in the provinces. The Jacobin ideology underlying the system was expressed by Prime Minister Crispi thus:[10]

> Since each Prefect has to represent in his province the totality of the powers of the central government, each province must have a Prefect who is the interpreter, the echo of the concepts of the central government. And since the central government is the interpreter of the ideas of the legislative assembly, there must be harmony between the one who legislates and the one who administers.

And it was found that career Prefects could perform the necessary partisan roles just as dependably as politicians. Successive governments did not find it necessary (even if legally possible) to turn out of office the Prefects of the former government and to replace them with their own supporters. They found the career Prefects to be sufficiently reliable, agile, and responsive to changing political circumstances. Few political Prefects had to be appointed, usually only in the major cities of the kingdom, and these would resign after a change in the cabinet, or be dismissed, or even be allowed to serve in some other post as a more or less permanent addition to the prefectoral career service. Most

8. This is the title of a famous work by Silvio Spaventa, *La Giustizia nell'amministrazione* (Turin, Einaudi, 1949).

9. Marchi, pp. 204–05.

10. *Atti Parlamentari, Legislatura XVI, Sessione 1886–1887, Camera, Discussioni*, p. 4466.

of the political Prefects were members of Parliament, although a very few were taken from the army, especially during periods of internal disorder, or from other state administrations.[11]

The responsiveness of the career Prefects was determined by several factors. They were recruited initially from the same classes that dominated the political institutions, and shared with ministers and deputies a community of outlook and interest. Prefectoral posts offered considerable prestige and power, rivaling posts in the military and diplomatic services in attractiveness to the nobility and upper middle classes. An increasing number of Prefects, however, had no independent livelihood and might fear an untimely retirement from the service. There were, on the other hand, significant rewards for faithful service such as promotion to increasingly prominent and influential prefectures or to the Council of State, the Court of Accounts, or (after seven years) to the Senate.

In the long climb from the lower ranks of the prefectoral career, aspirants were constantly reminded of the need for discovering the pleasure of ministers and deputies if they were to secure a prefectoral appointment before retirement. And once appointed, they made every effort to find out the wishes of the minister and the ministerial deputies before making decisions of any consequence. To prevent Prefects from establishing permanent or entangling alliances with the local ministerial deputies so as to resist transfer, they were rotated with great frequency before such alliances could be consolidated.

Thus if there was relative stability in the composition of the prefectoral corps, there was great instability in assign-

11. Marchi, pp. 212–13. The last major purge of the prefectoral corps took place in 1876 and is described in Silvio Spaventa, *Lettere politiche* (Bari, Laterza, 1926), pp. 139–46.

ments. In a ten-year period, there would be something like six different Prefects in a given province, and sometimes as many as ten or twelve. Tours of duty tended to last only one or two years.[12] Transfers or movements, sometimes involving all or nearly all prefectures, permitted new cabinets to adjust assignments to the shifts in national political orientation. Prefects who had been deeply committed to the old line could be transferred to provinces where they could start out with a clean slate. Before transfer, however, their appointments would be cleared with the local MPs and, during their stay, they would remain under the politicians' constant surveillance. The government could manipulate such movements to secure support or to neutralize opposition, threatening, for example, to appoint a fiery anticlerical Prefect to a pious province if the bishop did not support the ministerial candidates. Thus prefectoral administration was not only partisan, it was highly unstable.[13]

THE PREFECT AND LOCAL GOVERNMENT

Centralization—the allocation of governmental power in favor of the central government and intensive central controls over the lesser units of government—was an essential part of the political system. It provided the central government with a large share of the kinds of administrative satisfactions and penalties that could be bartered for legislative support and that deputies could, in turn, translate into electoral support.

The weakness of local governments, however, was relative; they still constituted important bases for local political

12. Smith, *Italy*, p. 200. For extensive data on prefectoral tours of duty, see the *Atti Parlamentari, Legislatura XIX, Sessione 1896–1897, Camera, Stampati*, No. 211–A, pp. 10–16.

13. Nasalli Rocca, passim.

leadership; they possessed some significant powers and duties in their own right, and since they were thus in a position to influence national elections, they could bargain with the central government for aid or protection. Despite repeated and widespread public commitments to decentralization and attacks on centralization as one of the major causes of "parliamentarism" and partisanship in administration, progress toward decentralization was slow and relatively limited in scope. The central government and its majorities were hesitant to surrender their power.

A major step in the direction of greater local autonomy was finally taken in 1889 when the local government or "administrative" electorate was enlarged to include about eleven per cent of the population as compared to about four per cent in 1865.[14] The same Consolidated Provincial and Communal Act (*Testo Unico* of February 10, 1889, No. 5921) provided for the election of mayors by the city councils of the larger communes. (The electoral principle was extended to the mayors of all communes by the Law of July 29, 1896, No. 346.) Crown appointment of mayors had been a major source of leverage in bargaining with local interests and it was abandoned with great reluctance.[15]

The same act removed the Prefect from headship of the provincial deputation and replaced him with a president elected by the deputation itself. But, as a corollary measure, the deputation's supervisory powers over communal government and public charities were transferred to a new body, the *Giunta Provinciale Amministrativa* (literally: provincial administrative junta) or GPA, a board chaired by the Prefect but with representation of local interests. It was felt that without the strong guidance of the Prefect as chair-

14. Luzzatto, p. 289.

15. Giuseppe Carocci, *Agostino Depretis e la politica interna italiana dal 1876 al 1887* (Turin, 1956), p. 475.

man, the provincial deputation could not be trusted to exercise tutelage powers on behalf of the state. But instead of the prefectoral council, which had no local representation and whose members were often too transient to be sufficiently acquainted with local interests, and instead of the courts, which were ill adapted to the largely political functions to be exercised, the legislature turned to a new type of body which provided representation of both local and central government interests.[16] Such boards were to become increasingly common in the next few decades.

Composed of the Prefect (chairman), two prefectoral functionaries, and four members (i.e. a majority) elected by the provincial council (until 1915) from outside of its own membership, the GPA assumed the power to rule on the *merits* of the major financial decisions of the province, the communes, and charitable institutions. It could veto such decisions, however, only after permitting the institution involved to state its case. Its vetoes could be appealed to the Minister of the Interior. It could reject new or increased communal taxation; it could refuse to sanction municipal budgets and require the drafting of more acceptable ones; it could deny requests to contract loans; it could veto schemes to municipalize public utilities; it could remedy the inertia of local authorities, such as their failure to pay employees or creditors, by superseding them in the exercise of their powers; under the direction of the Ministry of Finance, it set the minimum and maximum rates of local taxation and adjudicated appeals from local tax assessments.

The Prefect was left with the general power to veto the

16. Marchi, pp. 417–91; Gabriele Amendola, "La Provincia," pp. 100–01; Arnaldo De Valles, "Giunta provinciale amministrativa," *Il Nuovo Digesto Italiano*, 6 (1938), 345–46.

decisions of the province, municipalities, and charities only on grounds of illegality.[17]

The removal of the Prefect from the headship of the province *qua* semi-autonomous minor unit of government represented a departure from the prevailing Western European prefectoral systems, such as the French, the Belgian, and the Scandinavian, in which the prefect or governor is not only the representative and agent of the central government but also the chief executive of a distinct and semi-autonomous provincial self-government, and the prefecture serves not only for the purposes of central government administration but also to execute the policies of the provincial council.

With the establishment of a separate executive for the provincial council in the form of the president elected by the council to head the provincial deputation in the Prefect's stead, the province became a completely distinct unit of government with its own offices and staff completely separate from those of the Prefect, and outside of the prefecture. The prefecture and its staff became the servants exclusively of the state. The president of the provincial council and provincial deputation, rather than the Prefect, now directed the work of the provincial council, prepared and executed the province's budget, negotiated its contracts, regulated its personnel, and represented it in court. Now both the provincial council and the communal council elected their own chief executives and executive committees. But unlike the mayor, the president of the province did not become both chief executive of the province and state official: he remained only chief executive of the province, while the Prefect remained the general-purpose state official at the provincial level.

17. Marchi, p. 265.

Shortly after the GPA was created, Crispi put through another major reform, this time in the field of administrative justice, and in response to the demand for "justice in administration." Under the Law of May 1, 1890, No. 6807, the GPA (composed in this case of the Prefect, two councillors, and only two of the nominees of the provincial council, chosen by the Prefect) became the field agency of the newly created section of the Council of State that was established as the highest administrative tribunal. To the GPA *in sede giurisdizionale* (i.e. *qua* tribunal) were deconcentrated the judicial powers of the Fourth Section of the Council of State in matters concerning local government litigation.

The judicial functions of the GPA were considered originally as merely one part of its supervision of municipalities; but as a court of law, the GPA left something to be desired. Dominated by the Prefect, the GPA tribunal lacked the necessary independence from the executive power; nor did it always provide particularly competent judges.[18]

In any case, the GPA was just one instance in which the provincial council and deputation were systematically bypassed and weakened in favor of ad hoc prefectoral boards or committees.

The provinces as units for local self-government seldom became vital organisms. The obligatory functions of the provinces were limited to the maintenance of provincial roads (39 per cent of all roads) and care for the mentally ill and for foundlings. They lost the right to supervise municipal and charitable institutions. Powers that might have been devolved upon them were given instead to prefectoral boards or committees on which the provincial council had some, but gradually diminishing, representation, to the

18. De Valles, pp. 347–50.

chambers of commerce, or to state field offices such as the state labor inspectorates (1911), or to the provincial health office (a state office in the prefecture).

Provinces varied greatly in territory, population, and wealth, and the smaller, poorer provinces were incapable of performing even their existing functions satisfactorily. This inequality was aggravated by the tendency of the state to use the province as a convenient taxing device, i.e. to require the province to use its taxation powers to pay for matters formerly, or more properly, financed by the state itself. The list of compulsory provincial expenditures tended to grow as did the proportion of the list devoted to such matters as the provision of space for state field offices.[19]

Only the wealthier provinces were able to provide more services and contribute to the financing of other administrative ventures: they subsidized municipal, intercommunal, and charitable activities, the construction and maintenance of secondary schools. Some directly assumed the task of providing public utility services. Most were too poor to take on additional administrative functions, too weak politically to secure programs of state aid.[20]

Given the deficiencies of many provincial authorities, the expansion of state functions led to the creation of numerous ad hoc prefectoral committees, sometimes merely advisory, but sometimes with decision-making powers. In most cases, the composition of these committees reflected a desire to combine representation of local interests with the expertise of state technical officials and the policy guidance of the Prefect. Such boards were effective instruments for the adjustment of national policies in a growing number of fields to the particular needs and desires of the different

19. Amendola, pp. 106–89; Bolton King and Thomas Okey, *Italy Today* (2d ed. New York, Scribners, 1913), p. 268.
20. Amendola, p. 158.

provinces, yet under fairly close central control. Representation of local interests tended to decline as such boards came to handle more technical matters (as for example on the provincial health board).

The committees served to advise the Prefect on technical matters, on local reactions to national policies, and on local conditions in general. They also served to transmit national or prefectoral policy to the interested provincial groups. As the representation of state officials increased on these committees, the committees came increasingly to be dominated by their chairman, the Prefect. The staff work for the committees was performed by the prefecture.[21]

The most vital decentralized units of government, then, were the communes, which now had elective mayors and somewhat broader electoral bases in the community. Unlike the provinces, the communes did have important functions to perform in such varied fields as education, sanitation, poor relief, public works, and taxation. But their ability and willingness to exercise these functions was sharply limited by central government laws and regulations that made no distinction between urban and rural communes, between Naples, Rome, or Milan and remote mountain villages; by the increasing use of the communes by the state as taxation agencies to finance state activities and by the state's appropriation to itself of communal revenue sources in order to balance its own budget; by the lack of taxable resources in the poorer regions; by the negligence, lethargy, corruption, and financial extravagance of communal officials who enjoyed the protection of ministerial deputies; and by the dependence of many, if not most, communes on state aid.

The formal equality of communes stultified the enter-

21. Marchi, pp. 257–58; Amendola, pp. 103–60.

prise of the larger ones, while the provision for voluntary, and sometimes compulsory, intercommunal *consorzi* or associations was not particularly effective in compensating for the financial weakness of the smaller, rural local authorities.

The Prefect exercised his formal powers and informal political influence to control local governments according to the requirements of national politics, as interpreted by the Minister of the Interior and the "ministerial" deputies in the province. National politicians were usually closely allied to the factions contending for control of the province and its communes: it was the Prefect's job to ensure that the ministerial faction secured and maintained control, by rigging the elections and by promising and supplying state aid and protection to friendly factions. He harrassed the opponents by denying or cutting off state aid, investigating their administration, dissolving councils that they dominated, and appointing commissioners to run the communes or province until new elections and a more favorable outcome could be arranged.

The desire of national government officials and legislators to maintain centralization as a pillar of the political system and their unwillingness to remedy the weaknesses of local units of government resulted eventually in the assignment of the new, largely social and economic welfare functions to the central government.[22]

THE PREFECT AND THE STATE FIELD SERVICES

During the debate on the 1888 local government bill (which became the Consolidated Act of 1889), Senator Allievi, himself a former Prefect, described the existing relationships

22. Carlo Morandi, *La Sinistra al potere* (Florence, 1944), pp. 115–16; King and Okey, pp. 268–70; Amendola, pp. 189–219.

between the Prefect and the state field service and called for reform:[23]

> The Prefect . . . should be effectively and is [now] only in name the head of all the public security and the organ of the Ministry of the Interior. The financial offices, the offices of the Civil Engineers, the many inspectors of the Ministry of Agriculture and Commerce communicate directly with their respective ministries and act almost independently of the Prefect.
>
> It is correct to say [however] that neither the Prefect, nor these local officers of the other ministries can do anything in our administrative system. They have only authority to inform and to refer, but they do not decide anything.
>
> Everything depends on the approval of the Central Administration which approves [the appointments of] even the porters of the prefectures and police stations, which decides to award a gratuity of ten lire to an employee.
>
> There is no possible comparison, sirs, with the Prefect of the French administration. The latter is truly the chief of all the public services of the Province or Department. Within certain legal limits, he has authority to make contracts, authorize works, order payments; all the branches of the Administration are subordinate to him.
>
> He reports every day to his minister and the Court of Accounts, if money is involved, on the operations he performs under his own responsibility.
>
> Once the state budget is voted by Parliament, credits are opened for each Prefect to dispose of within the

23. *Atti Parlamentari, Legislatura XVI, Sessione 1887–1888, Senato, Discussioni,* pp. 2899–2900.

limits of the law and the general directives of the Minister.

In these conditions the [French] Prefect has really some power and consequently responsibility, and may truly represent the Government . . .

[Some Italian Prefects are influential in their provinces] but this they owe to their personal qualities, more than to the quality of the the office. Intellectual and personal superiority confers on them an ascendancy which does not derive from their functions.

The populations are in most cases unaware that there exists an on-the-spot representative of the Government, the Prefect. The representative of the Government is reduced to being a mere consultant, almost a passive agent.

If they want to be conscientious, the Prefects have to tell a citizen who wants a tobacco outlet concession or a humble employee who wants a promotion: write to your deputy because in this way you will be more successful.

Prime Minister Crispi, in his reply, admitted that[24]

the present system is not complete. In general, it is said the Prefects represent the executive power, but in reality they do not exercise all the powers which they would need to ensure regularity in the public services and (what is more important) without having to invoke at every instant the authority of the minister.

The Prefect must be the mandatory of all the central administration. The Ministry [Cabinet] must have in him its legal representative, except for judicial matters; a law is necessary for this and we will try to pre-

24. Ibid., pp. 2902–03.

pare one as soon as possible to complete the governmental organization of the province.

I must declare that, in general, I share the concepts of Senator Allievi but without enlarging the attributions of the Prefects as vastly as he would like and in accordance with the French system.

And indeed just over two years later, on January 20, 1891, Crispi presented two bills to the Chamber on the "Reorganization of the Prefectures and Subprefectures" and the "Reform of the Territorial Boundaries of the Provinces, the *Circondari,* and the Communes of the Kingdom."[25] The major feature of these proposals was the separation of the areas of provincial self-government from those of the state field services. Specifically, the bills would have created new areas, called *Distretti,* composed of two or more provinces, in each of which there would be a Prefect. The *Distretti,* no more than fifty in number, would have at least half a million people and constitute geographically, socially, and economically homogeneous areas. There would thus be fewer Prefects and prefectures and this, according to Crispi, would secure several advantages: (1) prefectoral government would be "stronger, more enlightened, and more impartial"; (2) prefectoral administration would cost less to the taxpayer; (3) with fewer Prefects, the central administration could deconcentrate many of its powers without fear of undue discrepancy or lack of uniformity in administration (here he referred explicitly to Minghetti's argument that there were too many Prefects for broad deconcentration); and (4) once these had been established, "many services which have distinct offices and locations and functions may be collected together in the Prefecture which will be-

25. Ibid., *Legislatura XVII, Sessione 1890–1892, Camera, Stampati,* III, No. 42.

come what it ought to be, the representative of the Ministry [Cabinet]."[26]

Such a scheme could be carried out, Crispi's report continued, since the Prefect was no longer the head of the provincial deputation. The criteria for drawing local government boundaries and field administration boundaries were not and should not be the same. The Subprefects, though often attacked as useless, would now take on important functions as the Prefect's agents, especially since the provinces and municipalities had been granted elective heads; they would also act as the agents for such ministries as Finance and War; their areas would have to be suitably redrawn so as to form units of at least 100,000 people with good internal communications. The offices of the Purveyor of Studies and of the Civil Engineers were to be placed in the new district capitals.[27]

The basic defect of both field administration and local government, in the Prime Minister's view, was the faulty drawing of the provincial boundaries. Provinces were either too large or too small; some had only 1,000 square kilometers and little over 100,000 inhabitants; some had 400 communes, others had only five. Boundaries would have to be redrawn to form viable provincial self-governments as well as to create suitable areas for prefectoral government.[28]

These proposals would, if enacted, have led to a much stronger prefectoral system, to a much greater degree of prefectoral integration of field administration. But they were never reported by a committee or even discussed. They were, in fact, one of the factors in the fall of the Crispi gov-

26. Ibid., pp. 1–2.
27. Ibid., pp. 3–4.
28. Ibid., p. 5.

ernment about a week later. The succeeding cabinet withdrew the bills from Parliament.[29]

Another attempt to modify the Italian prefectoral system was made again only six years later by Prime Minister Di Rudinì.[30] Introducing a bill on the "Reform of the Functions of the Governmental and Administrative Authorities in the Provinces," the Prime Minister recognized the widespread feeling that political protection and wirepulling were decisive in administration. Political meddling with administration had led to "administrative anarchy," contempt for the rule of law, and the discrediting of constituted authorities.

The second major defect of Italian administration, the Prime Minister reported, and closely connected with the first, was its extreme concentration: field officials were little more than reporters and transmission belts; they had little power or responsibility; they operated under stifling central controls; they had little general prestige and were anxious only to please local politicians. The central administration, on the other hand, was bogged down in matters of detail; it decided even minor cases, with little or no knowledge of local circumstances.

The third major defect, according to the Prime Minister, was "the disconnected, independent action of the various [state] offices . . . Until now each has aimed only at developing and extending its attributions, without taking into account the general conditions of the country or the effects of its decisions on those conditions."[31]

---

29. Roberto Lucifredi and Giuseppe Coletti, *Decentramento amministrativo: Commento della legge di delega 11 marzo 1953, no. 150* (Turin, 1956), p. 19.

30. *Atti Parlamentari, Legislatura XX, Sessione 1897–1898, Senato, Documenti, I*, No. 13.

31. Ibid., p. 1.

All three defects would be remedied, he thought, by the creation of a new prefectoral council, composed of the Prefect as chairman, two prefectoral councillors, the Intendant of Finance, the compartmental (regional) inspector or the chief engineer of the Civil Engineers, the Purveyor of Studies, and the chief accountant of the prefecture. The Prefect would be given authority to *direct* these service chiefs and thus become the effective, rather than merely the nominal, representative of all the ministers. Through the council, he would have regular contacts with the major field directors instead of the merely occasional, largely formal contacts he then had with them. He would have the right to inspect and investigate the operations of the various services so as to follow up on complaints and discover deficiencies. His responsibility for all state administration in the province would now be matched with commensurate authority to influence their activities. His supervision of the services would be institutionalized.

The various central ministries would then, the Prime Minister said, deconcentrate many powers to the Prefect; to exercise these powers the Prefect would have first to consult with his new council. In some cases, the decision of the council would be binding upon the Prefect. The council would not meet often; the service chiefs could send subordinates to represent them; thus they would not be distracted from their own jobs. But they would now be forced to sit down together with the Prefect every so often to study the general provincial situation, what the various services were doing, and how state action in the province could be improved.

The Prefect would appoint the lower grades of personnel in all the state services. The subprefectures would be abolished and replaced by provincial inspectors in the prefecture. The Interior would deconcentrate to the Prefects the power to suspend and dismiss mayors. The availability of appeals from prefectoral decisions to the ministry would be reduced.[32]

But, as with the Crispi proposals, Parliament again refused to approve this scheme to strengthen and institutionalize prefectoral control. Failure to revise the Prefect's area of operations and to institutionalize his supervision of the state services meant failure to check the trend toward complete autonomy of the various state field services. A "weak" prefectoral system was becoming even weaker. When forced to deconcentrate some of their authority, ministries and bureaus organized their own offices in the field, using the locations and areas which they deemed fit, tying these offices directly to themselves by exclusive channels of communication, by hierarchical dependence, and by intermediary inspective and supervisory echelons. They turned to the Prefects only when they had no agents of their own, when occasional political questions arose in particular provinces, when their programs required them to deal with representatives of provincial interests (whence ad hoc prefectoral boards), and when required to do so by old laws and regulations.

By the turn of the century a map of all the different administration areas used by the state services would have been a confusing maze of crisscrossing boundaries. Few of the services were using the province exclusively and some, not at all. Several kinds of regional or interprovincial offices had been established, seldom using the same set of areas as other services.[33]

In some cases, regional offices were established as an intermediary echelon in the chain of command between headquarters in Rome and numerous field offices at the

32. Ibid., pp. 1–2.
33. Marchetti, *La Formazione del regno*, pp. 231–424.

provincial or subprovincial level. These were designed to
reduce the span of central control, to act as the long arms
of the ministry or bureau in supervising lower level operations. Such, for example, was the task of the regional offices for civil engineering, direct taxation, indirect taxation,
cadastral surveying, prisons, telegraphs, postal inspection,
and military administration. Among these services, the number of regions varied from three to ten.

Some regional offices were established because there was
either no need or no funds to establish offices in each of
the sixty-nine provinces. Examples of this were the eight
treasury advocates who later became the State's Advocates,
the specialized legal corps that acted on behalf of all the
state administrations; the forty-five technical finance offices,
which acted as the engineering consultants of the Ministry
of Finance; and the eight regional lottery offices. The problems dealt with by these offices were spread fairly uniformly
over the country.

And then there were the regional offices whose location
and jurisdiction were adapted to the handling of problems
that existed exclusively or largely in certain parts of the
country. The customs, maritime, forest, and mining districts had to be specially drawn so as to bring the offices to
where the bulk of the work had to be done—to the frontiers,
the ports, the forests, and the mines.

Many of the services were organized at the regional level
and thus would be difficult to work into a scheme of prefectoral coordination. For which of the Prefects whose provinces were partly or wholly included in the different special-
purpose areas would exercise control?

The services that *did* operate at the provincial level
tended to free themselves from even the slight amount of
prefectoral control that existed at the foundation of the
kingdom.

In the case of the Provincial Civil Engineers, the Law of July 5, 1882, No. 874, and the implementing Regulations omitted all of the prefectoral controls that existed in the 1860s. The Provincial Engineers now operated under the close control of a regional inspector, who enforced ministerial directives, evaluated their performance, drafted the priority lists for the annual program proposals, examined technically all projects, and gave technical approval to those minor projects not subject to ministerial approval. The Provincial Engineer's dependence on the Prefect was now limited to matters involving condemnation proceedings, local government works, and certain regulatory powers in roads and streams.

Similarly, the legal provisions that tied the Intendant of Finance to the Prefect in the Decree of December 18, 1869, disappeared in the revised Regulations of August, 29, 1897, No. 512. The Intendant was now bound to defer to the Prefect only in matters of public order and the award of honors. As with the Provincial Engineer, the Intendant and the Prefect were still loosely connected by a miscellany of consultation requirements.

It will be remembered that the Purveyor of Studies, the state school superintendent in the province, was the only important state field official acting for a ministry other than the Interior who was placed under the hierarchical authority of the Prefect and located in the prefecture, i.e. the only one who occupied somewhat the same position vis-à-vis the Prefect of French specialist field directors. This exception to the general rule of functional hierarchy was based on the fact that the major responsibility for providing elementary education lay with the municipalities, which were, in a sense, the wards of the Prefect. The Prefect's authority would be needed, it was felt, to stimulate the communes to comply with their obligation. Some deference was paid to the principle of functional hierarchy by the provision for direct communication between the Purveyor and the Ministry of Public Instruction.[34]

Educationists were not, however, entirely content with having the Purveyor and education under prefectoral control. Such control involved the *Provveditore* with what was considered the domain of electioneering and police. Prefectoral officials were often too busy with other matters to devote sufficient attention to educational problems. They were slow to act, incompetent, sometimes partisan—or so the charges ran. Control by the Prefect meant control by the Interior rather than by the Ministry of Public Instruction, and between the two ministries there was often friction or inaction.[35]

It was also felt that the Purveyor's position was ambiguous: he was the representative of the Minister of Public Instruction in the province, yet just another official in the prefecture, and thus lacking appropriate dignity. He was treated by the other officials in the prefecture as a poor relation and had to be content with the administrative services that the other officials did not wish to take; he competed with them for supplies and secretarial assistance. The Prefect himself rarely bothered the Purveyor except to ask for an occasional political favor.[36]

Under the 1859 or Casati Education Act, the communes were required to provide elementary education; but no sanctions were specified for failure to do so or for the failure of parents to send their children to the schools, if opened. An Act of 1877 (July 15, No. 3968) provided penalties for noncompliant parents and authorized provincial deputa-

34. Filippo Virgilii, "Istruzione pubblica," in Orlando, *Primo Trattato, 8* (1905), 656–62.

35. Ibid., pp. 653–56.

36. Ibid., pp. 663–64.

tions to inscribe the necessary expenditures in the budgets of noncomplying communes. But it was only in 1886 that the state began to face the fact that the smaller communes, especially those in the South, could not comply without some form of state aid; the state began to contribute to the salaries of elementary teachers.[37]

The amount of state financial aid became significant, however, only after the turn of the century. The census of 1901 revealed that about half the national population was still illiterate; in the South and Islands, the rate of illiteracy was in many places still over 70 per cent. Further legislation provided for the establishment of elementary schools directly under state control in the neediest communes, mostly in the South, and for increased grants-in-aid.

All of these measures, however, were failing to provide a minimum national standard of education. Under local control, the development of primary education was being impeded by local factionalism, limited local resources, and local unwillingness to spend. For these reasons, an Act of 1911 (June 4, No. 487), took control of education away from communes except the capitals of provinces and *circondari*, transferring it to the state. The state would henceforth assume complete financial responsibility for primary education in all but the more important localities. (Centralization of all primary education was completed in 1931.)

Thus the primary raison d'être of prefectoral control disappeared. Accordingly the Purveyor, now responsible for the direct management of most elementary schools, was removed from the prefecture and given a separate office and staff, directly under the authority of the Ministry of Public Instruction.

37. Carlo Francesco Gabba et al., *Lex: 1911* (Turin, UTET, 1912), pp. 511–41, Smith, *Italy*, pp. 260–61; *Atti Parlamentari, Legislatura XXIII, Sessione 1910–1911, Camera, Documenti*, No. 331.

The Purveyor shared his powers with a new provincial school board, which he rather than the Prefect now chaired, composed of principals and teachers (now state employees) and two representatives of the communes. Above the provincial school board, the 1911 Act placed a new ad hoc prefectoral board to supervise its activities. With the 1911 Act, the only exception to the pattern of functional hierarchy disappeared.[38]

Within this pattern of functional autonomy, the Prefect could not very easily keep track of what the various services were doing. The various directors, with the backing of their central ministries, tended to act on their own, often failing to inform him of decisions affecting provincial interests, setting their own pace, and perhaps by inaction or conflict with local interests undoing his work in building a favorable image of the government in the province. Each ministry was tending, moreover, to distribute its patronage through its own field offices. To counteract the adverse effects of this uncoordinated activity, the Prefect could only act through the various hierarchical channels to disclaim responsibility for what had happened. In general, however, the Prefects were preoccupied with their own institutional concerns: manipulating elections to produce ministerial deputies and local councils and, once elected, moderating their demands and pressing them on the appropriate central departments; arbitrating their disputes; combating their enemies; and handling the complaints and disorders arising from their domination of prefectoral and local government.[39]

---

38. Camillo Quercia, "Istruzione elementare," *Il Nuovo Digesto Italiano,* 7 (1938), 318–30.

39. Marchi, pp. 263–64; Arturo Carlo Jemolo, "I Prefetti," *Il Mondo, 5,* No. 10 (March 9, 1954), 1–2; Ministero per la Costituente, *Relazione, 1,* 365–66; Oscar Scalvanti, "Il Decentramento amministrativo," *Rivista di*

THE BEGINNINGS OF THE WELFARE STATE

The Prefects were the major executors of the policies of repression with which the conservative, sometimes reactionary, governments of the 1890s sought to check the development of the incipient Italian labor movement. The rise of capitalism in northern agriculture and the belated growth of industry and masses of urban industrial workers in the triangle between Genoa, Turin, and Milan led to the formation of trade unions, labor chambers, cooperatives, mutual aid societies, and eventually a Socialist party. In the face of acute social distress and the growing social agitation of the agricultural and industrial proletariats, a series of authoritarian governments in the 1890s resorted to repressive military and police action, the dissolution of working-class organizations (both Catholic and Socialist), the arrest of radical leaders, the banning of left-wing newspapers, and declarations of martial law. The whole concept of constitutional government was endangered.

But the threat to what was, after all, an increasingly democratic and liberal constitutional system was countered by a surge of liberalism, which at the turn of the century brought Giovanni Giolitti into power.

It was Giolitti who brought about a radical change in governmental response to the developing sociopolitical power of the newly organizing industrial and agricultural workers. The state was no longer to resist social change, to ignore the distress of the working classes, and to crush the

---

Diritto Pubblico, 2 (1892), 477–88; Carlo F. Ferraris, *L'Amministrazione locale in Italia* (Padua, 1920), 1, 85–86; *Atti Parlamentari, Legislatura XVI, Sessione 1886–1887, Senato, Discussioni,* p. 1726; and Tommaso Bruno, "Discentramento," *Il Digesto Italiano, 9,* Pt. III (1898), 240–62.

manifestations of that distress: it was to become a neutral mediator in the conflict of socioeconomic interests and to attempt to bring the hitherto inarticulate, unrepresented interests into the political system. Again the Prefects assumed the leading role in implementing this new policy: they were no longer to side automatically with the industrialists and landowners in conflicts with labor and to bombard the government with requests for troops, but to mediate such conflicts from a neutral standpoint. Moreover, they were to seek to remove the causes of social distress and conflict by promoting improvements in the socioeconomic conditions of the working classes.

It took Giolitti's constant prodding, reprimands, exhortations, and detailed direction over a period of years to wean the Prefects from their traditional mental outlook and methods of operation. He forced them for the first time to study questions of prices and salaries, rather than quantities of troops, and to devise schemes for the improvement of social conditions. Public order was to be the result of preventive social policy rather than police action.

For the Prefects, the new policy required much more subtle and difficult action than the simple defense of the status quo. It meant breaking their traditional solidarity with the propertied classes. Many of them were reluctant to turn against their long-standing connections, protectors, and allies, to betray their own class. Many were unconvinced of the effectiveness of the new policy of giving free rein to the developing labor movement as a means of curbing its revolutionary tendencies. Many found it degrading to have to parley with "subversive" working-class leaders. As a result of their hesitations, Giolitti had to follow their actions closely, force them to accept their new role, convince them of its advantages, resist their demands for police action, advise them on just how far to tolerate agitation. It was only his pressure and support that sustained the Prefects, now deprived of their traditional allies without having as yet gained any new ones.[40]

Giolitti did not, however, break with the tradition of using the Prefects to manage elections and manipulate local government—far from it.[41]

> Under Giolitti's rule, the interference of the prefects with local government and elections reached unprecedented heights of brutality. Where the electorate was refractory to pressure and the elected mayors and town councillors refused to bow, the prefect not only dismissed them, but "managed" local and national elections. If an election had to be carried out, the police, in league with the Government supporters, enrolled the scum of the constituencies and the underworld of the neighboring districts. In the last weeks before the polls, the opponents were threatened, bludgeoned, besieged in their homes. Their leaders were debarred from addressing meetings, or even thrown into prison until election day was over. Voters suspected of upholding the opposition were refused polling cards. Those favoring governmental candidates were given not only their own polling cards, but also those of opponents, emigrants, deceased voters, and were allowed to vote three, five, ten, twenty times. The Government candidates were always the winners. Any deputy who dared Giolitti had to confront a bad time at his next election.

40. He did not, however, find it necessary (or perhaps possible) to make numerous dismissals and outside appointments. The prefectoral rolls for 1905, for example, show that none of the Prefects serving at the time had been admitted to the state service after 1893. See Ministero dell'Interno, *Elenco del personale, 1905* (Rome, 1905), pp. 59–64. On the Giolittian Prefects, see Nasalli Rocca, *Memorie;* Gaetano Natale, *Giolitti e gli italiani* (Milan, 1949), pp. 43–53, 89–91, 426–49; and Ernesto Ragionieri, *Un Comune socialista: Sesto Fiorentino* (Rome, 1953), pp. 98–111.

41. Salvemini, "Introductory Essay," pp. xii–xiv.

Giolitti applied these methods, however, only in southern Italy, and the southern constituencies regularly provided him with the bulk of his parliamentary majorities.

In northern and central Italy, local governments and the opposition were better protected by public opinion and given free or freer rein. (It was the Fascists who first applied such methods on a nationwide scale.) The rise of the working-class movement and the gradual entry of Catholic groups into active political participation, together with the gradual broadening of the local government electorate, brought about a great expansion in municipal activities in these regions. Representatives of the lower classes sought and often obtained control of local governments in order (1) to redistribute the incidence of local taxation, which was quite heavy and could hit either the lower classes through reliance on consumption duties or the upper classes by a shift to property taxes; (2) to subsidize labor exchanges; (3) to establish and improve elementary schools; (4) to improve sanitation and sanitary regulation; (5) to build public housing.[42]

Symptomatic of expanding municipal enterprise was the beginning in the 1890s of the movement to municipalize public utilities, under the inspiration of Socialist and Popular Catholic theories, and in reaction to the unsatisfactory performance of private utility companies. Municipalization, at first extralegal, was brought under state regulation and sanctioned in 1903 (the Law of March 29, 1903, No. 103). Between 1903 and 1912, 135 municipal utility companies were created, only eight of which, however, were in the South and the Islands.[43]

The Prefects' use of their powers over local government

42. King and Okey, pp. 275–76; Ragionieri, pp. 91–215.
43. Ufficio Centrale Formazione della D. C., *Il Comune democratico* (Rome, 1956), pp. 330–35.

was somewhat redirected in line with Giolitti's policies. They were no longer used to impede the expansion of local government activities on the part of Socialist or Catholic majorities, especially if the latter were protected by deputies whose support the minister sought in Parliament. National and local politics were closely entwined, given the high degree of centralization: only through the deputies could municipalities and provincial governments secure favorable action by the central government or its field representatives on its budgets or requests for state grants. A hostile Prefect could usually manage to have the municipal budget slashed in the GPA, and have municipal loans and new taxation rejected; the municipalities generally required the mediation of a deputy for reasonable bargaining power in the GPA and in Rome. The Prefects were urged to clean out municipal corruption as another means of reducing lower-class discontent.[44]

The growing power of the labor movement and Giolitti's concern to transform that movement into a constitutional, even conservative force was reflected in the establishment of a Labor Office in the Ministry of Agriculture, Industry, and Commerce in June 1902 with the task of gathering and publishing information on labor conditions and social legislation. The same law (June 29, 1902, No. 246) created an Advisory Council of Labor in that ministry, consisting of deputies, functionaries, and representatives of employers, agriculture, commerce, cooperatives, mutual aid societies, people's banks, and trade unions. This was tantamount to a de facto recognition of the hitherto illegal and extralegal development of labor unions, and it provided a forum for the peaceful articulation of labor's interests in the administration. The council became an active sponsor of much of

44. Ragionieri, pp. 127–28; Natale, pp. 478–81.

the social legislation that Giolitti successfully put through Parliament during this period.[45]

A series of laws on female and child labor, emigration, accident prevention, and compulsory holidays marked the tardy beginning of Italian protective legislation. Earlier legislation along these lines had been almost inoperative due to the lack of specialized enforcement officers and the fierce resistance of factory and mine owners. Responsibility for enforcement had been placed on the Prefects, the police, the mining and civil engineers, and local medical officers, but as an addition to their regular responsibilities. A Decree of April 3, 1879, No. 4828, had created two posts of Factory and Vocational Training Inspector in the Ministry of Agriculture and by the turn of the century these two inspectors and a chief inspector were supposed to enforce social legislation throughout the country.

It was only after an international agreement had been signed with France in 1904 that a serious effort was made at enforcement. In 1912, by the Law of December 22, 1912, No. 1361, a specialized Inspectorate of Industry and Labor was established in the Ministry of Agriculture, Industry, and Commerce with eight regional field offices, independent of the prefecture, and with a total staff of seventy-one employees.[46]

The same period saw the beginning of state programs in the field of social insurance. A Law of July 17, 1898,

45. John Clarke Adams, "Italy," in Walter Galenson, ed., *Comparative Labor Movements* (New York, Prentice-Hall, 1952), pp. 430–32; Francesco Arcà, "Legislazione sociale," in Orlando, *Primo Trattato, 6*, Pt. 1 (1907), 1–109; Enrico Roselli, *Cento Anni di legislazione sociale* (Milan, 1951), *2*, 115 ff.

46. Ministero del Lavoro e della Previdenza Sociale, *Relazione annuale sull'attività dell'Ispettorato del Lavoro: 1955* (Rome, 1957), pp. 1–5; King and Okey, p. 379; Gabba et al., *Lex: 1913*, pp. 7–9.

No. 350, established a National Fund for Old Age and Disability Insurance to administer a voluntary pension scheme for manual workers—outcome of a long battle between proponents of voluntary as opposed to compulsory schemes and between those who favored administration by mutual aid societies and savings banks, subsidized by the state, and those who preferred a single national fund under close state supervision.

The Fund was established as an autonomous corporation, managed by a president and board of directors appointed by the government. The mutual aid societies did not succeed in getting representation on the board but they did secure a provision in the act whereby they, together with savings banks, unions, public charities, and other institutions, might serve as the field agents of the Fund. The board was empowered, however, to set up its own field agencies in the form of local committees appointed on the advice of the Prefect. Local staffs, in any case, were to be centrally appointed and managed. The Ministry of Agriculture, Industry, and Commerce retained considerable control over the Fund.[47]

A similar but entirely separate National Fund for Labor Accidents was established as a semi-autonomous agency under the same ministry by Royal Decree No. 698 of June 5, 1913. The failure of voluntary industrial accident schemes had led in 1883 to the formation of the Fund on the basis of a convention between the government and major private banks. The voluntary scheme under the Law of July 8, 1883, No. 1473, was made compulsory in 1898, although the Fund was given a monopoly of industrial accident insurance only in 1926. The banks participating in the scheme

47. Istituto Nazionale della Previdenza Sociale, *Mezzo secolo di attività assicurativa e assistenziale (1898–1948)* (Rome, n.d.), pp. 1–15; King and Okey, pp. 218–19.

continued to be responsible for its administration under the reorganization of 1913.[48]

But working-class groups were not alone in pressing claims with some success upon the state. Other groups, in an increasingly differentiated society, were also pursuing their objectives through government—organized groups resulting from the processes of industrialization, urbanization, and developing national communications. In a period of prosperity and rising public revenues, the state was able to meet many of the demands for increased intervention in the form of tariff protection, fiscal exemptions, grants-in-aid, direct regulation, and provision of services. In many cases, groups were successful in obtaining state recognition and aid for institutions that had been developed privately or locally—chambers of commerce, agricultural societies, savings banks, cooperatives of all kinds, rural banks, agricultural extension units (*cattedre ambulanti*), agricultural experimentation stations, private *consorzi* of landowners for reclamation (*consorzi di bonifica*), and aqueduct and port authorities. Institutions of this kind, originally private or established by local authorities, and under private or local control, were becoming the typical instruments for the administration of state economic policy. Like prefectoral boards, they were instrumentalities that served to adjust the requirements and interests of the state and of local authorities and private groups. While more or less amenable to state direction, they could continue to be financed at least in part by the direct beneficiaries of the programs administered and could adapt their action to the needs of the particular communities that fostered them.[49]

But if reliance on private and local initiative, stimulated

48. King and Okey, pp. 215–17.

49. Enrico Presutti, "L'Amministrazione pubblica dell'agricoltura," in Orlando, *Primo Trattato*, 5 (1930), 1–40.

and regulated by the state, for the achievement of national policy objectives was well suited to the needs and possibilities of the North, it was doomed to failure in the South. For the South in the half century since unification had remained isolated from the process of social differentiation, the organization of interests, and the development of local initiative. The North had kept pace with the social and economic development of Western Europe, while the South remained firm in its semifeudal mold. Partly responsible for this stagnation was national policy and administration since unification. For decades the South was considered a naturally rich area that would automatically prosper under the enlightened rule of the new liberal state. Policies developed in the northern states were extended to the South, which suddenly found itself deprived of its former tariff walls and burdened with much higher levels of taxation than it had previously experienced or than it could reasonably be expected to pay. Several decades passed before northerners realized that the South was largely a destitute area, with poor land, tilled by masses of day laborers (*braccianti*) working for a few baronial landowners on extensive latifundia or divided into tiny strips cultivated by other masses of dependent smallholders; that there were few genuine cities but rather peasant slums, perched on hill and mountain tops to avoid the ravages of endemic malaria; that there was no industrial and commercial middle class, but only a class of lawyers and other baronial intermediaries.

Northern Prefects were sent to the South for punishment or initial experience and, if successful, were rewarded with a prefecture in the North. Prefects of southern origin, still by the turn of the century disproportionately few in number, were recruited from the class of landlords and lawyers and tended to share their outlook and to protect their interests. Prefects from both areas had to cooperate with the cliques of landlords and their clienteles who dominated provincial and communal councils and exploited them exclusively for their private purposes, but who also provided the government with faithful parliamentary supporters. For part, if not most, of the responsibility for southern stagnation lay with the traditional ruling classes of the South itself. It was they who failed to invest in their lands; who placed the burden of local taxation on the poor; who preferred to subsidize fireworks, theaters, and classical high schools rather than provide possibly dangerous elementary schools, or roads or sewers or other essential services; who refused to accept state subventions for such services when offered; and who maintained private systems of justice, such as the Mafia, which the state could neither destroy nor dispense with.[50]

Only the action of the state, then, could make up for

50. Francesco S. Nitti, "La Burocrazia di stato in Italia," *Riforma Sociale,* *10* (1900), 472–73; Smith, *Italy,* pp. 230–42. The prevalence of Piedmontese in the Ministry of the Interior is demonstrated in the following official statistics for the year 1875.

Region of birth	Total employees	Ministerial employees	Population per employee
Piedmont	632	73	5,923
Lombardy	571	24	5,554
Venetia	372	14	7,881
Central Italy	263	14	4,433
Ex-Papal States	407	17	8,382
Tuscany	307	15	6,451
Naples	778	23	9,222
Sicily	363	11	7,118
Sardinia	114	5	5,584
Abroad	47	2	——
Total	3,854	198	6,954 (average)

See Ministry of the Interior, *Statistica degli impiegati della amministrazione centrale e provinciale e degli ufficiali di pubblica sicurezza* (Rome, 1875), pp. 144–49.

defaulting private and local action in the South, and under Giolitti the state began to act. Laws were passed to provide state aid to particular regions: for the city of Naples (1904); for Sardinia (1897, 1902, and 1907); for Basilicata (1904); and one for the entire South and Islands (1906).[51] Naples was given special tax exemptions to encourage the establishment of industries. Calabria was given relief for those stricken by the earthquake of 1906, as well as state-financed public works, railroads, reforestation, and slope consolidation projects. Sardinia received state aid in the form of agricultural credit, reclamation, stream control, reforestation, and highways; its rural communes were required to constitute *consorzi* for the provision of public services. In Basilicata, the Prefect of Potenza was appointed civil commissioner for Basilicata, which then constituted a single province, with deconcentrated powers to administer the special act that provided for state and state-financed projects for flood and erosion control, slum clearance, agricultural credit, *cattedre ambulanti* (agricultural extension units), as well as private reclamation, rural housing, and farm improvement. It was three years, however, before this program for Basilicata was actually begun, such were the difficulties of administration in a primitive environment.[52]

Much of this legislation was hastily prepared and only meagerly financed. Many of the projects were never completed and many completed with incredible slowness.[53] Far more effective in relieving southern distress was the spontaneous exodus of emigrants, half a million of them in 1901, reaching 872,000 in the year 1913 alone.[54]

51. Gioacchino Volpe, *Italia Moderna: 1815–1915* (Florence, 1943–53), 2, 62–72.

52. Ibid., p. 387.

53. Ibid.

54. Smith, *Italy*, p. 239.

It was the First World War that undermined the bases of the liberal constitutional "prefectocracy." The war generated conflicting expectations and demands that the traditional system, under the impact of universal suffrage, proportional representation, and mass ideological parties, could not adjust or satisfy.

In the first two years after the Armistice, the peasants and workers took the political offensive. Their social and political power was mobilized in massive nationwide organizations—the Socialist General Confederation of Labor, which had grown in membership from 327,212 in 1913 to 2.2 millions in 1921; the Socialist party and the Catholic Populist party which in the general elections of 1919, the first under universal manhood suffrage, won 156 and 100 deputies, respectively.[55] These were disciplined parties with elaborate extraparliamentary organization and fairly rigid and cohesive ideologies: it was no longer possible to transform the opposition into ministerial deputies through patronage. In the local elections of 1920, the Socialists won control of 2,166 out of 8,327 communes and 26 out of 69 provinces. The Populists captured another 1,650 communes and 10 provinces.[56]

The labor movement displayed its power in those years in other ways. Its pressure forced the creation of a separate Ministry of Labor, by Decree Law of June 3, 1920, No. 700, to mediate the multiplying industrial and agrarian conflicts, to represent the interests of labor in the Cabinet, and to symbolize the importance of such interests in the nation. The trade unions, moreover, secured direct representation in one of the parastate agencies supervised by the new ministry, the Fund for Old Age and Disability Insurance.

55. Ibid., pp. 326–27; Adams, "Italy," p. 426.
56. Luzzatto, *Elezioni politiche*, p. 290; Gabriele De Rosa, *Storia del partito popolare* (Bari, 1957), p. 159.

In the Law of April 21, 1919, No. 603, which reorganized the Fund as the *Cassa Nazionale per le Assicurazioni Sociali*, or National Social Insurance Fund, both labor and management were given the right to select representatives on the central board of directors and the tripartite boards that were to represent the Fund in the provinces. The provincial directive committees were constituted in equal measure of ministerial appointees (including the chairman), representatives of the insured workers, and representatives of management. Considerable authority was deconcentrated from the central board to the provincial committees, although the professional staffs were to be centrally appointed. Ambiguities in the laws and regulations, however, led to frequent conflicts between the central and local boards concerning their respective spheres of authority: the provincial committees drove persistently toward greater autonomy.[57]

But Italian labor was not content with reformist achievements, with representation in Parliament, in local councils, and in the administration. Under the hypnotic effect of the Bolshevik Revolution, it aspired to total power, to the dictatorship of the proletariat. The Socialists refused to collaborate with bourgeois reformist parties in the institutions of the parliamentary monarchy. They and the labor leaders promoted and tolerated chronic industrial conflict and violence, the pillage of shops and warehouses, attacks on veterans and interventionists, paralyzing strikes in the public services, peasant invasions of uncultivated estates, and the culminating nationwide occupation of the factories.

The liberal postwar cabinets were ineffective in combating the mounting inflation, unemployment, and shortages and in maintaining order against left-wing vio-

57. Istituto Nazionale di Previdenza Sociale, *Mezzo Secolo*, pp. 64–70.

lence. Giolitti himself returned to power in 1920 in time
to face the high tide of the revolutionary challenge—the
occupation of the factories. Resisting demands to call out
the troops, he allowed the occupation to come to an incon-
clusive end. From this crest of revolutionary fervor, which
passed off without any move toward the conquest of the
state, the labor movement subsided into a state of demoralization. It had succeeded only in terrorizing the propertied
classes.

The Populists held the balance of power, but they could
not collaborate with a party of revolution and found it almost as difficult to work with the anticlerical liberals who
had dominated prewar Italy. Giolitti attempted to reduce
the forces of both the Socialists and Populists by dissolving
the Chamber and holding general elections in 1921. But
for once prefectoral manipulation did not work: if the
Socialists were slightly weakened, the Populists were returned in even greater numbers than in 1919. Once again
no firm majority could be constructed in Parliament. Giolitti's government resigned and was succeeded by a series
of weak caretaker cabinets.

The initiative passed from these cabinets with precarious
majorities to a counterrevolutionary movement of nationalist veterans and students, renegade interventionist Socialists, landowners, shopkeepers, and industrialists, grouped
into bands of Fascist vigilantes. From an epicenter in the
Po Valley, the Fascist squads began a systematic campaign
to terrorize the labor movement. Socialist and Populist
party and union headquarters were sacked and demolished;
their leaders were beaten, humiliated, and killed; their
town halls were stormed and their majorities forced to
resign.

With the outbreak of civil war, the government in Rome
gradually lost control of the country. The prefectoral ma-

chinery broke down: when Prefects were willing to repress
Fascist violence, they could not control their Subprefects
or the Carabinieri or the Royal Guards; nor could they prevent the military from furnishing the Fascists with muni-
tions, protection, and encouragement. The police refused
to act against the Fascists, who enjoyed widespread sympathies. Had not Giolitti himself included the Fascists in
his own electoral ticket in the 1921 campaign (when they
returned only thirty-five deputies) and thus conferred
legitimacy upon the movement? As for the army officer
corps, it was no longer the upper-class preserve of the prewar period, bred to a tradition of discipline, but saturated
with middle-class nationalists, highly susceptible to the
Fascist appeal.[58]

The liberal ministers made some attempts to stamp out
Fascist violence, but they failed to understand the nature
of the Fascist threat. They considered Fascist violence as
illegal activity to be repressed by the normal machinery of
justice, rather than what it actually was—a subversive in-
surrectionary challenge to the liberal state which could be
met only by an open counteroffensive with troops loyal to
the government. They could not conceive of using the same
methods of military repression traditionally used against
peasant and worker agitation also against sons of the pa-
triotic bourgeoisie. Nor did they have the solid parliamentary backing necessary for such drastic action.[59]

With the failure of the government to act against it, the
Fascist movement mushroomed and spread its control from
the rural areas to the largest cities. The Prefects were
ordered to urge the Fascists to stay within the law, but they
were not allowed to call in the troops. When too weak or

58. De Rosa, pp. 159–69; Luigi Salvatorelli and Giovanni Mira, *Storia
d'Italia nel periodo fascista* (2d ed. Turin, 1957), pp. 15–179.
59. De Rosa, pp. 166–67.

compliant with the Fascists, they were transferred. Thus the province of Parma in 1922 had six different Prefects! When they attempted to take action against the Fascists, the Fascists stormed their prefectures and forced them to leave the city.

By the summer and fall of 1922, the Prefects had been pushed to the periphery of provincial politics. The provinces were solidly under the control of Fascist action squads. The Prefects could only observe and wait and see. In October the Fascists occupied the prefectures and the telegraph offices and prepared to march on Rome. The cabinet prepared a decree of martial law. The army would still have responded to a call to obedience from the Throne. Victor Emmanuel III, from fear of or sympathy with the Fascists, refused to sign the decree and, upon the resignation of the cabinet, appointed Benito Mussolini to head his government.[60]

60. Ibid., pp. 170–296.

Chapter Four

THE FASCIST ERA (1922–43)

THE REFORMS OF THE
PSEUDOCONSTITUTIONAL PHASE (1922–24)

IN THEIR FIRST YEARS of power, the Fascists kept at least a semblance of constitutional regularity. Indeed, Mussolini's first cabinet included representatives of all the non-Marxist parties: the Fascists held only the Ministries of Justice, Finance, Interior, and Foreign Affairs, as well as the Prime Ministership. One of the first acts of the new government was to secure from a quiescent Parliament an enabling act which granted the government plenary powers "to reorganize the tax system with the objective of simplifying it and adapting it to budgetary necessities, and better distributing tax burdens; to reduce the functions of the state; to reorganize the public offices; and to diminish expenditures."[1] With the aid of this remarkably unlimited

1. Law of Dec. 3, 1922, No. 1601.

grant of power, expiring over a year later at the end of 1923, the government issued hundreds of decrees affecting every sector of public policy and administration.[2]

To a great extent, these reforms followed the recommendations of a parliamentary committee of inquiry in 1921. They often made changes that had been held up for a long time by legislative inaction. To promote economy and interministerial coordination, the number of ministries was reduced from fifteen to ten. Labor and Social Security, Agriculture, and Industry and Commerce were merged in a single Ministry of the National Economy. The Ministry of Posts and Telegraphs, the state railway and telephone directorates, and the Commissariat for Merchant Marine were integrated under a single Minister for Communications. The Ministry for the Reconstruction of Liberated Areas was abolished. The disappearance of a separate Ministry of Labor reflected the shift in political power of labor: it was no longer to have its own spokesman in the Cabinet. The parliamentary committee of 1921, while recommending the rest of the above changes, had not been willing to risk the repercussions of such a change.[3]

The reforms carried out in local administration were marked by a similar concern for economy and unified authority through integration. The powers of chief executives and executive committees were strengthened vis-à-vis the conciliar elements in provincial and communal government. State tutelage of local government was simplified, but made more penetrating. The Interior deconcentrated im-

2. Salvatorelli and Mira, *Storia*, pp. 222–37; Attilio Tamaro, *Venti Anni di storia, 1922–1943* (Rome, 1954), *1*, 369–77.

3. *Atti Parlamentari, Legislatura XXVI, Sessione 1921, Camera, Documenti*, No. 2-bis, *Relazione della Commissione Parlamentare d'Inchiesta sull'ordinamento delle amministrazioni di stato e sulle condizioni del personale (Legge 16 marzo 1921, N. 260), 1*, 52–54.

portant powers to the Prefects and transferred some prefectoral powers, in turn, to a reduced number of Subprefects.[4] The number of Purveyors of Studies was reduced from over sixty-nine to nineteen, raising these officials to regional jurisdiction with considerable deconcentrated authority.[5] Many provincial boards and committees were abolished or made strictly advisory. The tug of war between the provincial committees and the central authorities of the National Social Insurance Fund was ended by the transfer of the committees' decision-making powers to the professional provincial directors appointed by and responsible to the center.[6]

The Ministry of Public Works underwent a series of interesting reorganizations. Its eight functional bureaus were re-formed into three areal bureaus for northern, central, and southern and insular Italy, respectively. Each of the area bureaus was in turn subdivided into functional divisions (bridges and roads, hydraulic works, building construction, etc.). The regional inspectors of the Civil Engineering Corps were brought into the ministry to act as technical advisers to the administrators in charge of the bureaus. The reform was designed to permit the close coordination of planning and operations in the different functional fields to suit the particular needs of each area of the country. The ministry had long been besieged by demands from the South for more roads, for example, despite the fact that there was little traffic on those already built. The functional bureaus tended to consider the whole country as uniformly requiring more roads and would accede to southern demands, whereas it was hoped that a geographical bureau would discount such demands in favor

4. Royal Decree of Dec. 30, 1923, No. 2839.
5. Royal Decree of Dec. 31, 1922, No. 1679.
6. Istituto Nazionale di Previdenza Sociale, *Mezzo Secolo,* pp. 77–80.

of those kinds of public works of which the South had greater need.[7]

The area bureaus were to be given separate lump-sum appropriations which they were to allocate to the different sectors according to the particular needs of their area. Investment policy would be more flexible. And even more importantly, at least for a southern minister under pressure from southern politicians, areal budgets and appropriations would allay suspicions of regional disparities and would finally end the tendency to overinvest in the more prosperous and politically powerful North. Then, too, the geographical division of labor would permit more effective supervision of the provincial engineering offices. Under the functional division of labor, the Provincial Engineers often received contradictory directives from the different bureaus but were supervised by and sometimes contented none of them in particular. Under the new system, each Provincial Engineer came under the authority of a single bureau head.

Under the old system, moreover, the personnel office had often disregarded the particular needs of each bureau and the general need for stability in assignments and specialization in the problems of particular areas. Under the new scheme, the area bureaus would have to consent to the transfer of personnel out of their jurisdiction and could freely assign them within that jurisdiction.[8]

The reform was undone, however, by the next Minister of Public Works who insisted that the same kinds of matters, the same functions, should not be handled by different bureaus in different ways. He restored the old functional division of labor. He removed the inspectors from the bureaus and placed them again in the field as regional supervisors;

7. Carlo Petrocchi, *La Politica dei lavori pubblici* (Rome, 1926), pp. xix–xxi.
8. Ibid., pp. xxi–xxv, 230–50.

he abolished the requirement for previous field experience in central appointments and authority to send administrative personnel into the field. By so doing, he revived the old struggle for funds and personnel among the functional bureaus in which the strongest usually managed to expand their type of projects throughout the country despite the greater need for other types of projects in particular areas. By ending the interchange of ministerial administrators and field engineers, he exacerbated the persistent tensions between the two groups. By abolishing the area bureaus, he aroused the ire of the southern ministers in the Cabinet and was forced to create a central inspectorate for the South and Islands with responsibility for coordinating and supervising planning and operations in that area, but with little actual means of doing so.[9]

Still another change at the head of the ministry brought in a Venetian who was favorably impressed with the performance of the *Magistrato alle Acque* (or regional water authority) created in 1907 for his region, as well as sympathetic to southern problems. He worked out a scheme that combined elements of both approaches. The functional bureaus in the ministry were retained but most of their authority in southern and insular Italy was deconcentrated to a new set of regional *Provveditori alle Opere Pubbliche* or Purveyors of Public Works for the South and Islands.[10]

The new regional offices were patterned after the Venetian Water Authority but were given even broader powers: they took on most of the powers and duties of the central functional bureaus (except for new railway construction, utilization of public waters, and earthquake damage reconstruction) but also authority from other ministries. From National Economy, they were given operating responsibili-

9. Ibid., pp. xxv–xxvii, 251–70.
10. Ibid., pp. xxvii–xxxi, 276–307.

ties for irrigation, reforestation, erosion and flood control, and land improvement. The Interior devolved to them authority in matters of water supply, hospital construction, and other sanitation works. And from Public Instruction they received authority to handle special grants. At the same time, the advisory authority of the Public Works Advisory Council (*Consiglio Superiore dei Lavori Pubblici*) and of the Council of State was deconcentrated to technical-administrative committees under the chairmanship of the Purveyors.

Through the *Provveditorati,* organic programs of works adapted to particular regional needs could be prepared swiftly, yet (being at the regional level) somewhat removed from localistic political pressures; the programs of several ministries could be interrelated, planned, and executed under a single authority; the demands of the South for special treatment could be satisfied; projects would be planned and executed by specialists in the problems of particular areas; and the Provincial Engineers would work under the immediate supervision of a single superior, close enough to furnish realistic direction and stimulus.

Seven such *Provveditorati* were created by Decree of July 7, 1925, No. 1173, to administer a ten-year public works investment scheme for the South and Islands. Their authority expired finally in 1937 (1940 in the case of Sicily and Sardinia) and they were replaced by regional inspectors with only supervisory authority.[11] A similar temporary regional office was created for the Tuscan Maremma reclamation area, covering four central Italian provinces, in 1926.[12]

Shortly after the Purveyors' offices were created, the city council of Naples was dissolved for at least the fifteenth

11. Royal Decree of Sept. 2, 1937, No. 1633.
12. Royal Decree Law of Feb. 7, 1926, No. 192.

time since 1861 and the provincial council as well. The powers of the city and provincial councils, of the prefecture, and of the Purveyor of Public Works for the Campania region were fused in a single High Commissioner for the City and Province of Naples under Royal Decree Law of August 15, 1925, No. 1636. The new High Commissioner was also given the powers of the Naples Port Authority and of the regional Superintendent of Excavations.[13] He was made responsible for stimulating, coordinating, and directing all state and local activities designed to raise the economic and social standards of the city and its province. He was given the power to direct all state services except the judiciary, the military, and the financial offices. The office, however, was established for only a five-year period and after its authority had been extended for another such period, it was abolished and its powers transferred to the regular authorities.[14]

THE ESTABLISHMENT OF THE FASCIST DICTATORSHIP

It was only after the murder of Matteotti in 1924 and the resulting disaffection from Fascism that Mussolini established an outright dictatorship. The elections of 1924 had given the Fascists control of Parliament through a new electoral law, which gave a two-thirds majority in the Chamber to the party or coalition winning a simple plurality of the popular votes, through the traditional pressure of the Prefects, and through the violence and intimidation practiced by Fascist squads against anti-Fascists. Controlling Parliament, Mussolini put through a series of laws in

13. Royal Decree Law of Aug. 15, 1925, No. 1636.
14. Ministero per la Costituente, *Relazione*, 2, 389–91.

1925–26 which destroyed *de jure* the competitive liberal political system.

The Fascists made no formal change in the *Statuto* but transformed the traditional governing organs—the Crown, the Council of Ministers, Parliament, the civil, military, and judicial bureaucracies—into the allies or instruments of the dictator. Non-Fascist political forces were either suppressed, like the parties and Freemasons; brought under state and Party control, like labor, management, veterans, and other organized interest groups, and the press; or neutralized into benevolent support, like the Church. Alongside of or replacing the traditional organs and forces were created new instruments of control and domination: the Fascist Grand Council, the Militia (MVSN), the Fascist party (PNF) bureaucracy, and the Special Tribunal for the Defense of the State.

The *Gran Consiglio del Fascismo* or Fascist Grand Council, originally only a Party organ, replaced Parliament and the Cabinet as the supreme policy-making organ of the regime. Completely dominated by Mussolini, who alone could summon it into session, fix its agenda, and determine its membership, the Grand Council served as a forum for the discussion and ratification of major government policies, as worked out by the ministers and Party leaders who participated in its deliberations. Its supremacy was officially sanctioned in the Law of December 9, 1928, No. 2693, which confirmed its authority as "the supreme organ that coordinates and integrates all the activities of the Regime." The Council of Ministers was relegated to a less spectacular role.[15]

Mussolini gradually transformed the Fascist party into

15. Dante L. Germino, *The Italian Fascist Party in Power: A Study in Totalitarian Rule* (Minneapolis, University of Minnesota Press, 1959), pp. 33–34, 85.

a rigidly centralized hierarchical organization under his direct control. The Party came to perform an increasing number of important political and administrative functions on his behalf: (1) it controlled a series of dependent organizations, such as the associations of schoolteachers, civil servants, veterans; (2) it provided the dictator with organized political support in the most remote localities; (3) it created a vast network of interests vested in the preservation of the regime by the distribution of patronage; (4) it provided a check on the other bureaucracies, as well as surveillance over all public and many private activities; (5) it directed the youth organizations designed to inculcate Fascist ideals and allegiance to the dictator; (6) it shared in the direction of the Fascist labor unions and in the shaping of economic policy; (7) it provided services for propaganda, paving the way for acceptance of government decisions and reporting upon their reception by the public; and (8) it provided for the enforcement of a growing number of public policies, such as price control, wage reduction, etc.[16]

Party activities were directed by its National Secretary, who was directly responsible to the Duce. The National Secretary was eventually authorized to attend Cabinet meetings, made a Minister of State in his own right, and appointed to membership on the Supreme Defense Board, the National Council of Corporations, the Central Corporative Committee, and the Advisory Council on Education. In addition, he acted as secretary of the Grand Council, commanding general of the Fascist Youth (*Gioventù Italiana del Littorio* or GIL), and president of the associations of teachers and civil servants and of the *Opera Nazionale Dopolavoro* (National Recreation Agency). He also directed

16. Ibid., pp. 19–31; Arnold Zurcher, "The Government and Politics of Italy," in James T. Shotwell, ed., *Governments of Continental Europe* (2d ed. New York, Macmillan, 1952), pp. 258–61.

the operations of the Fascist labor, sports, and women's organizations. Through him and through the Party, the dictator was able to expand his reach into many hitherto private spheres of Italian life.[17]

The Party Militia (*Milizia Volontaria per la Sicurezza Nazionale* or MVSN) had been created in 1923 by incorporating the Blackshirt squads into an official paramilitary force. This transferred the cost of upkeep from the Party's financiers to the taxpayer and provided the dictator with the instruments of violence with which to suppress opposition. Militiamen swore allegiance to the Duce, rather than to the King, and served as independent combat units in Ethiopia and Spain. The MVSN was the reserve force of the Party against possible dissidence in the army and the police. In addition to the regular militia, there were special militias for policing frontiers, railroads, communications, ports, forests, highways, penal islands, and universities.[18]

A separate network of organizations was created to constitute the "corporative" system. These institutions developed into another of the bureaucratic arms of the Fascist party-state, in addition to the regular state administration; the parastate agencies; and the various hierarchies of the Party. A Ministry of Corporations was established in 1926, by Royal Decree of July 2, 1926, No. 103, to exercise governmental control over labor organizations and labor-management relations. The independent labor organizations were suppressed and replaced by unions whose leaders were selected and directed by the Party and the Ministry of Corporations. The unions and the employers' organizations were linked in 1934 into twenty-two "corporations" and in various corporative (i.e. labor-management) councils, ostensibly designed for the self-regulation of industry and

17. Germino, pp. 40–41.
18. Ibid., pp. 106–10.

agriculture, but actually used for the negotiation of collective agreements, the adjustment of conflicts of interest, and the development of recommendations on economic policy —all under close Party and state supervision and control.[19]

In 1929, the ministry took over the general responsibilities in industry and commerce of the defunct Ministry of National Economy, at the same time that a separate Ministry for Agriculture and Forests was restored. It was through the Ministry of Corporations that the state came to exercise most of its increasing control over the economy. The ministry stimulated the process of cartelization initiated during the world-wide depression. It spawned many of the parastate agencies that actually formulated the policy and exercised the economic controls that the corporative bodies were supposed to handle.[20]

The expansion of government activity under Fascism was reflected to some extent in the number of ministries, which, on the eve of World War II, had climbed back to fifteen. In the official order of precedence, these were Foreign Affairs, Interior, Italian Africa (ex-Colonies), Justice, Finance, War, Navy, Air (1925), National Education (ex-Public Instruction), Public Works, Agriculture and Forests (1929), Communications (1924), Corporations (1926), Popular Culture (ex-Press and Propaganda, 1935), and Foreign Trade (1937).

But a far more spectacular manifestation of the growth of public services was the proliferation of public agencies (*enti pubblici*) which pullulated in a bewildering variety of structure and function. Most of these agencies were created either for welfare purposes or to cope with such problems as salvaging bankrupt industries, developing the

19. Ibid., pp. 163–64.
20. Ernesto Rossi, *I Padroni del vapore* (Bari, 1955), pp. 157–82; Felice Guarneri, *Battaglie economiche* (Milan, 1953), *1*, 278–97.

Empire, regulating production, and managing credit institutions and import-export controls in an effort to fight the depression and make Italy self-sufficient and prepared for war. Aside from the thousands of public agencies operating only in particular localities or only in Rome, there were at least 260 of them which carried out their activities throughout the country. These were classified (somewhat vaguely) in an official postwar report as follows:[21]

1.	general administration	52
2.	education, fine arts, and tourism	77
3.	public health	11
4.	welfare	48
5.	economic control	80
		268

Such agencies multiplied incoherently to meet contingencies as they arose, under a variety of legal regulations, sources of finance, personnel systems, and relationships to the regular state ministries. Many of the new agencies were removed from the regular fiscal controls of the *Ragioneria Generale dello Stato,* the Court of Accounts, and Parliament. They were generally organized under their own statutes, approved by law or decree, with presidents, executive committees, boards of directors, boards of trustees, and directorates general—all of which could be dissolved and replaced at any time by a Government Commissioner. Control over such agencies was nominally vested in different ministries, but according to no coherent plan. Ministerial functionaries were placed on the boards of most of these agencies not only to exercise ministerial supervision and

21. Ministero per la Costituente, "Enti pubblici non territoriali; organizzazione sanitaria," *Relazione, 3,* 151–292.

provide technical expertise, but also as a lucrative supplement to their earnings.

Many of these agencies were grossly inflated with Party members in subaltern positions. The National Institute of Foreign Exchange (*Istcambi*), an agency of the Bank of Italy (itself since 1936 an agency of the Treasury), by 1937 had expanded its staff to about 1,300 employees, the vast majority in the lowest grades and with dubious backgrounds. When reorganized under the Ministry of Foreign Trade in 1937, the staff was reduced to about eight hundred employees, with no apparent loss in efficiency. But most of those eliminated were members of the Rome Federation of the PNF and many were "Fascists of the first hour." The *Capo del Governo* was flooded with anonymous letters; the personnel director of the Institute was denounced to the Party Federal Secretary and brought before a Party internal discipline board, which demanded his dismissal. The Minister of Foreign Trade had to appeal to the Party National Secretary to call off the action against his subordinate; so influential was the minister that he was successful in this and in promoting non-Party members, despite precise directions to the contrary given by the Party.[22]

Mussolini stood at the apex of all these ramifying hierarchies as the joint chief of Party and state. Ministers and Party leaders were appointed, transferred, and dismissed as just so many bureaucratic subordinates, who learned of their fate on the radio or in the newspapers. Mussolini mediated and sometimes, if he wished, settled the fierce internecine conflicts constantly arising among Party factions, ministries, and interest groups, adjusting the relative power of each so that no challenge could be made to his personal autocracy. Policies were either determined unilaterally by Mussolini, consulting no one, or thrashed out

22. Guarneri, *1*, 28–29.

under his presidency in the various arenas for bargaining such as the Grand Council, the Cabinet, the corporative councils, the Supreme Defense Board, cabinet committees, and his private office.

Democratic politics was replaced by bureaucratic politics. Open political competition in constituencies and Parliament was replaced by the covert conflict and bargaining among and within an increasing number of personal factions and public bureaucracies. Alongside of the state administration, itself divided into a growing number of vertical hierarchies, there were the newer organizations which competed with the older formations for power and resources, and maintained separate channels of accountability and access to the Duce.

Ministers were kept under control by frequent "changes of the guard," and by the surveillance of the Party and the secret political police (OVRA). Every morning Mussolini would have on his desk the transcripts of his ministers' telephone conversations of the day before. He would skim over these, mark out certain passages with red and blue pencil, and have them distributed to the different ministers with requests for explanation. Knowing that their calls were being tapped, ministers would sometimes exploit this unusual kind of access to influence the dictator's decision-making.[23]

But the dictator does not seem to have made effective use of his powers of coordination. Says the former chief of the secret police, Guido Leto:[24]

> Mussolini had no idea whatsoever . . . of administrative problems and took on the enormous weight of the

23. Ibid., 2, 384.
24. Guido Leto, *OVRA: fascismo–antifascismo* (2d ed. Bolgna, 1952), p. 146.

ministries of which he was the titular head. In practice the real minister was the Undersecretary of State. The most important questions were submitted to him [Mussolini] with the proposed conclusions—conclusions which he unfailingly approved.

But it often happens . . . that the administrative measures of one ministry interfere and sometimes profoundly conflict with the views and policies of other branches of the administration, so that with ever growing frequency the injured ministry, so to speak, submitted the same question to Mussolini with a solution diametrically opposed to the one adopted.

And Mussolini approved again.

Thus was born a conflict which sometimes assumed humorous forms because the heads of the administrations in conflict showed each other the note or memorandum—a real talisman—with the signature of Mussolini, which had been affixed to approve completely antithetical conclusions.

Further testimony on this point comes from Mussolini's Minister of Foreign Trade (1937–40), Felice Guarneri:[25]

Right after approving economies, [Mussolini] authorized, when he did not actually encourage, rapid evasions . . . He was led by the mobility of his spirit to strange contradictions so that it was not rare for him to sign on the same day two different memorandums, submitted separately in mutual ignorance by two of his collaborators who proposed for the same matter divergent and even opposed and contradictory solutions. Whence confusion, conflicts, and paralysis in the action of the Government.

25. Guarneri, *1*, 435.

THE PROVINCIAL BASES OF POWER

One of the major problems faced by Mussolini in establishing his dictatorship was to secure effective control of the provinces. In the early months and even years of the regime, the provinces lay under the semifeudalistic tyranny of the local and provincial Party bosses (called *Ras*), many of whom had entrenched themselves before the March on Rome. From the start, however, an effort was made to preserve and enhance the existing prefectoral network, which was tending to disintegrate under provincial Party pressures. Only by bringing the provincial Party leaders under tight central control could a modus vivendi between Party leaders and Prefects be brought about. Until this was done, the relations between them were marked as much by conflict as by cooperation.

From the very start of the regime, there were clashes between Prefects and Party bosses whenever Prefects resisted the drive for total provincial domination by the Party and Militia. The Prefects, most of whom had been left in office, attempted to serve the national Party and state leaders, while the provincial bosses were serving themselves. In these early years, the Prefect and the state police, on the one hand, and the Party and its Militia, on the other, represented the two methods of Fascist rule. The Prefects were used to establish the dictatorship through formal, legalitarian, conservatively respectable procedures: the dissolution of opposition parties and unions, the censorship and banning of the opposition press, etc. The Party *Ras* administered the informal, generally illegal means of coercion and terror, which were vital elements in the establishment of the one-party state.

The Prefect and the Party leader tended to have the diverging outlooks of the policeman and the vigilante. Both were useful instruments in maintaining power, although their relative prominence and authority had to be adjusted from time to time as shifts in public opinion dictated changes in emphasis from legalitarianism to "revolutionary" activism and back again.[26]

Prefects and Party leaders collaborated in suppressing opposition to the Fascist dictatorship. They collaborated in ejecting the opposition from local government and in securing the Fascist victory in the general elections of 1924. The Prefects allowed the Fascist *squadristi* to terrorize their provinces and protected them from reprisals; they themselves managed the elections by the old-fashioned administration of threats and bribes.[27]

It was only after the Matteotti crisis in 1924 that the provincial Party leaders were brought under the tight control of the Party's National Secretary, himself responsible only to Mussolini. Party statutes were revised to provide for central appointment of Party secretaries at the provincial and local level and for the concentration of control over Party activities in the secretarial network. The National Secretary gradually brought most of the provincial bosses into line by a combination of inspection, purges, and frequent rotation. Provincial Party secretaries were transformed from locally based politicians into professional Party functionaries regularly transferred, promoted, and retired in "changes of the guard." The largest movement of secretaries was carried out in 1934 when forty-four out of ninety-two were replaced or transferred and thirty-one new appointments made. This movement was made feasible

26. Leto, pp. 13–14, 147–48; Germino, pp. 10–11, 47–48.
27. De Rosa, pp. 336–468; Tamaro, 2, 8–123.

by the promotion of the older secretaries to seats in the Chamber of Deputies in the "elections" of 1934.[28]

But if the Party was now organized into a rigid hierarchy (with the exception of a few provincial bosses, with large national followings, who retained direct access to and influence with Mussolini), the problem remained of the relations between this hierarchy and that of the Prefects, just as between the Party Militia and the state police. Each of these hierarchies was responsible to a different central superior in Rome: the Party secretaries to the Party National Secretary; the provincial commander of the MVSN to the commanding general of the MVSN; the Prefects to the Minister or Undersecretary of the Interior; the *Questori* (the provincial state police chiefs) to the *Capo della Polizia* in the Ministry of the Interior.

Instead of merging the networks of Prefects and Party secretaries as was done later in Nazi Germany, Mussolini decided to maintain the two networks as separate hierarchies, each responsible ultimately to himself. "Personal union" of the state (prefectoral) and Party offices would have removed the friction between the two and obviated the need to define their respective spheres of authority. For his own power and safety, however, Mussolini preferred the policy of "divide and rule." Each of the hierarchies could serve as a check on the others and each might protect the dictator against the others. For the same reason, he maintained the independence of the various state police forces from the Party.[29]

But retaining both the Prefect's office and that of the Party secretary as separate ones, occupied by different func-

28. Germino, pp. 33–36.
29. Ibid., p. 83; Leto, p. 148. Cf. Alfred V. Boerner, "The Position of the NSDAP in the German Constitutional Order," *American Political Science Review*, *32* (1938), 1059–81.

tionaries, meant that some attempt had to be made to clarify their respective roles and authority. Mussolini decided for various reasons that the Prefects, rather than the Party secretaries, should be—at least on paper—the supreme authority in the province. Fascist ideology, for one thing, tended to stress the subordination of the Party to the state, in accordance with Mussolini's famous formula: "Everything in the State, nothing outside of the State, nothing against the State." Ideological and other considerations were brought out in a famous circular to the Prefects of January 5, 1927, issued in response to widespread demands for "normalization," for an end to the confusion and sometimes chaos in the provinces, and for the curbing of partisan excesses.

The circular rejected the idea of coequal but distinct spheres of prefectoral and Party jurisdiction. The Prefect was declared to be "the highest authority of the State in the province" and "the direct representative of the central executive power." "All citizens" and, above all, Fascist party militants owed "respect and obedience to the highest political representative of the Fascist regime, and must subordinately [sic] collaborate with him in order to facilitate his task. Wherever necessary, the Prefect must stimulate and coordinate the activities of the Party in its various manifestations."

Underlying the subordination of the Party to the Prefect was the concept that "authority cannot be shared" but is "one and indivisible." Responsibility had to be pinpointed in a single authority or the state would once more be completely disorganized and disintegrated: Fascism had come into power "precisely in order to give consistency, authority, prestige, and force to the State, to make the State one and untouchable." The Party was "only an instrument conscious of the will of the State."

The state through the Prefects was now, the circular continued, sufficiently strong in coercive power to remove the need or desirability of the vigilante methods of the Fascist squads. There were to be no more outbursts of squadrist violence (which by this time constituted an embarrassment to the regime): for the "era of retaliations, of devastations, or violence [was] finished."

The Prefect was to be "in charge of all provincial life" and give it "impulse, coordination, and direction."[30]

Unfortunately for the Prefects, central Party headquarters proceeded right after the issuance of the circular to sabotage it by issuing its own "interpretive" directives, and restoring the theory of coequality in distinct spheres.[31]

Relationships between the Prefect and the Party secretary (or *federale*) remained uncertain and unresolved throughout the Fascist period and continued to plague the Fascist Republic of Salò, set up under German auspices after the 1943 armistice. The Prefects and the *federali* continued to send in divergent and contradictory reports on events and the state of opinion and to pursue mutually defeating policies—reflecting in the field the basic differences that continued between the Ministry of the Interior and the Party. After a serious incident in Turin—when armed Fascists invaded a Court of Assizes to liberate a Fascist accused of common crimes, clashed with the Carabinieri, and wounded the chief magistrate himself—Mussolini, urged by the Prefect of Turin, sent off a telegram to the Chiefs of the Provinces (as the Prefects were renamed), subordinating the Party federations to direct prefectoral control

30. *Bollettino Parlamentare*, 2 (March 1928), 60–62. The 1927 circular is reproduced in Herbert W. Schneider and Shepard B. Clough, *Making Fascists* (Chicago, University of Chicago Press, 1929), pp. 138–39.

31. Eugenio Dolfin, *Con Mussolini nella tragedia* (Milan, 1949), pp. 121–22.

for "the entire duration of the war." That afternoon, the Party National Secretary informed Mussolini of the "deleterious impression" that the telegram would make on the *federali* and on Fascists in general. The Duce agreed to allow the Party to send out "interpretive instructions" which in practice nullified the original telegram. Mussolini's private secretary (a career Prefect himself) wrote in his diary: "The problem of the coexistence of the party and of the State, despite all our experiences, remains in its relationship of traditional uncertainty."[32]

The problem was partly eased by the gradual appointment of Fascist generals and Party leaders to prefectoral posts. In the early years of the regime, few career Prefects were dismissed or voluntarily resigned. Many Prefects shared the sympathy for Fascism, in its conservative aspects, which prevailed in the Court, and among other high state functionaries, large landowners, industrialists, the aristocracy, and many of the liberal politicians. The position of the Prefects in the early years was not enviable, but with the trend toward "normalization," and indications of increasing prefectoral power and prestige, Party members began to press for prefectoral appointments. The first group of Fascist Prefects, all generals, was appointed in 1923; every year afterward a new infusion of Party elements took place so that by the mid-thirties about half of all Prefects serving in the provinces were from outside the regular career service.[33]

32. Ibid., pp. 43–44, 121–22.
33. Edoardo Savino, *La Nazione operante* (3d ed. Novara, 1937), pp. 189–209. Of the sixty-five Prefects listed in this work, thirty-one were from the career service, thirty-four from the Party. The great majority of the career Prefects by this time were coming from the South, according to the same data, whereas the great majority of the political Prefects came from northern and central Italy. Of the thirty-four political Prefects, at least ten had engaged in vigilante activities; twenty-two had university degrees; thirteen

By 1926, in any event, those Prefects and prefectoral officials who had resisted pressure to become members of the Party had yielded to the minister's threat of dismissal unless they did so.[34]

Political Prefects were selected with very little concern for their educational qualifications but rather for their expected ability to dominate rebellious Party secretaries. Only political Prefects, it was felt, could check Party encroachment upon the state administration and suppress Fascist illegalities, without fear of denunciation as anti-Fascists. The appointment of political Prefects was carried out gradually so as to minimize the disruption of an administration already severely shaken by purges and Party attacks.[35] Some of the political Prefects performed respectably in the eyes of their career colleagues, especially those who left administrative matters in the hands of their career vice-prefects. Others were considered ignorant, prepotent, violent, and factious.[36] In any case, the political Prefects in

---

had been Party Secretaries; others had been career military officers, war heroes, officers in veterans associations, etc. Lasswell and Sereno in their study of the Italian elite found that twenty-two of the forty-nine first-class Prefects were outside appointees, and of these twenty-two, nine had participated in squadrist violence. See Harold Lasswell, *The Analysis of Political Behavior: An Empirical Approach* (London, K. Paul, 1947), pp. 158–72. That about half the prefectoral corps was composed of outside appointees is further confirmed by Marshal Pietro Badoglio who states in his *L'Italia nella seconda guerra mondiale: Memorie e documenti* (Milan, 1946) that about fifty non-career Prefects had to be purged from the service after the fall of Fascism (pp. 88–89). For the first outside appointees under Fascism, see the *Corriere della Sera* (Jan. 17, 1923), p. 2; (May 7, 1923), p. 1.

34. Arcangelo Cirmeni, "Il problema dei prefetti," *Il Corriere Amministrativo, 1* (1945), 10.

35. Leto, p. 15.

36. Carmine Senise, *Quando ero Capo della Polizia, 1940–1943* (2d ed. Rome, 1947), p. 170; Arturo Lentini, "Burocrazia, prefetti e prefetture," *Il Corriere Amministrativo, 2* (1946), 985–87.

Jayadeva, son of Bhojadeva.

জয়দেব গোস্বামীনী শ্রীশ্রীগীতগোবিন্দম্ / নৈহেলোম্ব হেম্বাক্চত্র: শ্রীনরোহরিহেম হেরাসিংহ. 1. সংস্করণ. নোম্বান, সংস্কৃত প্রকাশক মণ্ডল, 1967.

4, 210 p. 19 cm. 5.00

Running title: শ্রীশ্রীগীতগোবিন্দম্.
In Sanskrit; introductory matter and explanations in Manipuri.

Title romanized: Jayadeba Goswā-
migi Śrīśrīgītagobindam.

1. Krishna—Poetry.   I. Herāsimha, Nommāithema, tr.   II. Title.   III. Title: Śrīgītabobindam.

PK3794.J3G5   1967   74-902766

Library of Congress   72 [2]   S A

DC
317
.C58

DC
318 101
.W5

JV
2017. 103
.T3

practice were no more apt than their career colleagues to take a strong stand against Party corruption and violence: sometimes it was quite the reverse.[37]

As the Prefects' prestige and influence augmented, so did the ambition of Party functionaries to head a prefecture. To restrain such ambition and maintain the morale of the career service, it was necessary to issue a decree (Royal Decree of June 27, 1937, No. 1058) which required that three-fifths of all Prefects on the rolls be taken from the career service of the Interior.

The politicization of the prefectoral corps may have bolstered the Prefects' claim to superiority over the Party. It seems to have become the practice for the Party secretary to report to the Prefect every day and to receive instructions on the management of Party activities insofar as they interested the state: such instructions, however, could not infringe upon the "technical" discretion of the Party secretary. The Prefect's opinion and *nihil obstat* became basic elements in the central appointment of the Party *federale* and subordinate Party functionaries, and in central settlement of difficulties in provincial Party life. The relations between the Party secretary and the Prefect on the provincial level were apparently analogous to the relations between the Party's National Secretary and the Chief of the Government at the national level. Such at least was the state of affairs according to the former Prefect and Councillor of State, Renato Malinverno, writing in the standard legal encyclopedia of the period, *Il Nuovo Digesto Italiano*.[38]

37. Antonio Ciccia, "Prefetti e prefetture," *Il Corriere Amministrativo, 3* (1947), 960–61.
38. Renato Malinverno, "Prefetto," *Il Nuovo Digesto Italiano, 10* (1939), 154–55. Cf. Germino, *The Italian Fascist Party*, pp. 95–97.

"IL PREFETTO FASCISTA"

A Law of December 24, 1925, No. 2263, institutionalized Mussolini's political ascendancy over his ministers by creating the new office of "Chief of the Government Prime Minister Secretary of State," i.e. by expanding the powers of the President of the Council of Ministers. To the new *Capo del Governo* were given the King's powers to appoint and dismiss the ministers, who became responsible exclusively to Mussolini, and no longer to the King or to Parliament. And it was decided that just as Mussolini was the indisputable chief of all the ministers, so the Prefect should have clear supremacy over ministerial representatives in the province. The Prefect was to become an image in the province of what Mussolini was in Rome. For this purpose, a bill was submitted to the Fascist-dominated Parliament on November 27, 1925, on the "extension of the powers of the Prefects."[39]

The Minister of the Interior in presenting the bill declared that the Prefect's role as representative of the executive power under the Provincial and Communal Act had "remained in reality the mere affirmation of legislative intent without any practical efficacy." The result was that[40]

> the Prefect does not have any real influence (*azione*) or intervention (*ingerenza*) in the Administration and in the services which are not directly subordinate to him, not even for the purposes of the general vigilance which lies in the nature of his functions; and all the less [for the purpose] of a control and coordination of

39. *Atti Parlamentari, Legislatura XXVII, Sessione 1924–1925, Camera, Documenti*, No. 663.

40. Ibid., p. 1.

the action of the various specific organs of the State Administration—a control and coordination which are, however, indispensable in order that the activity of those organs be carried on with unity of orientation, in conformity with the general political directives of the Government, avoiding dissonances and disharmonies.

To make prefectoral oversight effective, the following legislation (which I quote in its final form) was necessary:

Law of April 3, 1926, No. 660: "Extension of the Powers of the Prefects"

Art. 1. In conformity with the general directives of the Government, the Prefects shall act to ensure unity of political orientation in the activities of the different State services and of the local authorities, within the territory of their respective provinces, coordinating the activity of all public offices and supervising their services, except for the administrations of Justice, War, Navy, Air, Railroads, and the Purveyors of Public Works for the South and Islands.

Nothing is hereby modified in the present organization with respect to the functions of the Prefects in matters included in the jurisdiction of the administration of the Interior.

Art. 2. To secure the objectives of the preceding Article, the Prefect shall summon to collegial conference, as a rule once a month or whenever he so desires, the following functionaries, in order to receive information on the general operations of the services which each superintends, and in order to issue opportune directives:

1. The Intendant of Finance;

2. The Purveyor of Studies in the provinces in which he is located and a functionary or school head delegated by him in the other provinces;

3. The Sub-Stewards of Vacant Benefices;

4. The Provincial Director of Posts and Telegraphs;

5. The Chief Engineer of the Civil Engineers;

6. The Forest Inspector;

7. The Directors of the Agricultural Extension Service;

8. The Chief Engineer of the Royal Mining Corps;

9. The Labor Inspector;

10. The Port Commanders of the major ports of call of the province.

The Prefect may summon to participate in the conferences the Royal Procurators of the Provincial Tribunals, for the administrative affairs in their charge, and as many other chiefs of offices which operate within the territory of the Province as he, the Prefect, may from time to time consider opportune to summon.

To secure the objectives of Article One, the Prefect may invite the above indicated functionaries to the prefecture individually as well.

Art. 3. Likewise to secure the objectives of Article One, and with the exceptions mentioned in that Article, the Prefect supervises all the personnel of the various state administrations within the province, but within the limits of Royal Decree of December 30, 1923, No. 2960, concerning the legal status of state employees.

The committee of the Chamber which reported the bill

revealed that the railway administration had been exempted from prefectoral supervision, despite the great need for close surveillance, because that administration used special areas of operation and it would be difficult in many cases to find the appropriate railway official for the Prefect to deal with.[41] The committee itself had rejected attempts to include other state officials in the list of participants in the Prefect's monthly conference, such as the university rectors, the emigration inspectors, or the vice-presidents of the recently created Provincial Economic Councils: it did not want the Prefect's conferences to "degenerate" into little parliaments. It denied that the law would change the figure of the Prefect in Italian public law by making him a "Viceroy" or "Governor" because, and this should be noted, the law left the specific functional hierarchies between technical field directors and their central ministries intact. Each technical director was to remain hierarchically subordinate only to his central superior: his "technical-administrative" activity would remain unaffected. The law aimed to achieve, in the committee's words,[42]

> the political coordination of all the action of the Government in the field . . . The provincial offices, of whatever species, are not watertight compartments, with no communications between them, as sometimes happens through jealous zeal in the performance of delicate functions; they are *organs,* members of a body, functioning and working toward a single end.

On the floor of the Chamber, a Fascist deputy acutely observed that there were several regional authorities and

41. Ibid., No. 663–A, p. 2. The railway administration was particularly suspect due to the frequency with which the railway workers had joined in strikes and aided the Socialists.

42. Ibid., p. 3.

that these would largely escape the effects of the law. He asked that such offices, such as that of the Purveyors of Studies, be transformed into provincial offices. He also expressed skepticism concerning the effectiveness of periodic conferences, suggesting that individual contacts would be more effective, and he regretted that the government had not had the courage to go one step further and place the state field directors under the hierarchical authority of the Prefect.[43]

The Minister himself elaborated on the purposes of the law during the Chamber "debate." By establishing unified political coordination of state administration through the Prefects, this law would implement "that fundamental principle of the ethical and political unity of the State which is among the main points of the doctrine and practice of Fascism." But, he noted, "political coordination . . . naturally does not imply invasion of individual spheres of technical jurisdiction (*competenza*) assigned to the various office chiefs. This technical jurisdiction remains autonomous." The newly created regional Purveyors of Public Works had been exempted from prefectoral control, the Minister continued, because they were to perform temporary functions of such a nature that prefectoral coordination would be "inopportune" and "incongruous."[44] (He was alluding, presumably, to the chaos that would have resulted if half a dozen Prefects attempted to issue directives to a single regional Public Works Purveyor.)

It should be explained that under Article Three of this law and the 1923 Decree to which it refers, the Prefect could not interfere with the right of hierarchical superiors directly to issue binding instructions to their subordinates in the field, to review and amend their subordinates' de-

43. Ibid., *Discussioni*, XII, Deputy Leonardi, 4981–83.
44. Ibid., p. 4987.

cisions, and to take disciplinary action against them. "Hierarchy," after all, was one of the main ideals of Fascism (it was the title of Mussolini's own political journal) and the law sought to protect the right of a minister to have complete charge of his field representatives through the functional chain of command. Presumably then, the Prefect's right to issue directives was limited by the amount of discretion left by the various ministries to their field representatives.

What was the effect of this law in actual practice? It is not easy to say. Curiously, no circulars seem to have been issued to interpret it for the guidance of Prefects and field directors. When the law was consolidated into the new Provincial and Communal Act of 1934, the Prefects' powers of "political" coordination were confirmed, but the regulations to implement the act, which would have elaborated on practical details, were never issued. The old *Regolamento* of 1911 continued to be operative. It would seem, in any event, that monthly conferences of state officials under prefectoral direction never became a standard practice.[45] But this law, together with the 1927 circular and other measures that enhanced prefectoral status, did have the effect of permitting the Prefects, when they so wished, to have their way with the various field directors insofar as the latter enjoyed discretionary powers.[46]

Renato Malinverno, however, in his authoritative and generally realistic article on the Prefects (cited above) stresses the great difference between the powers granted to the Prefects in the 1926 Act and those inhering in hierarchical supremacy, which remained with the central ministries:[47]

45. Interviews with personnel of the Ministry of the Interior, 1958–59.
46. Ibid.
47. Malinverno, p. 156.

It is usually the case that the authority of the Prefect is translated, when some conflict arises with another provincial or regional authority, into a referral to the central office to which the other authority is subordinate: a referral which is undoubtedly very authoritative and which is always given great consideration, but which normally must wait upon the concrete measures of the central authority. Only in extraordinary and absolutely urgent cases, when a decision is immediately indispensable can the Prefect substitute himself for the other provincial authority, even sending in a commissioner, without waiting for the higher-level decision, in which case he assumes all the responsibility for the substitution. This is obviously not a frequent hypothesis since in all the specific provincial offices there are organs which may deputize for the chief of those offices.

Conflicts between Prefects and other field directors appear, however, to have been rare, such were the prestige and influence of the Prefects. For the Prefects were the direct agents of the Minister of the Interior and the Minister of the Interior, except for the two years between 1924 and 1926, was Mussolini himself. The Prefects were thus closer than any other state field official to the *arcana imperii*.

The status of the Prefects under Fascism was enhanced in several ways. Sumptuous new buildings were constructed to house the prefecture and on all prefectures, except in Rome, was inscribed "Palazzo del Governo" or "Government House." The Prefects were raised in the official order of ceremonial precedence at Court and at public ceremonies (in their province) to one of the highest categories, bringing with it the title of "Excellency" and precedence over the presidents of the Courts of Appeal and the commanding generals of army corps. The periodical Grand Report of the Prefects to the *Capo del Governo* became one of the outstanding events of the regime. They were frequently summoned individually or in groups to receive the personal instructions of the dictator, who kept close watch on their activities. They began to make highly publicized tours of their provinces, rivaling in ceremonial splendor the circuits of the bishops.[48]

The technicians, given the Prefect's status and influence, seldom questioned prefectoral judgments as to how state aid was to be allocated and how regulations were to be enforced. Cooperation rather than conflict seems to have characterized their relations—cooperation based on the fact that both were hamstrung by the extreme concentration of administrative power in the central ministries and agencies. Prefects and technical directors tended to unite forces in order to compete with the officials of other provinces for limited central attention and resources. The Prefect's support was often essential to a technical official in winning or expediting central ratification of his proposals. The deconcentrating tendencies of 1922–24 were sharply reversed with the establishment of the dictatorship. The central ministries, largely staffed and directed by functionaries who had spent little or no time in the field, held on even more jealously than before to their decision-making powers and their posts in Rome. Authority in such matters as hiring of personnel, even of the lowest grades, the obligation and disbursement of funds above certain very limited amounts, and the allocation of state funds as between individuals, groups, and localities in the province was reserved to the center. The inclination of field officials, including Prefects, to shun responsibility and initiative and to refer matters

48. Arturo Carlo Jemolo, "I Prefetti." Finer, pp. 274–76; Guido Zanobini, *L'Amministrazione locale in Italia* (2d ed. Padua, 1930), pp. 42–44.

of any importance to Rome was encouraged. The decisions in the various services which the Prefect could influence were therefore in the nature of recommendations and proposals for central action. Since the last word lay with the ministries on matters of any significance, they could scarcely resent prefectoral intervention.[49]

The prefecture, in any case, did not become the center of provincial administration. Offices continued to be set up outside of it and not dependent upon it for assistance and direction. The various ministries continued to set up regional and provincial offices administratively independent of the prefecture, sometimes even to take over functions hitherto performed by the prefectures. The technical ministries and bureaus were left with complete control over their field offices, which they set up in functionally adapted areas. They continued to communicate directly with their field offices, to control them through central or regional inspectors, to delegate authority directly to them, and to give them their own administrative staffs for accounting and secretarial purposes.

The proliferation of agencies in Rome to administer programs designed to mitigate the effects of the depression and later to prepare the country for war led to a similar development in the provinces. New field services, however, were seldom grafted on to existing offices but set up independently, despite the greater administrative costs. There were three policy sectors in which the dispersion of authority, personnel, and funds was most marked: social welfare, economic control, and police. In each of these sectors there arose a multitude of separate central offices, each with one or more sets of field establishments. By 1943, for example, in the sector of social welfare, there were separate field of-

49. On the concentration of administrative power, see, e.g., Camillo Quercia, "Istruzione elementare," p. 322.

fices and installations for (a) old age, disability, tuberculosis, and unemployment insurance, and family allowances (INPS); (b) workmen's compensation (INAIL); (c) health insurance (INAM); (d) local government employees' insurance (INADEL); (e) state employees' insurance (ENPAS); (f) war invalids' assistance (ONIG); (g) war orphans' assistance (ONOG); (h) maternal and child welfare (ONMI); (i) emergency relief (CRI); (j) assistance to deaf-mutes (ENS); (k) assistance to the blind (ENLC); (l) veterans' assistance (ONC and ANC); (m) agricultural workers' social insurance (SENLUCA); (n) poor relief (ECA); (o) tuberculosis care (Provincial Antituberculosis Consortia); (p) the eradication of malaria (Provincial Antimalaria Committees); etc. In addition to these specialized agencies, there were the welfare activities conducted by (a) the ministries and their field offices; (b) the provinces and communes; (c) the Fascist party and its ancillary organizations such as the Fascist Youth (GIL) and the workmen's recreation agency (*Opera Nazionale Dopolavoro*); (d) the public charitable institutions (*opere pie*), especially hospitals and orphanages; and (e) public agencies for assistance to particular groups in particular areas.[50]

The multiplication of welfare institutions, each with its own policies, procedures, structure, and staff, meant that the limited resources of a relatively poor country were drained off into many channels, with no organs for the overview of whole sectors of activity, that benefits under each program were meager, and that considerable proportions of welfare funds were absorbed by administrative overheads. But Fascism, which possessed the dictatorial power to integrate programs and agencies, found greater

50. Amministrazione Aiuti Internazionali, *Organi ed enti di assistenza pubblica e privata in Italia* (Rome, 1953), passim; Leto (p. 55) reports that there were about twenty different police forces operating under Fascism.

propaganda value in a showy façade of activity—in a manifold of ad hoc initiatives—than in a coherent economical organization of effort.

Fascism then did not reinforce the Prefect's powers of political coordination by placing the growing number of agencies under his administrative control, instead of in substantial independence from the prefecture and from each other. Yet whatever links seemed to be required among the various agencies were provided by the Prefect in the form of prefectoral committees. Where particular programs required the coordinated efforts of different services in the field and also of local authorities and interest groups, representatives of services, authorities, and interests were brought together in a growing number of committees under the Prefect's chairmanship. Such committees were created, for example, for the purposes of (a) assessing contributions to corporative organizations; (b) assessing contributions from landowners for agricultural workers' social insurance; (c) allocating quotas for the compulsory delivery of agricultural products; etc. These committees usually included not only the directors of interested state or parastate field agencies and representatives of labor-management organizations, but also a member of the PNF, appointed by its National Secretary.

A number of technical field directors were periodically assembled by the Prefect in the Provincial Economic Councils established in the Law of April 18, 1926, No. 731. The councils were actually the old chambers of commerce, to which were added representatives of agriculture, industry, Fascist labor unions, and state and parastate field offices. The chambers of commerce had till then been autonomous institutions directed by councils elected by the merchants of the province and possessing their own offices and staffs. The state had exercised only limited powers of supervision over them, based on the fact that they were legally recognized and empowered to levy contributions on provincial businessmen. The chambers, however, had been weakened after the war by the development of specialized trade and employer associations which tended to take over the tasks of representation.[51]

In accordance with Fascist authoritarian principles, however, such autonomous bodies could not be tolerated. They were therefore transformed into organs of the state just as the formerly autonomous organizations of labor and management. The Provincial Economic Councils were given the powers and duties of the chambers of commerce but also of the provincial agricultural committees, provincial forest committees, provincial livestock committees—thus unifying in the province the same matters that were unified, until 1929, in the Ministry of National Economy.

The council included in its membership the representatives of the officially recognized labor and management organizations as well as a number of state officials: the Prefect (chairman); the Labor (after 1928, the Corporative) Inspector; the director of the *cattedra ambulante* (the semi-autonomous agricultural extension body which was to be transformed into the Provincial Agrarian Inspectorate, a direct field office of the state, in 1935); the Regional Agrarian Inspector (appointed in 1929 to administer the "Integral Reclamation" program); the Provincial Commander of the Forest Militia (the old State Forestry Corps, militarized in 1926); the Chief Engineer of the *Genio Civile;* the Provincial Veterinarian (a state official in the prefecture); a representative of the National Recreation Agency, the *Opera Nazionale Dopolavoro;* a representative

51. Camera dei Deputati, Legislatura XXVII, *La Legislazione fascista, 1922–1928 (I–VII), 1,* 1517–22; "Consiglio provinciale delle corporazioni," *Il Nuovo Digesto Italiano, 3* (1938), 919–35; Guarneri, *1,* 278–97.

of the social security agency (INPS); a representative of the workmen's compensation agency (INAIL); the Provincial Emigration Delegate; the Port Emigration Inspector; and as vice-president, the Federal Secretary of the PNF.

The work of the council was directed by a presidential committee which included the Prefect (president), the Party secretary (vice-president), and the presidents and (Party) vice-presidents of the various sections into which the council was divided (agriculture, labor, industry, commerce, etc.).

In 1927 the staffs of the former chambers of commerce and other similar economic bodies were absorbed into Provincial Economic Offices, designed to act as the direct field offices of the Ministry of Corporations and (after the Ministry of National Economy was abolished) the Ministry of Agriculture. The new Provincial Economic Offices acted as secretariats of the council and acted for the central ministries by observing and reporting on provincial economic conditions and administering economic regulations. The higher officials of the offices became state functionaries, subject to the hierarchical authority of the economic ministries via the Prefect. The council, or rather the participating labor and management organizations, however, paid for the maintenance of these offices.

The Provincial Economic Council (renamed the Provincial Council of the Corporative Economy) was given authority under the Law of September 20, 1934, No. 2011, to coordinate all economic activities in the province. It was to act as a two-way transmission belt, providing the government with advice from provincial economic interests and transmitting the government's information and directives to those interests. It was also to coordinate the welfare activities of labor and management organizations; stimulate the development of production; advise state functionaries on the issuance of regulations on trade, markets, communal agrarian rights (*usi civici*), and rural police; impose restrictions for the conservation of woods and forests; administer the stock exchanges; and ascertain and codify standard agarian and commercial practices.

As president of the council and of its presidential committee, the Prefect performed his traditional role of mediating between the government and provincial interests. He acted as the council's legal representative; convened, presided over, and set the agenda of its meetings; approved or rejected the representatives designated by the labor and management groups; and approved or vetoed the decisions of the various sections.

But in this developing field of state economic control, the Prefect had to contend with the rival roles assigned to the Party's Federal Secretary and the confused allocation of responsibilities as among the prefecture, the Provincial Economic Office, the syndical (i.e. labor and management) organizations, and the specialized state field offices.

For almost ten years it appears that an informal Party committee—the intersyndical committee—chaired by the *federale* and grouping representatives of labor and management played a much more important role than the Provincial Economic Councils.[52] For it was these intersyndical committees that exercised such important powers as settling labor disputes, negotiating and enforcing collective labor agreements, fixing prices and wages, and appointing the leaders of the labor and management organizations. The Party's National Secretary did, however, allow the vice-prefect to sit as a regular member of this committee as the representative of the Prefect. The intersyndical committees were created extralegally by the Party in 1927 to reduce

52. Germino, pp. 42–44; Malinverno, pp. 155–58.

prices so as to cushion the effects of the nationwide wage cuts determined that year. Under the protection and encouragement of the Party, the committees assumed most of the important duties that the Provincial Economic Councils (PECs) were supposed to perform. The Ministry of Corporations and the Party engaged in a long battle to destroy each other's committees. Until 1937 (and perhaps even later), the intersyndical committees made the important decisions affecting provincial economic life, while the Provincial Economic Councils were restricted to somewhat academic discussions and the sending of their minutes to the responsible ministries. It was only in 1937 that the Party's price control powers and duties were transferred to the presidential committee of the PEC, in an at least apparent victory for the Ministry of Corporations.

There was a similar duplication and conflict of jurisdictions between the Prefect's own *Ufficio Sindacale Corporativo* and the Provincial Economic Office and between the offices of the agricultural workers' unions and landowners' associations, on the one hand, and the regular state field offices in agriculture.[53]

Many of the services created in the drive for economic self-sufficiency ("autarky") and in war mobilization were attached to the Provincial Economic Council as the general headquarters for economic administration. Such was the case, for example, with the Provincial Food Sections (SEPRALs) created as sections of the economic councils under the Law of December 18, 1939, No. 2222, to administer the food supply and distribution system for the Ministries of Agriculture and Corporations. They were headed by a directive council, chaired by the Prefect, with representatives of various state field offices and of the labor and man-

53. Malinverno, pp. 158–59.

agement organizations involved in the production, distribution, and sale of foodstuffs. In practice, this council did little deliberation on its own, acting instead to implement the directives of the central ministries as transmitted by the Prefect. In the first years of the Second World War, about ten other offices were attached to the food sections: the provincial consortium of meat slaughterers, the office for the distribution of food oils and fats, the office for the distribution of cereals, flour, and noodles, etc. Each of these offices was given the usual corporative façade by being placed under councils with representatives of labor and management, ostensibly to permit the economic groups involved to regulate themselves. This had the advantage of other corporative institutions: they relieved the state budget of the costs of administration by shifting those costs to the regulated groups in the form of "syndical" contributions. But as with most corporative institutions, the councils and worker representation were merely the window dressing for a new form of financing agencies which were in practice merely the executors of ministerial decisions. Despite the paraphernalia of presidents, bipartite boards, and the formal traits of public law autonomy, the corporative institutions were completely under central ministerial authority and for all intents and purposes acted as regular state field offices through their full-time professional functionaries, often absorbed en masse from the trade associations.[54]

The expansion of the Ministry of Agriculture's activities in the form of direct regulation of agricultural production and programs of financial aid led to the transformation of the *cattedre ambulanti* (literally "mobile professorial chairs") into direct state offices—the Provincial Agrarian

54. Fierio Corsi, "I Servizi dell'alimentazione," *Rivista Trimestrale di Diritto Pubblico, 3* (1952), 457-93.

Inspectorates under the Law of June 13, 1935, No. 1220. These technical assistance bodies in agriculture had in most cases been established by local governments and private organizations. They had, however, come to be recognized and regulated by the state, which devolved an increasing number of administrative functions upon them, for lack of any specialized agronomic state service. They were located in nearly all provincial capitals. Regional Agrarian Inspectorates had been established as direct arms of the ministry in 1929 to administer the technical aspects of the "Integral Reclamation" law, in collaboration with the *Genio Civile,* reclamation consortia (local organizations of landowners), and the Prefects.[55] But with the growing number of regulatory and assistance programs, the ministry felt the need for directly controlled offices at the provincial level. The *cattedre* had the necessary technical specialists; they enjoyed the confidence of farmers through their promotional activities; and they had accumulated detailed knowledge of local agricultural conditions. They could be taken over by the state yet continue to be financed by local authorities and groups. Ideological considerations were also taken into account, for, as the Minister of Agriculture declared in Parliament, "One cannot permit in a political system which requires everything to be subordinated to the State that the function of assistance and control in the field of agricultural production be entrusted to organs which are not subject or only imperfectly subject to hierarchical bonds to the State, and which are in large part autonomous, legally and financially."[56]

55. Royal Decree Law of Nov. 18, 1929, No. 2071. See the *Atti Parlamentari, Legislatura XXVIII, Camera, Documenti,* No. 413 and 413–A.

56. *Atti Parlamentari, Legislatura XXIX, Camera, Documenti,* No. 621, pp. 1–2; "Ispettorati provinciali della agricoltura," *Il Nuovo Digesto Italiano,* 7 (1938), 222–30.

Thus another set of formerly autonomous bodies became direct organs of the state. (In some cases at least the Fascists had already removed the presidents and directors of *cattedre* who were not of the correct political persuasion.)[57]

The provinces and communes suffered the same fate as the other formerly autonomous institutions and were transformed into agents of the theoretically omnipotent state. Initially the Fascists had been content to dissolve most of the councils elected in 1920 and to hold rigged elections in which Fascists were assured of victory. But the continuation of elections to provincial and communal councils was not only in contrast to authoritarian principles of fascism but also either consolidated the power of local Party bosses or provoked internecine disputes within the Party. Mussolini decided therefore to abolish all elective provincial and communal authorities and to replace them with central and prefectoral appointees. Two laws of 1926 (Royal Decree Laws of February 4, 1926, No. 273, and September 3, 1926, No. 1910) abolished communal elections and provided for the state appointment of *Podestà* who assumed all the powers of the former mayors, executive *Giunte*, and councils. The *Podestà* were given strictly advisory *Consulte*, with members designated by labor and management organizations and ratified by the Prefect. A law of 1928 (Royal Decree Law of December 27, 1928, No. 2962) applied the same authoritarian principle to the less important provincial administration, replacing the elected president and provincial deputation with a centrally appointed *Preside* and the council with a centrally designated *Rettorato*. The Prefect's recommendations for appointments to these posts were usually ratified by the Minister of the Interior.[58] It is note-

57. *Corriere della Sera* (Jan. 17, 1923), p. 2.

58. Ministero per la Costituente, *Relazione*, 2, 382–99; Malinverno, pp. 161–62; H. Finer, p. 328.

worthy, however, that the Prefect was not himself made the chief of the provincial administration, as he had been before 1888: this is still another instance of the Fascist tendency to disperse administrative, as opposed to political, authority.

Most of the *Presidi* and *Podestà* were in practice chosen from among the traditional aristocratic and bourgeois ruling classes, thus excluding the representatives of the peasants and industrial workers from the major source of governmental-administrative power that they had been able to win since the unification of the country. All formal governmental power in the commune was now located in the *Podestà*, although, like the Prefects, they had to contend with the rival political authority of the Party's representatives, in this case, the communal Political Secretaries. Governmental control over communal affairs was further increased in 1928 when the professional Communal Secretaries—the chief communal civil servants—became functionaries of the state, freely transferable from one commune to another and subject to the direct hierarchical control of the Prefect, bypassing the *Podestà*. The Communal Secretaries had been major political figures especially in rural communes where they were often the only local notables with training in public affairs.[59]

A law of 1925 authorized the Prefects to purge local government staffs of employees guilty of activities "incompatible with the general political directives of the government." In 1933, Party membership was made a prerequisite to local government employment. The provincial Secretaries became state functionaries, with a single national roll, in 1942. Thus the chief professional functionary of both the province and the commune came to be hired and fired not by the local authorities but by the state. This develop-

59. Ministero per la Costituente, *Relazione*, 2, 392–94.

ment was generally welcomed by the provincial and communal secretaries who thus achieved both greater prestige as state employees and a measure of independence from local political conflicts.[60]

The GPA was retained with its powers of tutelage over provincial and communal administrations but its composition was changed by Royal Decree of December 27, 1928, No. 3123, in accordance with *étatiste* principles to include five state officials (the Prefect, the vice-prefect inspector, a prefectoral councillor, the chief accountant of the prefecture, and the Intendant of Finance) in addition to one member of the Fascist party, designated by its National Secretary.

Increased prefectoral control over local government, however, had to be exercised so as not to offend the Party. When one prefectoral official attempted to prevent the tax collector of a commune, who was also its PNF Political Secretary, from diverting communal revenues to private purposes, he was transferred under the pressure of the *federale*, despite the six months' resistance of the career Prefect to such a transfer. The same prefectoral official was transferred some time later when he attempted to stop a Political Secretary, who was also the chief engineer of a commune, from padding the figures in public works contracts and retaining the difference for himself and the Party treasury. One word from the Party secretary to the Prefect, a political appointee, secured this transfer within twenty-four hours. It appears that Prefects had to be quite tolerant of the widespread tendency of Fascist provincial and communal authorities to enrich themselves at public expense.[61]

Action was finally taken on the long-standing question of the Subprefects and provincial boundaries in 1927. Un-

60. Ibid., pp. 641–50; H. Finer, p. 276.
61. Ciccia, pp. 960–61.

der the Law of January 2, 1927, No. 1, all subprefectures were abolished and their staffs and functions transferred to the prefectures. To soften this tremendous blow to the prestige of hundreds of minor provincial towns, some seventeen new provinces were created, increasing the number of prefectures and provinces to a total of ninety-two as opposed to the sixty-nine of before the First World War. Some new provinces had been created in the territories acquired after the war (Trieste, Trent, Fiume, Pola, and Zara) and two *circondari* had been transformed into provinces for the cities of La Spezia and Taranto, the population and importance of which had grown enormously since they had become the major Italian naval bases. Seventeen new provinces were now carved out of existing provinces, further reducing the Prefects' areas of operations.

Several general factors played a part in this reform: (a) the improvement in communications, permitting the Prefects to control their provinces without the aid of Subprefects; (b) the intensification of state controls over local governments through the banning of political opposition, the system of central appointment to replace elections, and the creation of fulltime prefectoral officers (the provincial inspectors or vice-prefect inspectors) responsible for continuing inspection of local government operations (under Royal Decree Law of October 23, 1925, No. 2113); (c) the need to increase prefectoral staffs without budgetary increases; (d) traditional criticism of the subprefectures as useless bottlenecks; (e) occasional conflicts between Prefects and Subprefects in evaluating local situations, requiring central settlement; (f) the political feasibility of abolishing the subprefectures in a dictatorship over the protests of the towns deprived of income and prestige; (g) the abolition of elections and the need for Subprefects as electoral agents; (h) a desire to check the growth of large cities by creating a larger number of centers of attraction; (i) the possibility of satisfying a greater number of Party secretaries anxious to obtain appointment as Prefects.[62]

Particular factors entered into the creation of certain provinces, such as Bolzano. A separate province was carved out of the larger province of Trent in order to isolate the German-speaking population for the purposes of "Italianization." In this way, the German minority (a majority in the new province) could be watched more closely and brought into closer contact with the political and administrative agencies of the regime. The establishment of many state field services would augment the size and influence of the Italian minority.[63]

Two other provinces were created in the 1930s, Littoria and Asti (1934–35). The provincial capital of Littoria was a completely new town, founded in the heart of the Pontine reclamation district. The name was inspired by the major Fascist symbol, the fasces carried by the Roman lictors. Finally, in 1939 the four provinces created in Libya were assimilated to those in the homeland, making a grand total of ninety-eight provinces on the eve of the Second World War. One province, Caserta, was absorbed into the province of Naples in 1927.

The many and profound changes in local government institutions necessitated the elaboration of a new Consolidated Act or *Testo Unico* of the Provincial and Communal Law, which was promulgated by Royal Decree No. 383, dated March 3, 1934. Under the new law the Prefects were empowered to review not only the legality of local government decisions, but also their merits or con-

62. Malinverno, p. 148; Salvatorelli and Mira, *Storia,* pp. 356, 391–94; Ministero per la Costituente, *Relazione,* 2, 382–88; Arturo Lentini, *L'Amministrazione locale* (2d ed. Como, 1953), pp. 21–22.

63. Tamaro, 2, 163–64.

venience, subject to appeal to the Minister of the Interior. This destroyed whatever formal autonomy remained to the provinces and communes. The Prefect's emergency powers were vastly expanded: he could now make and unmake local and national laws and act as he saw fit in cases of "necessity" or "urgency." At the same time, the Party succeeded in securing four out of nine posts on the GPA for its appointees, the other five consisting solely of prefectoral officials.

Article 19 of the 1934 Act reformulated the definition of prefectoral powers in accordance with the 1926 Act and the 1927 circular to the Prefects. The Article runs as follows:

> The Prefect is the highest authority of the State in the Province. He is the direct representative of the Executive Power.
>
> The Prefect is in charge of the life of the province which receives from him impulse, coordination, and direction.
>
> In conformity with the general directives of the Government, the Prefect acts to ensure unity of political orientation in the activities of the different State services and of the local authorities, coordinating the action of all public offices and supervising the services —with the exception of the services of the Ministries of Justice, War, Navy, and Air and the Railway Administration.
>
> He exercises the powers devolved upon him by the laws and promotes, when necessary, the settlement of jurisdictional conflicts between the administrative and the judicial authorities.
>
> He takes, in case of necessity or urgency, those measures which he believes indispensable in the public interest.

He supervises the operations of all public administrations and their personnel within the limits of the general norms on the legal status of State employees and with the exception of those administrations indicated in paragraph three of this article.

He orders the investigations which he believes necessary with respect to the administrations subject to his supervision.

He appoints special commissioners to carry out legally obligatory decisions in the case of delay or omission on the part of the ordinary local administrative bodies and to run such bodies whenever for any reason they cannot function.

He supervises public order and superintends public security, commands the police forces, and may request the intervention of the other armed forces.

He presides over the Prefectoral Council and the Provincial Administrative Junta.

Under Fascism the Prefects had reached the zenith of power and prestige. Through them, the dictatorship extended its control to every aspect of Italian life and carried out its episodic "battles" to reshape the Italian people and land in the Roman Imperial image. Through them, it directed the press and enforced political conformity, Italianized German toponymy in Bolzano and confiscated the property of the Jews under the 1938 racial laws, removed offensive street names and prevented rural workers from migrating to the cities, repressed agitation arising from acute social distress and administered summary political justice, propagandized the "works of the regime" and distributed sustenance to the ruling middle and upper classes.[64]

64. Michele La Torre, "Prefetti e prefetture," *L'Amministrazione Italiana,* 3 (1948), 311.

But if Fascism made the Prefect powerful in the province, it also took steps to ensure his subservience to the dictator. The Prefect continued to work, in the words of a former career Prefect who served during the period, in the same "crowded theater of ambitions under pressure," to perform the same "harlequinades in delirium" as before Fascism. But under the dictatorship, this same official reveals, the Prefects were brought under the surveillance of several officials: (1) the provincial commander of the Carabinieri, who reported directly to the commanding general of the corps, who in turn reported directly to the Duce; (2) the *Questore,* or provincial police chief, often a political appointee, who reported directly and in person to the Chief of Police (the former director general of public security in the Ministry of the Interior), who, in turn, despite the opposition of the Undersecretary of the Interior, also reported directly to Mussolini; (3) the regional inspectors of the OVRA, or secret political police, with their thousands of informers located in every office, public or private, on trains and trolleys, in factories, etc., who reported exclusively to the Chief of Police in Rome and were explicitly independent of the prefectures and *Questore;* (4) the provincial and regional political investigation offices of the Fascist Militia (MVSN), which reported directly to their commanding general, who in turn had direct access to the Duce; (5) the Party Federal Secretary, so often anxious to get the Prefect's job, who reported directly to the National Secretary, who again had direct access to the dictator; and (6) the private inspectors of the Chief of Police himself.[65]

This surveillance and the deliberate insecurity of prefectoral tenure were to some extent self-defeating, for Prefects became afraid to report anything to Rome that might

65. Domenico Soprano, "Prefetture," *Il Corriere Amministrativo, 14* (1958), 480–81.

displease the Party or Mussolini, which might expose them to charges of being unenthusiastic about government policy or even anti-Fascist. Thus they tended to gloss over adverse reactions to government measures and to refrain from reporting the growing disgust with Party corruption in the late 1930s and the pervasive dismay at Italy's entrance into World War II.[66]

66. Leto, pp. 147–48; Arturo Lentini, "Prefetti e Prefetture," *Il Corriere Amministrativo, 4* (1948), 1020–22.

Chapter Five

THE REPUBLIC

THE COLLAPSE OF FASCISM AND THE DRIVE TO REPLACE THE CENTRALIZED STATE (1943–46)

ONCE AGAIN IN ITALIAN HISTORY involvement in war, instead of consolidating the existing political regime, undermined its bases and caused its collapse. The initial unpopularity of the war and the alliance with Nazi Germany, military defeats in the Balkans, Russia, and Africa, the loss of the Empire, the massive bombardment of practically defenseless Italian cities, the Allied conquest of Sicily and imminent invasion of the mainland combined to produce mass disaffection from the Fascist regime and the demoralization of the ruling Party itself. The way was paved for the previous allies of the regime—the King, the army, and the police—with the aid of dissident Fascist leaders, to remove Mussolini from power in July 1943, and to replace the Fascist totalitarian dictatorship with a traditional monarchical autocracy.

The King appointed a government of high functionaries

under Marshal Badoglio which attempted to meet popular demands for an end to the war and for sanctions against Fascists, yet without provoking a massive German invasion, Fascist counterrevolution, or a popular uprising. On the one hand, therefore, it declared that the war would be prosecuted; proclaimed martial law, with the transfer of responsibility for internal security to the military and military tribunals; maintained the racial laws and censorship of the press; and banned organized political activity for the duration of the war. On the other hand, it dissolved the Fascist party, the Fascist Grand Council, the Chamber of Fasces and Corporations, the Special Tribunal for the Defense of the State, and the secret political police (OVRA); established a special court to confiscate the illicit personal gains of Fascist hierarchs and their sympathizers; absorbed the Militia into the regular army; and placed the property and organization of Fascist party ancillaries—such as the labor and management organizations, the Fascist Youth (GIL), and the recreation agency (the *Dopolavoro*) in the hands of government commissioners. It also began a modest purge of the state bureaucracy.[1]

Characteristically, none of the Fascist Prefects offered to resign and many implored the new government to maintain them in their posts.[2] And indeed, the first Minister of the Interior in the Badoglio Cabinet, a career Prefect, with the backing of the King and of the Chief of Police, another career Prefect, who had served as Chief of Police between 1940 and February 1943, proposed to remove only eight Fascist Prefects, all more or less incompetent and serving in very minor provinces. The rest of the Cabinet rebelled at such timidity and Badoglio was forced to install a new Minister of the Interior, who proceeded, much

1. Salvatorelli and Mira, *Storia*, pp. 965–1061.
2. Senise, *Quando ero Capo*, p. 207.

against the King's desires, to replace about fifty Prefects who had been appointed from outside the career service.[3] The new Prefects were taken from the career service and from the regular army. Marshal Badoglio preferred, however, to govern through the territorial military commanders, who were ordered to fire upon any demonstrators without the traditional three blasts of the trumpet. To the Prefects, he issued terse military "service orders" to prevent any political activities, to carry out gradual purges in local administration, to arrest dangerous Fascist hierarchs, and to make some preparations to cope with the massive Allied bombardments. In practice, however, neither military commanders nor Prefects attempted to prevent the popular demonstrations against Fascism which broke out immediately after the coup of July 25 or to check the emergence of anti-Fascist political organizations and activities. They did remove many of the Fascist *Podestà*—those who did not, like most prominent Fascist leaders, go into hiding.[4]

The first Badoglio government, however, lasted only forty-five days; for, after the armistice was finally concluded with the Allies in September, the King and Badoglio fled south, without warning or informing the other ministers, to seek Allied protection from Italy's erstwhile ally. This marked the utter collapse of the centralized Italian state. The army, left without orders, disintegrated. German armies, which had been pouring over the Alps during the forty-five days, proceeded to occupy most of the peninsula and for twenty months to resist tenaciously the gradual and painful Allied advance up the mountainous peninsula. During this time, the country was divided in two: on either side of the zone of combat, there was an Italian government

3. Ibid., pp. 214–15; Badoglio, *L'Italia*, pp. 88–89.
4. Dolfin, *Con Mussolini*, pp. 216–17, 257–58.

dominated by foreign military authorities. Rome itself fell into German hands.

North of the German lines there was confusion and uncertainty, looting and disorders until the German military governors reimposed a measure of order and provided the conditions necessary for the resumption of economic activity and the public services. Those Prefects who had remained at their posts lost any hold of the situation: the careerists appointed by Badoglio waited nervously until they should be retired and replaced by those whom Badoglio only a few weeks before had purged. Many of the careerists had fled to the South; others remained and were arrested by the Germans and sent to concentration camps in Germany. It was only on September 23 that a regular Italian government in the form of the Fascist Social Republic was re-established under German auspices. The ministries in Rome were brought to the North and scattered among several towns and cities. The Prefects serving the Fascist Republic were forced to contend with the demands of the local German commanders, with the problems of civil government in a society ravaged by wartime hardships and civil war, with the lawless operations of the numerous formal and informal police forces, with the sabotage and terroristic violence of the anti-Fascist Resistance, with the hopeless tasks of recruiting a new Fascist army and a labor force to work in Germany.[5] Most of the Prefects were Party leaders, chosen on the basis of Party seniority and fidelity to Mussolini; almost none of them had the usual college degree; some had backgrounds of corruption and violence.[6]

In the South, the legitimate government, the King's government under Marshal Badoglio, re-established an em-

5. Ibid., pp. 216–17; Franz Turchi, *Prefetto con Mussolini* (Rome, 1950), passim.

6. Dolfin, pp. 216–17, 257–58.

bryonic central administration in the town of Brindisi, with the protection of the Allies and the aid of the few Italian civil servants who had managed to flee to the "Kingdom of the South."[7] Under the supervision of the Allied Control Commission established on November 13, 1943, the Badoglio government attempted to make contact with the Prefects of the seven provinces initially under its control (four in the southeastern part of the peninsula—the region of Apulia—and three in Sardinia). Through them, it attempted to round up the available state functionaries, to restore the services and personnel of the local governments, to aid the refugees streaming across the line of combat, to curb the black market and allocate food supplies, and to restore a minimum of public order—all despite the paralysis of transportation and communications.

In February 1944, the Italian government was permitted to establish itself in Salerno, with control over ten provinces south of Naples, the provinces of Sardinia, and those of Sicily. Communications with the two islands were so poor, however, that the government was forced to deconcentrate considerable ministerial authority to two High Commissioners, one for Sardinia[8] and one for Sicily,[9] with appointed representative advisory committees and power to supervise and coordinate the work of the Prefects and of the other state services. The Allies had restored the pre-Fascist local government officers—the mayors and the presidents of the provincial deputations. This measure was generalized to all provinces under Italian control by the Badoglio government. Royal Decree Law of April 4, 1944, No. 111, authorized the Prefects to replace the *Podestà* and *Presidi* with the traditional mayors and presidents, together with their

7. Badoglio, pp. 279-98.
8. Royal Decree Law of Jan. 24, 1944, No. 21.
9. Royal Decree Law of March 8, 1944, No. 91.

respective executive committees, and to appoint four locally prominent citizens to replace the representatives of the Fascist party on the organs of tutelage, the *Giunte Provinciali Amministrative*. The Prefects were also authorized to appoint five-man juntas to run the Chambers of Commerce, Industry, and Agriculture, which replaced the Fascist Provincial Economic Councils.[10] Under another law, the office of *Capo del Governo* became once again the traditional Presidency of the Council of Ministers.[11]

The Badoglio government of bureaucrats was replaced in April 1944 by one representing the spectrum of anti-Fascist political parties that had emerged in the summer of 1943. The six parties ranged from the Liberals on the right, a weakly organized party of eminent personalities (its leader was Benedetto Croce), close to the monarchy and to the traditions of the pre-Fascist regime which they had dominated; the Labor Democrats, the largely southern followers of some pre-Fascist political leaders, akin to the French Radical Socialists; the Christian Democrats, the heirs to the pre-Fascist Populist party; the Actionists, a new party of left-of-center, republican intellectuals; the Socialists; and the Communists. These parties were also represented on self-designated local, regional, and national Committees of National Liberation (CLNs), with equal representation of all parties until elections should demonstrate the effective popular support of each one. In the CLNs, as in the government, the unanimous consent of all parties was required for decision-making. By the summer of 1944, the six-party Cabinet was governing from newly-liberated Rome.

10. Royal Decree Law of Jan. 27, 1944, No. 23. The Ministry of Corporations was renamed the Ministry of Industry, Commerce, and Labor by Royal Decree of Aug. 8, 1943, No. 718. The Ministry of Popular Culture was transformed into an Undersecretariat for Press and Information by Decree Law of July 3, 1944, No. 163.

11. Royal Decree Law of May 16, 1944, No. 136.

Committees of National Liberation had also been formed to direct the Resistance against the Nazi-Fascists in northern and central Italy. Only in the North was there a full development of the armed Resistance in the form of partisan brigades. Only there did the CLNs acquire great prestige and power as the leaders of a mass movement involving all groups and classes. And only there did the CLNs develop their revolutionary demands for profound social and economic reforms and the establishment of a new state-form, based on the CLNs rather than on the old bureaucracy.

Carlo Levi has described the atmosphere of these times in *L'Orologio:*[12]

> Rome signified together all the negative aspects of a false and bankrupt world: the name meant centralization, the inept and parasitic bureaucracy, nationalism, fascism, the Empire, the bourgeoisie, the monarchy, clericalism; and also the common defects, the lack of courage and initiative, cynicism, indifference and fanaticism, the fear of liberty . . . But, in a certain period, this meant a positive will, something genuine. Thus, for example, during nine months, from the dramatic days of its liberation to the end of the war, the entire city of Florence, down to the last artisan and boy, had been together in a daily battle against Rome, in the name of liberty. No one wanted to hear any more talk of Prefects, of those who then were called "the proconsuls of Rome in the provinces," and who came, it was said, with the mission of sabotaging the recovery of the city, which, just as it had liberated and defended itself with its own forces, wanted to administer and reconstruct itself. The Prefect, who landed in that incandescent world like an undertaker at a wedding ban-

12. Carlo Levi, *L'Orologio* (Turin, Einaudi, 1950), pp. 216–17.

quet, was an old Sicilian nobleman with a beak-like nose and bags under his eyes, broken in for all possible regimes, remote from any impulse of enthusiasm. He tried not to annoy anyone, to make himself as small as possible, to pass unobserved, in order to resist: and in the end, he was the strongest and he won. But meanwhile all the walls were filled with writings. "Away with the Prefect! Partisans, a new enemy, the Prefect! Get away while you still have time! Go back to Rome!" could be read in coal, in chalk, in paint, on the houses of San Frediano and the Cure, on the walls of the fifteenth-century palaces in the center, on the banks of the Arno, everywhere.

The Prefect did not leave his house, even though no one had it against him personally, but only against the institution he represented. All the parties were in agreement amidst the growing popular ferment: within the walls of the city, which felt rejuvenated as in the times when its palaces were new and brilliant, no one dared to defend the centralized state and its anachronistic instruments. The Committee of Liberation met, discussed and approved a moderate and reasonable draft in which they asked the abolition of the Prefects or at least consent that the Prefects be named not by Rome, but by the local organizations; and it decided to go in its entirety, with all its members, to present the draft to the Government to have it approved.

But demands of the Tuscan CLN to abolish the prefectures or to allow the CLNs to appoint the Prefects met with the suspicion and hostility of the conservative parties in Rome—the Liberals, the Labor Democrats, and the Christian Democrats—who feared that the leftist CLNs of central and northern Italy were the prototypes of Soviets, portending the revolutionary destruction of the re-emerging centralized state.[13] The Cabinet, therefore, agreed only to give the matter its consideration: the time, it was said, was not right for such profound reforms.[14]

The underground CLNs of the North were more successful in a way: they succeeded in securing from the Rome government and the Allied Commission (in an agreement of December 27, 1944) the right to govern the liberated provinces until the arrival of Allied troops. But at the same time, they would have to give up their powers and place the partisan brigades under Allied command.

When the Allies eventually broke through into northern Italy in the spring of 1945, they found Prefects, vice-prefects, mayors, vice-mayors, *Questori,* and provincial presidents already appointed and, in the provinces liberated by the CLNs, already governing. The various posts were distributed so as to give each party represented a roughly equal share of power in the various regions. When the Allied Military Government (AMG) officials arrived, they investigated the CLN appointees and usually ratified the appointments. Thus in the North, the Prefects in charge of the provinces were not appointed by the central government, but sponsored by one of the Resistance parties, accepted by the provincial CLN, and appointed by the provincial Allied Military Governor. The AMG officers brought with them the *Gazzetta Ufficiale,* with all the laws and regulations of the Roman ministries, but they permitted the CLN Prefects considerable latitude in enforcing them. The Prefects in the North were not therefore the representatives of the Roman government, but of the Committee of National

13. Norman Kogan, "The Italian Action Party and the Institutional Question," *Western Political Quarterly, 6* (1953), 286–89.
14. Levi, pp. 218–19.

Liberation that sponsored them. The Roman government, consequently, had no direct control over the northern provinces except through the mediating diaphragm of the provincial and regional Allied Military Governors. With AMG support, the Prefects could resist instructions from Rome or go far beyond what Rome allowed. AMG control was close at hand: prefectoral decisions could be ratified quickly and with knowledge of local problems and circumstances, unlike the traditional system in which prefectoral decisions required the sanction of the remote government in Rome.[15]

With the end of hostilities, a new cabinet had been formed after lengthy negotiations between the northern Resistance leaders, the ministers in Rome, and the Allies. It was composed of representatives of the six CLN parties as before, but headed by Ferruccio Parri, one of the major leaders of the northern Resistance. The Republicans, still another pre-Fascist party, refused to serve in any government under the monarchy. For five and one-half months, from June to December 1945, the Parri government struggled with the problem of restoring central government control over a prostrate, misery-ridden country, torn apart by the autonomistic CLNs in the North, separatist agitation in Sicily, Sardinia, Aosta Valley, and Trent, and an almost complete breakdown in transportation. In the end, the Parri government—in which the northern CLNs had placed their hopes of radical reform—was brought down by the conservative Liberals and Christian Democrats and gave

15. Carlo Garrone, "Vita, morte e miracoli di un prefetto politico," *Il Ponte*, 2 (1946), 861–76. Giuseppe Romita, Socialist Minister of the Interior from December 1945 to July 1946, asserts that by the time he took control of the Ministry, it was an act of courage to send out a circular to the Prefects—so undemocratic had that act of routine administration come to appear! See Romita's memoirs, *Dalla monarchia alla Repubblica* (Pisa, Nistri-Lischi, 1959), p. 32.

way to the first of a long series of cabinets under the leadership of Alcide De Gasperi, the head of the Christian Democrats. The two key issues involved in the fall of the Parri government were the leftist drive to purge the bureaucracy of Fascists and rightist efforts to replace the political Prefects of the Resistance with career Prefects responsible to the government in Rome. Both of these questions involved the much broader one of the restoration of the pre-Fascist state as opposed to revolutionary decentralization of power to the Committees of National Liberation. De Gasperi, with the solid political and military support of the Allies, the backing of the Liberals and his own Christian Democrats, and the anxious pressure of conservatives generally, pledged himself to the reconstruction of the old centralized state and to the establishment of (central) law and order throughout the country.[16]

Throughout the period of the Parri government, the CLN Prefects had struggled with the overwhelming problems left in the wake of the war: destitution, unemployment, and inflation; the collection of taxes and the enforcement of laws; the adjustment of the manifold conflicts between newly autonomous social groups and between those groups and administrative authorities; the reconstruction of damaged cities; the restoration of essential public services; the repression of the black market, with the aid of the courts; the confiscation of illicit profits; compulsory agricultural deliveries; relief measures to veterans, refugees, and the general population, including the distribution of UNRRA aid; rationing and price controls; and the restoration of public tranquillity.[17]

16. Leo Valiani, *L'Avvento di De Gasperi: Tre anni di politica italiana* (Turin, 1949), pp. 1–40.
17. Garrone, p. 871.

It was on this last point that conservatives were most critical, for in many areas in the North, the CLN Prefects seemed unable or unwilling to take strong action against left-wing disorders and outright terrorism. Political Prefects, it was claimed, could not act against the forces responsible for their appointment. Nor could they be trusted to act as the impartial guardians of life and property after the impending withdrawal of the Allied Military Government on January 1, 1946. Increasing political tension was expected to develop during the first electoral campaigns to be held in a generation—the local government elections in March 1946—which were to be followed in June by the election of a Constituent Assembly and a nationwide referendum on the fate of the monarchy. Conservatives did not feel that the Prefects responsible to the CLNs would be sufficiently neutral in the impending political struggle.

The *élan* of the northern Resistance, its drive to preserve the authority of the CLNs as new organs of government (appointing Prefects and *Questori* and mayors and provincial presidents), was weakened by the agreement of December 1944, whereby the real authority in the North was transferred to the AMG, which in turn could yield up its powers to the central government in Rome; by the fact that the authority of the CLNs did not rest upon popular elections; and by the determination of the Allies to prevent a revolutionary movement in the North and to restore the authority of the centralized state. There was also a massive reaction of the country south of Rome against the CLNs and their radicalism. The South had not, after all, experienced the months of Nazi-Fascist occupation and terror and its own CLNs had not therefore acquired the prestige and influence of their northern counterparts. Finally, opposition to CLN control came from the Liberal and Christian Democratic representatives on the northern CLNs themselves, and from the Roman bureaucracy anxious to reassert the complete control of traditional state machinery over the country.[18]

Thus in early 1946, upon the withdrawal of AMG control in the North, all of the CLN Prefects were called to Rome and offered the alternative of incorporation in the regular prefectoral career service and subjection to the discipline of Rome, or dismissal. The Socialists and Communists accepted the abolition of the CLN Prefects and their replacement by Prefects responsible to Rome because they were still at that time represented in the government and expected to have considerable voice in the issuing of directives to the Prefects. And in fact it was a Socialist Minister of the Interior who presided over the transfer of control over the Prefects from the CLNs and the AMG to the government in Rome. The Left expected that it would soon gain control of the entire machinery of the state through the coming general elections.[19]

Almost no CLN Prefects agreed to join the career service and become the functionaries of the Ministry of the Interior. Most of them returned to their former occupations, some, however, choosing instead to become members of Parliament. By March 1946, there was thus only a handful of Resistance Prefects still in service; almost all prefectures were now in the hands of professional career officials, all of whom had served as Prefects or vice-prefects under the Fascist regime.[20]

18. Ministero per la Costituente, *Relazione*, 2, 616–17; Mario Bendiscioli, "La Resistenza: Gli aspetti politici," in Aldo Garosci et al., *Il Secondo Risorgimento* (Rome, 1955), pp. 353–59; Panfilo Gentile, "La Restaurazione della democrazia," in ibid., pp. 384–88.

19. Valiani, pp. 40–43. See also Romita's memoirs.

20. Ministero dell'Interno, *Ruoli di anzianità del personale delle amministrazioni dipendenti: Situazione al 1° gennaio 1947* (Rome, 1947). As of Jan. 1, 1947, there were only eight out of 133 Prefects who had entered the state service after Fascism fell.

SHAPING THE INSTITUTIONS OF THE REPUBLIC

In June 1946 the referendum was held on the form of the state and it marked the only major accomplishment of the anti-Fascist Resistance. The Republic was established by the narrow margin of 12,717,923 (largely in the North and Center) for the Republic, as against 10,719,284 votes (largely southern) for the monarchy. The same lack of consensus was displayed in the simultaneous election of a Constituent Assembly to draft the constitution of the new Republic. Three mass parties emerged with 75 per cent of the popular vote—the Christian Democrats, the Socialists, and the Communists—the rest of the vote being fragmented among a miscellany of minor parties. (See Table 8.) These three parties formed a new government, again under De Gasperi, and, despite the extreme divergencies between them, managed to agree upon the terms of the new republican constitution.

The new Constitution, promulgated on January 1, 1948, reflected an attempt to establish the framework for a viable social democracy in antithesis to the totalitarian regime that had ruled Italy for over two decades. It provided for a standard parliamentary system of government, based on universal suffrage, but also for a series of checks on the power of the parliamentary majority: constitutional guarantees of civil and political rights; an independent self-governing judiciary; bicameralism (based on constituencies of different size and electorates of different ages); a President of the Republic elected by Parliament but possessing a practically unlimited right to dissolve either or both houses of Parliament, to appoint the Council of Ministers, to send messages to Parliament and request Parliament to re-examine its legislation, and to command the armed forces; national referenda to pass on constitutional amendments and certain

TABLE 8 Postwar Italian Elections (1946–63)

Parties	1946 % pop. vote	1946 Chamber seats	1948 % pop. vote	1948 Chamber seats	1953 % pop. vote	1953 Chamber seats	1958 % pop. vote	1958 Chamber seats	1963 % pop. vote	1963 Chamber seats
Neo-Fascists	5.3	30	2.0	6	5.8	29	4.7	25	5.1	27
Monarchists	2.8	16	2.8	14	6.9	40	4.8	23	1.7	8
Liberals	6.8	41	3.8	19	3.0	13	3.5	16	7.0	39
Christian Democrats	35.2	207	48.5	305	40.1	263	42.2	273	38.3	260
South Tyrol Populists	—	—	0.5	3	0.5	3	0.5	3	0.4	3
Republicans	4.4	23	2.5	9	1.6	5	1.4	7	1.4	6
Social Democrats	—	—	7.1	33	4.5	19	4.6	23	6.1	33
Socialists	20.7	115	} 31.0	} 183	12.7	75	14.2	84	13.8	87
Communists	19.0	104	} 31.0	} 183	22.7	143	22.7	140	25.3	166
Various	5.8	20	1.8	2	2.2	0	1.4	2	0.9	1
TOTAL	100.0	556	100.0	574	100.0	590	100.0	596	100.0	630

Sources: Lucio Luzzatto, *Elezioni politiche*, pp. 131, 150, 180; *Il Giorno* (Milan), May 28, 1958, p. 1; *Rinascita*, May 4, 1963, pp. 5–6.

kinds of legislation, as well as popular legislative initiative; a Constitutional Court with the powers of judicial review; a sovereign, independent, but established Church with powers based upon the Lateran Pacts of 1929; the rigidity of the Constitution itself, amendments requiring absolute majorities in both houses and a majority in a nationwide referendum, or a two-thirds majority in Parliament; and finally, the decentralization of legislative and administrative power to regional governments.[21]

The reaction to Fascist centralization, so strong after the fall of the regime, carried on into the period of the Constituent Assembly. Centralization was blamed for the victory of Fascism and for all the misfortunes that Fascist policy had incurred for the country; it was identified with (again in Carlo Levi's words) "the inept and parasitic bureaucracy, nationalism, fascism, the Empire, the bourgeoisie, the monarchy . . .," with Fascist misgovernment and corruption, with the national collapse. The war had stimulated the development of aspirations for local self-determination by disrupting and destroying communications and transport and weakening the ability of the central government to help with local problems. It had seen the emergence of local political groups, the Committees of National Liberation, which had taken on the full burden of liberating their provinces by military means and governing them once they had been liberated. It had fostered a tendency for the less damaged areas to dissociate themselves from the national disaster and to hoard their resources for local use. Finally, it had provoked in the outlying areas of the country—the physically isolated islands of Sardinia and Sicily and the border areas, such as Aosta Valley and Bolzano,

21. For a general analysis of the Constitution, see Giuseppe Maranini, "Le Istituzioni costituzionali," in Giuseppe Maranini et al., *Aspetti di vita italiana contemporanea* (Bologna, 1957), pp. 3–51.

with sizable ethnic minorities long oppressed by Fascist policies of forced Italianization—a desire for outright separation from or at least autonomy within the Italian state.

Aspirations toward decentralization took the form of proposals to establish more or less autonomous regional self-
governments. The major sponsors of regionalism were the
Christian Democrats, who revived the pre-Fascist Populist
demand for local autonomy. The Christian Democrats in
general were in favor of the constitutional diffusion of power in accordance with their corporatist ideal of autonomous
social groupings. Even more extreme decentralization was
demanded by the Republicans, who proposed the adoption
of an outright federalistic scheme.

Opposing the decentralizers were the parties at both ex-
tremes of the existing political spectrum. The Liberals
(with some notable exceptions), carrying on the tradition
of the strongly centralized liberal state, stressed the un-
wisdom of devolution in the face of the enormous tasks of
reconstruction. The Socialists and the Communists, on the
other hand, were opposed to any derogation to the sovereignty of the parliamentary majority; they opposed regionalism, just as they fought the President's unlimited right of
dissolution and the power of judicial review lodged in the
Constitutional Court. In the Jacobin tradition, they were
concerned lest regionalism impede the execution of far-
reaching economic and social reforms. They were, moreover, fairly sanguine concerning their chances of winning
a parliamentary majority in the first general elections under
the new Constitution and sought therefore to avoid the
creation of any checks on their future powers. Together
with the Liberals, they succeeded in watering down the
Christian Democratic proposals.[22]

22. Mario Einaudi, "The Constitution of the Italian Republic," *American
Political Science Review, 42* (1948), 661–76; Mario Einaudi, "Christian Democracy in Italy," in Mario Einaudi and François Goguel, *Christian De-*

The resulting compromise was a mild form of decentralization, indeed.

Title V of the Constitution divided the territory of the Republic into regions, provinces, and communes.[23] There were to be five regions with special statutes: Sicily, Sardinia, Trentino–Alto Adige (the provinces of Bolzano and Trent, otherwise known as Tridentine Venetia), Aosta Valley, and Friuli–Venetia Julia (which included the territories with a large Slavic minority, disputed with Yugoslavia and containing the city of Trieste).[24]

The rest of the country was to be divided into fourteen ordinary regions, listed as follows with their probable capitals: Piedmont (Turin), Lombardy (Milan), Venetia (Venice), Liguria (Genoa), Emilia–Romagna (Bologna), Tuscany (Florence), Umbria (Perugia), the Marches (Ancona), Latium (Rome), Abruzzi–Molise (L'Aquila), Campania (Naples), Apulia (Bari), Basilicata (Potenza), and Calabria (Reggio Calabria or Catanzaro). The boundaries were not specified by the Constitution itself, but left to the determination of the future Parliament. It was generally under-

---

mocracy in France and Italy (Notre Dame, 1952), pp. 47–49, 60–61; and Ministero per la Costituente, *Relazione, 2,* 217–55.

23. There had been general agreement among the parties to abolish the provinces as self-governing institutions, but this plan had to be dropped in the face of a storm of protest from provincial authorities and employees. See Ruggero Grieco, "Il Prefetto," *Rinascita, 8* (April 1951), Supplement, pp. 1–4.

24. The Regions of Sicily and Aosta Valley were created *before* the Constitution went into effect by Decree Laws of May 15, 1946, No. 455, and Sept. 7, 1945, No. 545, respectively. Both of these decree laws were ratified by the Constituent Assembly in Constitutional Laws of Feb. 20, 1948, No. 2 (Sicily) and No. 4 (Aosta Valley). Constitutional laws of the same date created the special Regions of Sardinia (No. 3), and Trentino–Alto Adige (No. 5). Creation of the fifth special Region, Friuli–Venetia Julia, was delayed until 1963 in part because of the difficulties concerning Trieste and conflicts among the provinces of the future Region. On this Region, see "Regione Friuli–Venezia Giulia," *L'Amministrazione Civile, 4* (Sept. 1960), xv.

stood that these boundaries would coincide with the grouping of provinces traditionally used in official government
statistics for decades. Regional capitals were presumably
to be determined by the regional councils since the latter
had jurisdiction over the location of regional offices.[25] The
special and ordinary regions are listed in Table 9.

The regions were to be organized as self-governing areas
with elected councils, executive committees, and presidents.
The powers of the councils in the special-statute regions
were to be particularly broad as determined in the statute
of each one. The councils of the ordinary regions were to
enjoy legislative powers in the following matters, as specified in Article 117:

> (a) the organization of Regional offices and adminis-
> trative bodies; (b) communal boundaries; (c) urban
> and rural local police [merely the enforcement of com-
> munal ordinances]; (d) fairs and markets; (e) public
> charities, and medical and hospital assistance;
> (f) handicrafts and vocational education, and educa-
> tional assistance; (g) museums and libraries of local
> authorities; (h) town planning; (i) tourism and the
> hotel industry; (j) trolley and bus lines of regional in-
> terest; (k) highways, aqueducts, and public works of
> regional interest; (l) lake navigation and ports; (m)
> minerals and thermal waters; (n) quarries and bogs;
> (o) hunting; (p) freshwater fishing; (q) agriculture and
> forestry; (r) handicrafts; and (s) other matters eventual-
> ly decentralized in constitutional laws.

The list of powers in the original draft included the far

25. Comitato Nazionale per la Celebrazione del Primo Decennale della
Proclamazione della Costituzione (27 dicembre 1947–27 dicembre 1957),
Guida alla costituzione (Rome, 1958), p. 237; Aldo Sandulli, *Manuale di
diritto amministrativo* (4th ed. Naples, 1957), p. 197.

TABLE 9 The Italian Regions

Regions (Capitals)	Number of communes	Area (sq. km.)	National area (per cent)	1951 Population	National population (per cent)	Number of provinces
OSTA VALLEY (Aosta)	74	3,262	1.1	94,140	0.2	1
RENTINO– ALTO ADIGE (Trent)	336	13,613	4.5	728,604	1.6	2
RIULI– VENETIA JULIA (Trieste)	217	7,847	2.7	1,226,121	2.6	3
ICILY (Palermo)	379	25,707	8.5	4,486,749	9.4	9
ARDINIA (Cagliari)	334	24,089	8.0	1,276,023	2.7	3
IEDMONT (Turin)	1,207	25,399	8.1	3,518,177	7.4	6
OMBARDY (Milan)	1,522	23,804	7.9	6,566,154	13.8	9
ENETIA (Venice)	582	18,377	6.1	3,918,059	8.2	7
IGURIA (Genoa)	234	5,409	1.8	1,566,961	3.3	4
MILIA–ROMAGNA (Bologna)	336	22,126	7.4	3,544,340	7.5	8
USCANY (Florence)	280	22,990	7.6	3,158,811	6.7	9
IMBRIA (Perugia)	151	8,456	2.8	803,918	1.7	2
IARCHES (Ancona)	216	9,692	3.2	1,364,030	2.9	4
ATIUM (Rome)	366	17,170	5.7	3,340,798	7.0	5
BRUZZI–MOLISE (L'Aquila)	438	15,231	5.1	1,684,030	3.5	5
AMPANIA (Naples)	540	13,595	4.5	4,346,264	9.1	5
PULIA (Bari)	249	19,347	6.4	3,220,485	6.8	5
ASILICATA (Potenza)	127	9,988	3.3	627,586	1.3	2
ALABRIA (Catanzaro)	407	15,079	5.0	2,044,287	4.3	3
	7,962	301,181	100.0	47,515,537	100.0	92

Source: *Annuario Parlamentare* (1957–58), pp. 398–407.

more crucial sectors of industry, commerce, mining, credit controls, public education, and public health, but the Liberal-Communist alliance forced the Christian Democrats to remove these from regional jurisdiction.

The regions were also to take over from the state the responsibility for the tutelage of provinces, communes, and other local government authorities. But strictly local autonomy was to be protected by limiting the regional tutelage organs to the supervision of legality: they could only request the re-examination of decisions of doubtful expediency.

The regions were supposed to be primarily legislative bodies. The Constitution exhorted them to exercise their decisions in the field not through their own staffs but through the provinces and communes. Article 118 runs as follows: "The Region normally exercises its administrative functions by delegating them to the Provinces, to the Communes, or to other local authorities, or making use of their offices." If regional field services had (in some undefined sense) to be created, they would have to be recruited, if possible, from among existing state and local civil servants who would be transferred to the regional services by national laws in the particular sectors of regional jurisdiction. The regions were forbidden to grant more favorable treatment to their services than that granted to the state civil service. The regional services would be directed by the regional presidents and juntas, elected by the regional councils. The presidents of the regions would be responsible to the central government for the administration of matters within state jurisdiction which were merely delegated to them by national law.

The regions were to have financial autonomy within the limits of national laws coordinating state, regional, and local finance. They were to be given their own taxes, as well as shares in state taxes. The state might make special grants-in-aid to the poorer regions for such purposes as economic development. The regions, moreover, would be given their own domains and property.

The state, that is, the Cabinet and Parliament, retained considerable control over the regions. Regional laws in the various sectors specified in Article 117 had to be in accord with the "fundamental principles" of national legislation, as established in a series of "framework laws" (*leggi-cornici*). Regional laws could not conflict with "the national interest or that of the other Regions." The national legislature was also to determine the degree of financial autonomy of the region in its tax laws, its grants-in-aid programs, and its award of domains and patrimonies. The national legislature had to approve the statute of each region. In each of the regions there was to be a resident Government Commissioner whose signature was required to validate regional laws; the Commissioner could send any law back to the regional council for reconsideration and if it was passed again by an absolute majority, the law could be challenged by the government before the Constitutional Court on grounds of illegality or before Parliament on grounds of conflict with the national interest or that of other regions. Parliament could therefore, in practice, overrule any regional law without much difficulty. The Government Commissioner was also to head a Government Control Commission to review *all* of the formal administrative decisions of the regional president and his junta; the Control Commission could disallow any such decision it deemed illegal and request reconsideration of any other; the Government Commissioner was also authorized to supervise the state services within the region and to coordinate state and regional administrative activities.

Finally, the President of the Republic was empowered to dissolve a regional council when it makes decisions contrary to the Constitution or grave violations of the law, or does not comply with the invitation of the Government to replace the Junta or President who shall have made such decisions or violations.

It [the Regional Council] may be dissolved when, through resignations or through the impossibility of forming a majority, it shall not be capable of functioning.

It may likewise be dissolved for reasons of national security.

A new regional council, however, had to be elected within three months.

It was assumed by most of the drafters of the Constitution that the prefectures would be abolished as soon as the regional councils were elected. The Prefects, as such, were not mentioned in the Constitution itself, but most of the members of the Constituent Assembly, having transferred the control over local government from the Prefect (and the GPA) to the regions, considered that the Prefects no longer had any raison d'être. The committee of the Constituent Assembly that drafted the provisions on decentralization (Section I, Local Autonomy, of the Second Subcommittee, Organization of the State, of the Committee of Seventy-Five) voted unanimously for the abolition of the Prefects. There were no replies to attacks on the institution in the plenary assembly.[26]

The Prefects as an institution had fallen low in public esteem. Exalted by Fascism, they were bound to be identified with its oppression and to share its fall from grace.

The most famous attack on the prefectoral system was written in 1944 by Luigi Einaudi, one of the leading Italian

26. Grieco, pp. 1–2; La Torre, "Prefetti e prefetture," p. 311.

scholars, a prominent anti-Fascist and spokesman of the Liberal party, who was to serve as President of the Republic between 1948 and 1955, the first President to be elected under the new Constitution. These are some passages from his widely publicized article, "Away with the Prefect!"[27]

To propose in Italy and in some other European countries the abolition of the "Prefect" seems to be extravagance worthy of an insane asylum. A venerable institution, which has come down to us from the earliest times (*la notte dei tempi*), the Prefect is almost synonomous with government and, with him gone, nothing else would seem to exist. Who commands and executes outside of the capital? How does the public administration operate? In truth, the Prefect is a disease which was inoculated into the Italian body politic by Napoleon . . . The new Italy, anxious to cement together the *membra disiecta* of the former states into a single body, imagined that federalism was the enemy and extended the prefectoral system even to those parts of Italy, such as the former Austrian provinces, which the disease had infiltrated in attenuated form. They believed they were establishing liberty and democracy, but they were forging the instrument of dictatorship.

Democracy and the Prefect are deeply repugnant to each other. In Italy, France, Spain or Prussia there has never been nor will there ever be democracy as long as there exists the type of centralized government of which the Prefect is a symbol . . . Elections, free choice of representatives, chambers, parliaments, constituent assemblies, responsible ministers are a lugubrious farce in countries with centralized governments of the Na-

27. Reprinted in Luigi Einaudi, *Il Buongoverno: Saggi di economia e politica* (Bari, 1954), pp. 52–59.

poleonic type . . . Democracy begins in the commune
. . . Therefore the *delenda Carthago* of liberal democracy is: Away with the Prefect! Away with all his offices
and his dependencies and his ramifications! Nothing
must be left standing of this centralized machine; not
even the stool of the porter. If we allow the porter to
survive, soon there will arise next to him a mushroom
growth of huts and sheds which will transform themselves into the old overshadowing *Palazzo del Governo*.
The Napoleonic Prefect must go, with his roots, his
trunk, his branches and his leaves. Fortunately indeed
in Italy today [1944] the centralized administration
has disappeared. It has shown itself to be a nullity; an
instrument without its own life, which the first ad-
venturer who happened along could seize and manipulate at his pleasure. Nothing evil will happen if we
do not reconstruct the already broken down and rotten
machine. The unity of the country is not provided by
the Prefects or the Purveyors of Studies or the Intendants of Finance or the Communal Secretaries or the
circulars and authorizations from Rome. The unity of
the country is made by the Italians. By the Italians
who learn at their own expense, committing mistakes,
to govern themselves . . .

THE REGIONS: VICTIMS OF THE
POLITICAL STRUGGLE

Today, fifteen years since the Constitution went into effect,
much of it remains a dead letter, including the provisions
for regionalism. The structure of the centralized state has
remained intact (except for the special regions) and the
Prefects have remained as essential instruments of central

control. The explanation for this lies in the nature of the postwar political struggle.

Italy after the war became a principal arena of international conflict. Domestic political forces emerged which reflected and participated in the struggle between the postwar superpowers. The Italian Communist party became the strongest Communist party in the West, with control over most of organized labor; about twenty per cent of the popular vote; a party membership of over two million; indirect domination of the Socialist party, with another twenty per cent of the voters; governing power, with the Socialists, in about one-third of Italian communes, including the cities of Milan, Genoa, Turin, Bologna, and Florence; control of a series of front organizations and of a flourishing network of cooperatives; and a nationwide disciplined apparatus, with cadres, skills, and weapons acquired during the Resistance.[28]

The formation of an anti-Communist coalition was undertaken by the forces close to the Catholic church—the only organization (aside from the army, the police, and the Communist underground) that had continued to operate with some corporate independence under Fascism. The Catholic forces filled the vacuum left by the collapse of Fascism as an antirevolutionary, conservative bulwark. Political leadership of the anti-Communist coalition was assumed by the Christian Democratic party, with the active support of the United States, the Catholic clergy, Catholic interest groups (such as Catholic Action, the Catholic trade unions, and the Catholic farmers' organization), the secular democratic parties (the Liberals, the Republicans, and the Social Democrats), and conservative interest groups, such

28. Aldo Garosci, "The Italian Communist Party," in Mario Einaudi, Jean-Marie Domenach, and Aldo Garosci, *Communism in Western Europe* (Ithaca, 1951), pp. 188–218.

as the Confederations of Industry and of Agriculture. In May 1947, De Gasperi dropped the Socialist and Communist ministers from his government and later in the year formed a new government, with representatives of the four democratic parties of the center—the Christian Democrats, the Liberals, the Republicans, and the Social Democrats. With this centrist alliance he entered the campaign for the election in April 1948 of the first Parliament under the new Constitution. The result of these elections was an astounding victory for the anti-Communists: the Christian Democrats alone secured 48 per cent of the popular vote and an absolute majority in the Chamber of Deputies.

Once firmly in power, however, the Christian Democrats, who had been the stanchest proponents of regionalism, turned their backs upon this and upon all of the other constitutional checks and balances that the Constituent Assembly had left to the future Parliament to create. Regionalism, after all, had developed as a plank in the program of the Populist party—a party of opposition seeking to reduce the power of the pre-Fascist liberal state whose legitimacy it challenged. It was taken up by the Christian Democrats partly as a sincere democratic reaction to Fascist centralization, and partly because of the uncertainty concerning future control of the central government. Having secured control of that government, the Christian Democrats, with the backing of their Liberal and Social Democratic allies, became reluctant to implement those provisions of the Constitution that would have limited their power in the legislature and the executive.

The left-wing parties, on the other hand, performed a similar *volte-face* after 1948 and began a campaign for the creation of the regions, the Constitutional Court, and the other independent centers of power that they had opposed before. The implementation of the Constitution became one of their major propaganda slogans. The fact that they became such ardent proponents of regionalism gave pause to the regionalists in the democratic camp.

The Constituent Assembly, leaving much of the responsibility for implementing the Constitution to the future Parliament, had provided no penalties for its failure to do so. It was easy therefore for the centrist coalition dominating the First Republican Legislature (1948–53) to do practically nothing in the way of creating the new republican institutions and revising Fascist legislation in accordance with the new constitutional precepts.

Given the prevailing geographical distribution of relative electoral power, the left-wing parties would have won control in at least three of the fourteen ordinary regions: Emilia–Romagna, Tuscany, and Umbria—a solid belt of territories cutting across north-central Italy from the Ligurian to the Adriatic Sea, with about seven and one-half million people (or 16 per cent of the national poulation). In these regions, the Marxist opposition would have been gratuitously afforded additional platforms for propaganda and leadership and more power and patronage with which to consolidate its power at the expense of the democratic center parties and the latters' often terrorized adherents in the "Red belt." To the mass of authoritarian, conservative voters who had flocked to the Christian Democratic party as the bulwark against revolution, this would have seemed an inadmissible concession to the Left.

To these general factors working against the establishment of the regions, one might also add the resistance of the state bureaucracy to the loss of power and prestige which regionalism involved, by transferring policy control in some areas to the regions and obliging some state civil servants to become members of less prestigious regional civil services; the general indifference and hostility to regionalism revealed in surveys of public opinion; conflicts and rivalries between the sections and cities of some future regions, some sections insisting upon separate regional autonomy and many cities opposing the elevation of their rivals to a superior status as regional capitals; fears in the South that regionalism might mean less national commitment and effort to aid in southern economic development; concern with the disruption in the national financial system, administration, and political equilibrium that regionalism would entail; and, finally, the availability of alternative forms of devolution, especially deconcentration of power within the state administration.[29]

The elections of 1953 opened a new period in postwar Italian politics—a period marked by increasing cabinet instability and the closely related breakdown of the bipolar political struggle between the Communist and anti-Communist coalitions, here again reflecting a parallel development in world politics. In the elections of 1953 the Christian

29. Piero Calamandrei, "La Costituzione e le leggi per attuarla," in Achille Battaglia et al., *Dieci anni dopo: 1944–45: Saggi sulla vita democratica italiana* (Bari, 1955), pp. 227–79; John Clarke Adams and Paolo Barile, "The Implementation of the Italian Constitution," *American Political Science Review, 47* (1953), 61–83. In a survey of Italian public opinion in March 1952, 53 per cent of those interviewed had never heard of the Regions; another 20 per cent thought the problem of slight importance; and only 23 per cent considered the problem of the Region "rather" or "very" important. Regionalism appeared most important to businessmen, professionals, white-collar employees, and those just left and right of center; it appeared least important to supporters of the Christian Democrats and the right-wing parties. When informed of what the regional scheme involved, one-fourth of those interviewed could not understand it; one-fourth could not tell whether the scheme would be a good thing; one-fourth thought it would be a good thing; and the last fourth opposed it. When informed about the scheme, northerners and supporters of the left-wing and center parties tended to favor it, while southerners and those with rightist sympathies tended to oppose it. See Pierpaolo Luzzatto Fegiz, *Il Volto sconosciuto dell'Italia: Dieci anni di sondaggi Doxa* (Milan, Giuffrè, 1956), pp. 425–29.

Democrats and their centrist allies suffered a severe setback, with a decline from 62 to 49 per cent of the popular vote. The major beneficiaries were the neo-Fascist and monarchist parties of the extreme Right, which advanced from 5 to almost 13 per cent of the vote. The Marxist Left also advanced, from 31 to 35 per cent. Conflict within the center coalition and within the Christian Democratic party became acute. At the heart of the conflict in the ruling parties was the question of the most effective means of anticommunism. On the right of the coalition, there was a propensity toward economic laissez faire, the discriminating allocation of patronage, and police repression; on the left, a drive to undermine the appeal of communism through social reform, government intervention in the economy, and implementation of the Constitution. For each of these policies a different alliance was necessary, but the Christian Democrats, who have remained the single largest party and the necessary nucleus of any governing alliance, have been unable to form a lasting alliance on either the Left or the Right. Factional struggles within the Catholic movement have tended to become more intense, especially since the death of De Gasperi in 1954 and since the gradual swing of the Socialists away from the Communists to a firm commitment to constitutional democracy under the impact of relaxing cold war tensions, the Khruschev report in February 1956, and Soviet intervention in Hungary later that year. Characteristic of the gradual breakdown of the bipolarity of 1948–53 was the election to the Presidency of the Republic in 1955 of a left-wing Christian Democrat by an ad hoc coalition of the Marxist parties, right-wing Christian Democrats, and members of the extreme Right.

The same year saw the beginning of a gradual movement to implement some of the key provisions of the Constitution, such as the establishment of the Constitutional Court

(1955), the National Council of Economy and Labor (1957), the Superior Council of the Magistracy (1957), and the revision of Fascist legislation—often with the aid of the Socialists.

The balance of political forces did not change significantly in the general elections of 1958. The stalemate between the forces of the left-center and right-center has persisted, provoking continual cabinet crises and impeding any major policy decisions. Regionalism continues to be a major issue in Italian politics and has constituted one of the major subjects of interparty negotiation. It is one of the many sources of cleavage within the Christian Democratic party and within the center coalition. The Christian Democratic party has never formally rejected regionalism or called for the amendment of the Constitution to modify or eliminate the pertinent clauses. It has preferred amendment by inaction, i.e. failure to implement the Constitution. Its party programs continue to call for the "gradual" establishment of the regions.

Important measures of social reform and constitutional implementation must wait upon an eventual coalition of the Christian Democratic party with the left-wing Socialists. Recent attempts at the formation of such a coalition have met with the veto of the Italian clergy and the threat of schism within the Catholic party. It is doubtful, therefore, whether the regions will be established before the clergy and allied interest groups modify their hostility toward an alliance between the Catholics and the Socialists.*

*Since this manuscript was completed, in the spring of 1961, events of major historical importance have occurred. The alliance between the Christian Democrats and the Socialists, which I indicated as a prerequisite to major institutional reform, was formed in February 1962 with the appointment of the fifth Fanfani government. This government, composed of Catholics, Republicans, and Social Democrats, and supported in Parliament by the Socialists, was pledged to the enactment of the following basic reforms:

TABLE 10 Italian Cabinets since World War II

		Premier	Appointment	Resignation	Governing coalition
		1 PARRI	June 21, 1945	Dec. 8, 1945	DC, L, A, S, C, LD
		2 DE GASPERI I	Dec. 10, 1945	July 1, 1946	Idem
First Constituent Legislature Assembly		3 DE GASPERI II	July 13, 1946	Jan. 28, 1947	DC, R, C, S
		4 DE GASPERI III	Feb. 2, 1947	May 31, 1947	DC, C, S
		5 DE GASPERI IV	May 31, 1947	May 23, 1948	DC
		6 DE GASPERI V	May 23, 1948	Jan. 14, 1950	DC, L, R, SD
		7 DE GASPERI VI	Jan. 27, 1950	July 19, 1951	DC, R, SD
		8 DE GASPERI VII	July 26, 1951	July 7, 1953	DC, R
Second Legislature		9 DE GASPERI VIII	July 16, 1953	Aug. 2, 1953	DC
		10 PELLA	Aug. 17, 1953	Jan. 12, 1954	DC
		11 FANFANI I	Jan. 18, 1954	Feb. 8, 1954	DC
		12 SCELBA	Feb. 10, 1954	July 2, 1955	DC
		13 SEGNI I	July 2, 1955	May 15, 1957	DC, L, SD
		14 ZOLI	May 19, 1957	June 19, 1958	DC
Third Legislature		15 FANFANI II	July 1, 1958	Jan. 26, 1958	DC, SD
		16 SEGNI II	Feb. 16, 1959	Feb. 24, 1960	DC
		17 SEGNI III	March 9, 1960	March 21, 1960	DC
		18 TAMBRONI I	March 25, 1960	April 11, 1960	DC
		19 FANFANI III	April 14, 1960	April 22, 1960	DC, SD
		20 TAMBRONI II	April 23, 1960	July 19, 1960	DC (MSI)
		21 FANFANI IV	July 27, 1960	Feb. 2, 1962	DC, L, SD
		22 FANFANI V	Feb. 10, 1962	May 16, 1963	DC, SD, R (S)

DC—Christian Democrats   SD—Social Democrats   R—Republicans
LD—Labor Democrats   L—Liberals   S—Socialists
MSI—Neo-Fascists   C—Communists

Source: *Italian Affairs, 6* (1957), 1799–1810.

Opposition to the regions continues to be strong. The operations of the four special regions, established in 1946–48, have provided the opposition with ammunition. The existing regional governments have been criticized on several grounds: for their tendency toward factious conflict with the national government, toward unproductive expenditures and the general augmentation of public spending; for their tendency to centralize decision-making in the regional capitals and refusal to decentralize functions to the provinces and communes, thus defeating the aim of bringing decision-making closer to the public; for their tendency to increase the complexity and instability of national politics and to increase the tensions and conflicts within and between the parties; for their emphasis on patronage, perquisites, and pork-barrel legislation, and their tendency to hire incompetent administrative staffs on the basis of party sponsorship; for their tendency to exacerbate animosities toward Rome and the Italian state; for their poor performance in reducing social tensions through reform and economic development (as, for example, with the

---

(1) the nationalization of the electrical industry; (2) the establishment of the Friuli–Venetia Julia region; (3) economic planning; (4) the transformation of the land reform agencies into agricultural development agencies; and (5) the creation of the regions.

Submission of the bill creating the regions was held up several months due to the demand by the Catholics, Social Democrats, and Republicans that the Socialist party pledge itself not to establish Popular Front alliances with the Communists in such regions as Emilia, Tuscany, Umbria, and the Marches, but instead support the same kind of left-center government in those regions which then governed the nation. Parliament appeared finally about to consider bills establishing the regions submitted by the Fanfani government when the national secretary of the Christian Democratic party declared (Jan. 8, 1963) that Italy lacked sufficient political stability for such a venture. In April 1963, general elections were held (see Table 8, p. 226) which, by weakening the Christian Democrats and advancing the Communists, made further Catholic-Socialist collaboration and, with it, the prospects of the regions, even more problematical than before.

ineffective agrarian reform program in Sicily); for their lack of stability; for their unwarranted modifications of national policy, creating zones of privilege which, it is felt, should not exist (as, for example, with the abolition of the registration of stock holdings for purposes of taxation in Sicily); and for their lack of financial self-sufficiency.[30]

Much of this criticism misses the mark. It fails to take into account the wide variation in performance of the four regions. The two regions in the North, Aosta Valley and Trentino–Alto Adige, have not been as guilty of the foregoing charges as have Sardinia and, especially, Sicily. It would be unfair, however, to expect Sardinia and Sicily, with their relatively undeveloped economies and traditions of misgovernment, to conform to the standards set by their northern counterparts. The tendency of the regional governments toward factious conflict with the central government has been matched by an equally strong tendency of the central government to obstruct and hinder the operations of the regional governments. It should also be noted that regional–state conflict, and conflict between regional and national elements within the parties and interest groups, is much more apt to receive public attention than instances of quiet cooperation.

The tendency of parties and interest groups within the regions to assert their autonomy from their respective national headquarters has often stemmed, moreover, from a refusal to allow stalemate over the great national issues to interfere with the settlement of the lesser issues of regional development: a refusal, in other words, to allow national immobilism to block regional progress.

All of the regional governments have served as active

30. Michele Monaco, *La Regione: sintesi storica dell'autonomia regionale in Italia* (Rome, n.d.), pp. 91–150; *La Stampa* (May 15–20, 1959); *Gazzetta del Popolo* (June 26, 1957).

forums and centers of initiative for the planning, deliberation, and execution of programs of welfare and development. These programs have been carried out by administrative staffs specializing in the problems of their areas and
not disrupted by constant transfers from one end of the
peninsula to the other, as in the national field services. The
regional governments have engaged in some experimentation in techniques of social action—experimentation that
the national government has rarely been willing or able to
conduct. These governments have also been effective as
pressure groups in securing larger shares of national resources for their constituents. In the cases of Sicily and
Sardinia, at least, this has meant that a greater proportion
of the national budget has gone to these regions than they
would have secured through less organized pressure. And,
finally, if the regional leaders exacerbate feelings of hostility toward Rome and the national government, they also
serve to draw off some antigovernmental sentiment upon
themselves. A famous Sicilian anti-Fascist and Christian
Democratic leader, Don Luigi Sturzo, once remarked that
it was perhaps an improvement for Sicilians to be grum-
bling about Palermo, rather than Rome.[31]

THE SURVIVAL OF THE PREFECTS[32]

Many of the factors that account for the failure to establish
the ordinary regions have also operated to preserve the prefectoral institution from abolition: the challenge of communism; the unsettled conditions of the postwar period
with its inflation, unemployment, hunger, and poverty; the

31. *La Stampa* (March 26, 1958); Monaco, pp. 120–50.
32. Unless otherwise attributed, the following information on the contemporary prefectoral system is derived from a series of personal interviews
in the Ministries of the Interior, Labor, Agriculture, Public Works, Finance,
and their respective field offices between February 1958 and June 1959.

restoration of political freedom—freedom to organize and articulate the group interests repressed for a generation under Fascism—and the resulting clash of social and political interests; and lack of consensus on basic political institutions or on policies to resolve the problems inherited from Fascism and war.

Given these circumstances, with the inherent risks of civil strife, revolution, or electoral defeat, successive governments have been unwilling to dispense with the aid of the Prefects as their representatives in the province. The Prefects have continued to serve these governments and the political coalitions sustaining them in several ways.

General political representation

The Prefect performs the functions typical of diplomatic representation, involving the symbolic personification of the government, with attendant ceremonial duties; the collection of information and reception of claims and demands and their evaluation and transmission to Rome; the maintenance of contacts and negotiation with provincial group leaders; and the protection and furtherance of government interests. The Prefect submits monthly reports to the Ministry of the Interior on political events, public order, business conditions, unemployment, and labor disputes. Special reports may be required in particularly tense periods, such as during critical phases of the land reform program or during election campaigns.

The Prefect jointly plans election campaigns on behalf of the government parties with the provincial Christian Democratic party secretary, under the central guidance of the Christian Democratic national party secretary. During the campaigns, the Prefect negotiates agreements with local notables, based on promises of state aid or threats of deprivation. He arranges the necessary campaign alliances and in the case of local government elections, attempts to maintain those alliances for the purposes of government. He provides guidance to the government and its candidates on the suitability of various appeals and the activities of the opposition. He distributes relief directly or through government supporters. He is also responsible for the maintenance of order, the allocation of facilities for campaign speeches and propaganda, and the administrative management of registration and balloting.

The Prefects' impact on the outcome of elections in a system of heavily populated constituencies, highly organized parties, and proportional representation is presumably slight as compared to that of the Prefects in the contrasting circumstances of a century ago. It is probably greater in the South and in rural areas, where political life has not been modernized, where there is greater fluidity in partisan allegiances, and where there are fewer politically relevant organizations outside of the state bureaucracy itself than in northern and urban areas.[33]

33. *Avanti!* (April 22 and May 9, 1958); *L'Unità* (May 17, 1958). The Prefect's influence over elections is by no means negligible. The little that is known concerning the motivation of Italian voters shows the great saliency of local, rather than national, international, or ideological issues. Italian voters apparently have a more pragmatic approach to politics than attention to campaign themes and party programs would indicate. Questions of "sewers, schools, road maintenance, local graft or corruption" are often the decisive issues, and the party that succeeds in solving these problems, regardless of its national ideology, stands to win the elections. See Joseph La Palombara, "A Decade of Political and Economic Change in Italy," *World Politics*, 9 (1957), 429.

The Prefect, of course, is much involved in precisely this aspect of local government. Incidents such as the following are common in rural areas, especially in the South, at election time. In one tiny hamlet in the mountains of Calabria, which lacked such public services as passable roads and a cemetery, the population became so exasperated with the failure of the Prefect to maintain his promise of state aid that it decided to abstain en

SURVIVAL OF THE PREFECTS 249

The protection of provincial safety

The Prefects have continued to be responsible for maintaining public order and security in the provinces, upholding confidence in the government's ability to protect life and property and to enforce the law, and ensuring the minimum level of order for the execution of government policies. They act therefore to ensure the continuity of essential public services and the provision of basic necessities during disasters and strikes; to repress banditism and political violence; to anticipate and prevent disorder arising from epidemics, mining disasters, heavy snowfalls, floods, and earthquakes; to mediate conflicts between social groups, such as labor and management, farm tenants and landowners, local governments and their employees, or between provin-

---

masse from the general elections of 1958. It held out until the last few hours before the polls closed when a rumor spread that mass abstention would be considered rebellion against the state. This frightened the population of the village into submission.

In a nearby village, the population decided upon the same tactic and all abstained from voting except for the parish priest and about nine others out of the 1,200 eligible voters. A few days before the elections, the vice-prefect had come to explain that the fault for their not receiving a long-promised road lay with former Prefects, especially the next-to-last one, who was now Prefectoral Commissioner for the City of Naples. The new Prefect, the vice-prefect claimed, was a fine man who would make up for the neglect of his predecessors. The Captain of the Carabinieri also visited the town and assured his sergeant, who had reported the planned mass abstention, that the town would vote in the end. Late on election day, when it appeared that no one was going to vote, the Christian Democratic leader of the village ran through the streets, crying (to no avail):

> Friends, I assure you that the new Prefect is a person worthy of your esteem and all your confidence. He doesn't deserve the wrong you are doing him. I know him. After the elections, I will lead you to him and together we will explain to him your needs. But vote!

These stories are reported by Bruno Malatesta in "San Nicola e le elezioni," *Il Mondo, 9* (Sept. 2, 1958), 5–6.

cial groups and a state service (such as between professional groups and the Intendant of Finance; the medical association and the government health insurance agencies) or between local governments and state field services (such as between a commune and the Superintendent of Monuments).

Violent or illegal agitation is a normal form of articulating group demands in a relatively poor society with many competing claims upon limited resources: only through such agitation, it is often felt, will officials pay attention to a claim and convey it to the government. The Prefect gets wind of impending agitation through the police, through the deputations which daily arrive at the prefecture and occupy much of his time, and through his contacts with provincial and interest group leaders.

How the Prefect handles such agitation depends on the nature of the agitators. Sometimes it is an entire commune that has revolted against the government for failing to build a long-promised road or aqueduct, or for threatening to remove a state field office, or for refusing to support the commune's demand to become a provincial capital. Sometimes all of the provincial party representatives in a town severely repressed by the Fascists during the war are united against allowing a neo-Fascist to speak. Sometimes Catholic trade unionists and even the local clergy participate in or support the illegal occupation of a factory or an uncultivated estate. In these cases, those in which government supporters are involved in the agitations, the Prefect assumes the neutral role of peacemaker and moderates the zeal of the police in repressing the illegal activity.

In most cases, however, violent and illegal agitations have been carried out by groups led by members of the left-wing opposition: demonstrations of the unemployed or those threatened with lay-offs; actual or symbolic occupations of uncultivated estates; violence against government supporters in the Red belt (the famous "triangle of death" in the Po Valley); "political" strikes against the Marshall Plan, NATO, and American "imperialism"; attempts to sabotage the execution of government programs, such as land reform and the establishment of a state monopoly of employment exchanges. These are repressed with severity.

In the early postwar years there was some fear of a left-wing attempt to overthrow the regime by violence, which would have involved a civil war such as was taking place in neighboring Greece. Until 1948, a left-wing coup seems to have been averted by left-wing expectations of electoral victory combined with the threat of Allied military intervention. By 1948, however, the police forces, which had been demoralized and shaken by the wartime collapse and purges, had been reorganized, re-equipped, purged again, and expanded so as to cope with any revolutionary coup and with left-wing attempts to make the country ungovernable. Violence or the threat of violence, however, remained the major tactic of the left-wing groups, which have been systematically cut off from regular peaceful access to the centers of power. The groups in power have sought to exclude their opponents from any access whatsoever to these centers, leaving the frustrated opposition little recourse save to the traditional methods of direct action developed during the long period when the lower classes were deprived of any legal influence over policy-making under the pre-unification absolute monarchies and the restricted suffrage of the pre-Fascist unified state.[34]

Left-wing agitations have served to maintain something

34. Joseph La Palombara, "The Utility and Limitations of Interest Group Theory in Non-American Field Situations," *Journal of Politics*, 22 (1960), 38.

of the revolutionary fervor of party and union militants, to make real the Marxist conception of the state as a tool of the bourgeoisie, and to enable the Left to claim credit for government-sponsored reform and welfare measures as uniquely the result of left-wing pressure. Such agitations have also served to create a tense political climate in which the Communists are represented as the only important opposition and the Christian Democrats as the only effective bulwark against them; in which the Communists have been able to capitalize on any and all group protests; and in which the authoritarian elements on the right and right-center have succeeded in blocking the implementation of the institutional and socioeconomic provisions of the Constitution.

Thus the Prefect has retained most of the police powers granted to him under the Fascist regime and, as an agent of the ruling parties, has exercised those powers largely against the opposition groups of the Left: banning peaceful demonstrations and propaganda against the government and its policies and repressing the unauthorized protest rallies that normally ensue; arresting the leaders of unauthorized parades and rallies, and of land occupations; suspending mayors and dissolving communal councils for "reasons of public order"; preventing left-wing organizations from distributing relief in disaster areas, etc. One of the major tests of the Prefect's performance has been his ability to maintain firm control over his province, to stand up to left-wing agitators, to administer the proper dosage of threats and violent repression, avoiding if possible embarrassing bloodshed and death. In some instances, a government has felt that only a general could provide the necessary impression of its determination to maintain control of public order and has appointed a general as Prefect in northern provinces where the Leftists are particularly assertive and powerful.[35]

It is not surprising, therefore, that the political functions of the police have received much more attention in the postwar period than their effectiveness in combating nonpolitical crime. The structure of the police system has remained roughly what it was under Fascism, except for the abolition of the Fascist Militia and secret police, with the continued duality and overlapping jurisdictions of the Ministry of the Interior's Corps of Public Security Guards and the Ministry of Defense's Carabinieri. These are aided in the maintenance of public order by the Finance Guards of the Ministry of Finance and, in exceptional cases, by regular army detachments. The police forces of the communes (the corps of *vigili urbani*) have no public security functions and are limited to the enforcement of communal regulations, traffic direction, etc. Police functions of any importance have remained under the direct control of the central government. The constitutional provisions calling for the transfer of full and exclusive control of the judicial police (including both Public Security and Carabinieri units) to the courts (the Procurators General) have not been implemented.

Control of local government

The Prefect has continued to serve the central government (and the forces sustaining and protected by it) through the exercise of formal controls over local government—controls which, under the Constitution, were to be reduced and

35. Giulio Andreotti, *De Gasperi e il suo tempo: Trento-Vienna-Roma* (Milan, 1956), pp. 268–69; *L'Unità* (Feb. 6, March 18, 22, 1950; Jan. 7, 8, 1953).

transferred to the regions. The provinces and communes have become major arenas for the national political struggle. With the return of local elections and the victory of the conservatives at the national level, the Left has been able to secure governmental power only at the regional, provincial, and communal levels. The government parties have sought to exclude the Left from such power through electoral laws and electoral competition. They have attempted to prevent left-wing local governments from utilizing their power so as to increase the electoral strength of the Left in parliamentary elections by the discriminatory administration of supervisory controls and programs of state grants-in-aid. Centralization has once again become a vital element in the democratic political system.

The system of intensive state controls over provincial and communal governments under the Fascist Provincial and Communal Act of 1934 has remained in effect, except that the Prefect has lost the power to overrule decisions on grounds of inexpediency.[36] However, given the considerable obsolescence, confusion, and ambiguities in the legislation covering local government, the Prefect's authority to veto illegal decisions has afforded him considerable leverage in controlling local government decisions. What is more, he continues to dominate the *Giunta Provinciale Amministrativa* (GPA) which retains its authority to veto and require the modification of all significant financial decisions of the local authorities.[37] The composition of the GPA was reformed to include six state functionaries (the Prefect, the Intendant of Finance, the vice-prefect inspector, two prefectoral councillors, and the chief accountant of the prefecture) and only four members elected by the

36. Law of June 9, 1947, No. 111.
37. See above, pp. 128–31, 151, 205, 208–09, and 217, for the previous evolution of the GPA.

provincial council.[38] Thus decisions whose legality cannot be challenged can be vetoed on their merits by the agents of the central government. The Prefect has retained many of his traditional powers, among them the general power of inspection; the right to appoint commissioners to carry out legally obligatory decisions that local authorities refuse to make; the right in "emergencies" to supersede local authorities in the exercise of their powers; the right to suspend mayors for serious reasons of public order or for persistent violations of their legal duties and to replace them by commissioners to carry out their functions *qua* officials of the state during the period of suspension; the right to approve the establishment of *consorzi* or unions between local authorities, to supervise these unions, to dissolve them for reasons of public order or violation of their obligations, and to appoint commissioners to administer them in the event of dissolution; and the right to suspend and bring disciplinary action against local authority employees.

These controls, and those reserved to the central ministries, have generally been exercised in a partisan fashion. The Prefects in Red provinces have been required to give aid and protection to pro-government minorities, to compete with Red provincial and communal authorities for the support of the population, and to harass the left-wing authorities in every possible way. The decisions of the provinces and communes in these zones (and throughout the country) are closely scrutinized for possible illegalities— which are not difficult to find, given the obsolescence and confusion prevailing in the local government legislation. Red governments are prevented not only from diverting local revenues into party coffers, but also from taking welfare initiatives that might strengthen their hold over the

38. Decree of April 4, 1944, No. 111.

electorate. The Prefects use their powers over public charities (such as hospitals and orphanages) to remove them from
the control of left-wing communes. They suspend mayors
from office for such various reasons as allowing communal
employees to engage in electoral propaganda, refusing to
kiss the bishop's ring, lowering the flag on the anniversary of
the Lateran Pacts, participating in political demonstrations,
and leading unauthorized agitations.[39] Thus in the period
between July 1, 1954, and April 26, 1955, for example,
forty-four mayors were suspended; another sixty-three were
suspended only from their functions as state officials; four
were removed from office.[40] Between 1946 and June 30,
1958, eighty-one mayors were removed from office for reasons of public order alone. In the same period, thirty-eight
communal councils were dissolved for the same reason.[41]
Prefects also attempt to prevent left-wing communes from
shifting the burden of local taxation to the wealthier classes, building public housing, opening municipal pharmacies,
and expanding municipal relief, as well as from passing
resolutions on foreign and domestic policy.[42]

The tactics of harassment may backfire, however: left-
wing councils deliberately court the veto of welfare schemes;
secondly, they sometimes succeed in appeals against pre-

39. Renato Nicolai, *Il Sindaco e la città* (Rome, 1956), passim; Achille
Battaglia, "L'Insidia dei prefetti," *Il Mondo, 8,* No. 24 (June 12, 1956), 1–2;
L'Unità (Jan. 6, May 10, 16, 1953); *Il Messaggero* (May 13, 1958), p. 6; *ROMA*
(Feb. 18, 1959), p. 2; *L'Espresso* (June 26, 1960), p. 2.

40. *Atti Parlamentari, Legislatura II, Documenti, Camera,* No. 1427–A,
p. 12.

41. Ibid., *Legislatura III, Documenti,* No. 159–A and 159–bis–A, (Oct. 6,
1958), pp. 26–27. There were, as of Dec. 31, 1956, 7,962 mayors and communal councils (ibid., p. 27). Between 1900 and 1922, forty-seven mayors
were removed from office for reasons of public order, and 1,185 communal
councils dissolved for the same reason (ibid., pp. 26–27).

42. Nicolai, passim.

fectoral decisions to the Council of State; and thirdly, under close prefectoral surveillance, they have avoided the scandals that have occurred in many of the centrist and right-wing communes and have produced the most respected local government performance in the country.

The Prefects, of course, make every attempt to prevent the Left from gaining control of local governments at election time and in the period following the elections, when the governing coalitions are arranged. To this end, they attempt to discredit existing leftist governments, to work out agreements among the anti-Communist parties for joint electoral campaigns and governing coalitions, and to demonstrate how much the allocation of state aid is geared to the political complexion of the local authority.

In the provinces in the North where the Catholics are extremely strong, such as in Lombardy and Venetia, the Prefect's task requires greater diplomatic ability and less toughness of character than in the Red provinces of Emilia and Tuscany. In the latter provinces, the political line is clear and straightforward, but in the strongly Catholic provinces where almost all of the political leaders are government supporters, there is no such clear demarcation between those to be favored and those to be fought. In these provinces, the political struggle is much less overt and takes place not in the *piazza* and at the hustings so much as privately, though often no less fiercely for being private. Here the Prefect must maneuver amidst shifting factions whose positions are never clear or fixed: all of these factions have some claim to prefectoral favor, all have local and Roman protectors who may influence the Prefect's career.

In such provinces, the Prefect has the ungrateful task of seeing that the law, however cumbersome and unpopular, is enforced, at least to the point of preventing discrediting scandals. His legal interpretations will be generous; his scrutiny of local government decisions will not be intensive; and initiatives will not be unduly cramped and impeded. Local governments in these areas are generally enterprising, wealthy, technically competent, and resentful of central restrictions and delays. The Prefect must see to it that they are not unnecessarily hampered by outdated laws and regulations and exasperated by the slow motion of the central government machinery. He must also attempt to satisfy the various parties and factions which, while united on a national scale, may be in competition locally.

South of Rome, the Prefects enjoy much greater status and influence than in the central and northern provinces, for there are few strong organizations outside of the bureaucracy itself. The political struggle often involves not the provincial branches of nationwide parties and interest groups, but rather personal bands of clients—cliques only tenuously related to the central organizations whose labels they use. Here the local governments tend to be centrist or right-wing in orientation, poor in resources and services, disrupted by personal feuds, utilized as instruments of personal aggrandizement, and greatly dependent on central aid.

Thus prefectoral tutelage policy has to be adapted to the sociopolitical complexion of the local government authorities, strictly in accordance with the requirements of national politics. The most spectacular example of this involved the commune of Naples which, between 1953 and 1957, was given *carte blanche* to commit all kinds of irregularities in tax assessments, the award of contracts, the administration of relief, the hiring of staffs, and general financial policies. The mayor of Naples was also the leader of one of the monarchist parties in Parliament and the votes of this group were occasionally necessary to the Christian Democratic governments. On the eve of the 1958 elections, the Christian Democrats decided that they could perhaps capture the clientele of this monarchist party in the coming elections and, in February 1958, the government dissolved the city council and placed the city under a prefectoral commissioner (who remained in office for over two and one-half years).[43] Similar irregularities have been tolerated in other communes under pro-government party control.

Large numbers of municipal councils and some provincial councils were dissolved following the local elections of 1956 due to the impossibility of forming governing majorities.[44] Local elections are held throughout most of the country at the same time; the campaigns are directed by the national party organizations, with the active participation of ministers and members of Parliament; campaign themes involve for the most part national political issues; the outcome is regarded as a test of national party strength; candidates are dependent upon national party and interest group organizations which provide the necessary funds, party labels, and other resources necessary for election: in return, the national party executives attempt to impose a nationwide pattern of alliances on their local representatives. In many localities, therefore, no majority can be formed since the national executives will not permit certain alliances to be formed; the councils are accordingly dissolved and prefectoral commissioners brought in to manage the local government until the government finds it convenient to call new elections. Thus, even the leading cities of the country may be deprived of elective leadership for long

43. *ROMA* (Feb. 18, 1958); *Corriere della Sera* (May 10, 1958); *Il Messaggero di Roma* (Feb. 15, 1958).

44. About sixty-five communal and four provincial councils were dissolved between 1956 and Sept. 30, 1958, because of the impossibility of forming a governing majority. See the *Atti Parlamentari, Legislatura III, Camera, Documenti,* No. 159–A and 159–bis–A, p. 27. On the 1956 local government elections, see Roy Pryce, *The Italian Local Elections 1956* (London, 1957).

periods of time due to the rigidity of the centralized multi-party system.

The effectiveness and autonomy of local governments have also been sharply limited by the failure to reform the legislation on local finance, under the provisions of which these governments have inadequate revenues to meet their multiplying burdens, remain saddled with the expenses of many state services, and become increasingly dependent upon central government aid and supervision. The disparity between demands for local services and available resources has been particularly serious in the largest cities, many mountain communes (those without large woodland patrimonies), and southern communes generally. But the badly needed general reform of local government finance has been held up by the failure to work out and establish the allocation of functions and resources under the regional system, as well as by the difficulties in reforming the finances of the state. These financial considerations have been one of the major factors impeding the decentralization of authority, functions, and resources to the existing units of local government.

The constitutional provisions calling for decentralization of power to the provinces and communes have been implemented only on a very minor scale. Within the basic centralized structure (which will remain until the regions are established) an attempt was made in 1953–56 to transfer some responsibilities from the state to the existing units of local government. A general enabling act was passed by Parliament in 1953 authorizing the government to devolve central government functions in a large number of specific policy sectors to either local government units (by way of decentralization) or to the state field services (by way of deconcentration).[45] The result was a number of legislative

45. Law of March 11, 1953, No. 150. See Lucifredi and Coletti, *Decentramento amministrativo,* cited above on page 139.

TABLE 11 Control of Local Institutions

Local institution	Pre-Fascist and post-Fascist control
Orphanages	a. Before Fascism, the municipal council appointed the president and the board. b. Today, the Prefect appoints the president and the board members are appointed by the Purveyor of Studies, the Bishop, the Provincial Federation of the ONMI (National Maternity and Child Welfare Agency), the local medical association, as well as by the provincial and communal councils, with a predominance of appointed members.
Hospitals	a. Before Fascism, the municipal councils appointed the presidents and boards of directors. b. Today, the boards are named by the Prefect, the ONMI Federation, and the medical association, in addition to the provincial and communal councils.
Chambers of Commerce	a. Before Fascism, the boards of directors were elected by the membership. b. Today, the presidents are named jointly by the Ministers of Industry and Agriculture and the board, by the Prefect subject to the approval of the Ministry of Industry.
Savings Banks	a. Before Fascism, the boards of directors were elected by the shareholders. b. Today, the presidents and vice-presidents are appointed by the Prime Minister.
Communal Relief Agencies (ECAs)	a. Before Fascism, the communal councils appointed the presidents and boards of the "Congregations of Charity," over which the Prefect had no hierarchical control. b. Today, the Prefect may veto the appointments of the communal councils; can dissolve the ECAs and place them under commissioners; and allocates most of their funds.

Source: *Atti Parlamentari, Legislatura II, Senato, Discussioni,* October 8, 1952.

decrees which, while deconcentrating some central ministerial powers to the field services, effected practically no decentralization at all, despite the efforts of the Union of Provinces and the Association of Communes.

In the case of many local institutions, there has not even been a return to the degree of autonomy and local control of the pre-Fascist period, as can be seen in Table 11.

THE PREFECT AND THE STATE FIELD SERVICES

The Prefect's major powers and responsibilities stem from his position as representative of the government and chief field agent of the Ministry of the Interior. His powers, derived largely from Fascist legislation, far from being abolished, have been only slightly modified and have even been increased, despite the widespread postwar hostility to the institution. But it is predominantly the role of the Prefect as controller of public security and local government that has been controversial—his powers to affect personal rights and local autonomy—rather than his role in coordinating state field administration within the province. The latter role, as we have seen, has been relatively unimportant in the Italian prefectoral system. Even the Fascist laws of 1926 and 1934 did not break substantially with the tradition of functional autonomy, of direct lines of command and communications between the central ministries and their field offices. And in the postwar reaction to Fascism, even the limited amount of prefectoral intervention sanctioned by these laws came under attack.

The dominant attitudes in the immediate postwar period toward prefectoral coordination can be seen in the recommendations of a study group established in 1945 to prepare the work of the Constituent Assembly. This official study group, the Commission for Studies Pertaining to the Reorganization of the State, summarized its recommendations as follows:[46]

> A. The political powers of the Prefect, where they cannot be separated from his strictly administrative powers, should be considerably reduced, both in subject matter and in scope, and be restricted to the tutelage of public order, hygiene, and health; they must, however, still include reserve powers to deal with emergencies in which the central government cannot intervene in time.
>
> B. The administrative powers of the Prefect should likewise be reduced. Those functions which lie within the institutional jurisdiction of ministries other than the Ministry of the Interior which have in the respective sectors specialized technical or administrative functions and can thus act with a greater sense of responsibility and freedom from political concerns should be transferred to the field offices of those ministries.
>
> C. The coordination of the activities of the various field organs can be achieved through the creation of collegial organs composed of the representatives of each interested ministry, with the possible participation of citizens expert in the different subject matters.

These recommendations were not, of course, incorporated into the new Constitution which is "silent" insofar as the prefectoral institution is concerned. They were, however, reflected in the Law of March 8, 1949, No. 277, which amended Article 19 of the Provincial and Communal Act (1934)—the basic operating charter of the Prefects. This amendment was at least of symbolic importance in that it

46. Ministero per la Costituente, *Relazione, 1,* 370.

restored the description of prefectoral powers prevailing before Fascism and canceled out the authoritarian features incorporated into the Provincial and Communal Act by the Fascists. The major objective of the amendment was to reduce the scope of prefectoral emergency power until such time as the fate of the Prefects should be determined.[47] The new version of Article 19, which is still in effect, runs as follows:

> Article 19 of the Provincial and Communal Act approved by Royal Decree of March 3, 1934, No. 383, is abrogated and replaced by the following:
>
> The Prefect represents the executive power in the province.
>
> He exercises the powers devolved upon him by the laws and regulations and secures, when necessary, the settlement of jurisdictional conflicts between the administrative and the judicial authorities.
>
> He watches over the operations of all public administrative authorities and, in case of urgent necessity, takes those measures indispensable to the public interest in the various branches of the service.
>
> He orders the necessary investigations to be carried out with respect to the local administrative authorities subject to his oversight.
>
> He appoints special commissioners to the administrations of the territorial and institutional local authorities in order to carry out, in case of delay or omission on the part of the regular organs (previously and promptly invited to comply), those decisions which are obligatory under law; or to direct them for the strictly necessary period of time whenever they cannot function for any reason.

47. *Atti Parlamentari, Legislatura I, Senato, Documenti*, No. 162, p. 1.

He protects public order and superintends public security, may employ the police forces, and may request the use of the armed forces.

He presides over the consultative, supervisory and judicial organs located or sitting in the prefecture.

That the prefectures will *not* be abolished even if the ordinary regions are established was apparently decided in the first and so far only piece of legislation to implement the constitutional provisions on regionalism—the Law of February 10, 1953, No. 62, on the operations of the regional organs. Article 64 of this law provides explicitly for the retention of the prefectures to carry out such functions as the dissolution and suspension of provincial and communal councils and the removal and suspension of mayors *qua* state officials; it also confirms the Law of March 8, 1949, No. 277, and the prefectoral powers under that act.

With the abrogation of Article 19 of the 1934 Act (and implicitly of the 1926 Act absorbed into it), there has been a return, at least as regards formal structure, to the traditional unintegrated or "weak" prefectoral system: one in which the Prefect has no statutory authority to direct or coordinate the various state services in the province, that is, to intervene in the various chains of command running from the ministries in Rome to their specialized field offices.

The Prefect enjoys general powers of command and intervention only with regard to the services of his own ministry—over the functionaries of the prefecture itself, over the *Questura* (or police headquarters), over the Provincial Fire Brigade (*Vigili del Fuoco*), and over the mayors *qua* state officials. He has only recently lost such powers over the Provincial Medical and Veterinary Officers, who have become the field agents of a separate Ministry of Health.

When the independent Ministry of Health was established in 1958, the proponents of autonomy for medical specialists were successful in freeing the field services of the new ministry from prefectoral control.[48] The field organs of the ministry were to be the Provincial Medical Office, the Provincial Veterinary Office, and the municipal health offices. Most of the powers of the Prefect as chief of public health in the province were transferred to the Provincial Medical Officer and Provincial Veterinary.

The Prefect managed to retain some of his powers, however. He will continue to preside over the provincial health board. He will continue to exercise the power to dissolve public institutions with public health and medical care activities and to supervise their *administrative* activities through chairmanship of the provincial committee of assistance and charity and through direct powers of inspection. He will also continue to enjoy the power to issue emergency ordinances in the field of public health, after consulting the Provincial Medical Officer. And finally he will have explicit, if ambiguous, authority to "coordinate" the activities of the Provincial Medical Officer and the Provincial Veterinary Officer, without any elucidation being given in the statute of what "coordination" actually involves.

The Provincial Medical and Veterinary Officers were given the Prefect's authority to supervise the *technical* activities of public health agencies in the province, and "all the other powers of the Prefect in matters of public health," except those few mentioned in the preceding paragraph.

Sentiment among the newly independent Provincial Medical Officers was mixed. On the one hand, as technical specialists, they were now free from the supervisory author-

48. Law of March 13, 1958, No. 296.

ity of the nonspecialist Prefects; they would not be cut off from their own central department by an intervening non-expert from another central department; they would no longer have to compete with the other units in the prefecture for limited administrative resources: clerical, fiscal, legal, etc.; they would now (or as soon as funds from the Ministry of Health were available) have independent offices and full command over their own funds, accounts, and staffs.

On the other hand, the Provincial Medical Officers had found close connection with the Prefect vital to the performance of their task in the past and might now, being external and remote, have more difficulty in securing the attention and support of the Prefect for their programs. The Provincial Medical Officers have few direct operational duties; most of their functions involve the supervision of provincial, municipal, and public health institutions. In the task of supervising these locally based authorities, the aid and support of the Prefect have been essential, for only the Prefect can enforce compliance with health regulations and urge authoritatively the expansion and maintenance of health facilities. Now the Prefect's aid and assistance in directing the health activities of the local authorities may be more difficult to obtain.

Furthermore, the Provincial Medical Officers may find themselves increasingly absorbed in the administrative tasks of directing autonomous field offices; they will have to fend for themselves in getting what they want from their own central department and from the local authorities.

There is, then, in neither law nor practice the concept of the Prefect as the general director of the state services in the province. Only the ministries are considered the directors of their respective field services. Control over the operations and personnel of the various services is lodged directly in the ministries: it is the latter, and not the Prefect, who control the careers of their field officers; who set the standards of behavior and performance; who supply and withhold funds; who may overrule decisions and impose sanctions. In almost all cases, the various ministries and agencies have established their field offices outside of the prefecture and are not dependent upon it for authority, funds, administrative services, or office space. Lines of command have been almost strictly vertical and functional, by-passing the prefecture. Communications have flowed freely and directly between the central ministries and their field counterparts. Ministries have commonly delegated authority directly to their field agents.

But this is not to say that Italian field administration is closer in design to the strictly functional American pattern than to the French pattern of prefectoral integration. For the existence of the prefectoral institution does affect in significant ways the operations of the other field services of the state.

Description of the Prefect's relations with the various state services is difficult since these relations are for the most part not prescribed by laws or regulations and are not formally institutionalized as they are in France. For this reason, this aspect of prefectoral behavior is almost completely ignored in Italian discussions of administrative law and administration generally.

Prefects no longer enjoy the prestige and influence they enjoyed vis-à-vis the various state field directors (or other institutions) under Fascism, when hierarchy and command were in style and the Prefect was the representative of the dictator himself. The Prefect, so the older Prefects and other officials recall, was then more successful in getting what he wanted from directors general, mayors, and field directors.

Some of this dependence on the Prefect remained in the

immediate postwar period when many provinces were entirely cut off from the central government. The Prefect's influence and prestige were bound to suffer with the return of normal communications, the restoration of political competition and elective authorities, the reaction to Fascist authoritarianism, and the movement to abolish the prefectures. Ministries reasserted control of their field subordinates; local authorities asserted an independence based directly on the sovereign electorate; and field directors asserted old claims to functional autonomy.

At the least, the Prefects had to change their style, to adapt their manner to the more diplomatic requirements of pluralistic democracy. The Interior tended to become just another ministry among several; the Prefect, just another field director among several. The Prefect's relations with the field directors became more remote, more occasional, more difficult. Field directors became more prone to resent what they considered prefectoral *menomazione* or attempts to diminish and impair the directors' dignity and authority.

The Prefect, however, never did become just one field director among many. He continued to enjoy status and influence unique among Italian officials serving in the provinces: a status and influence deriving from his fundamental role as political representative of the current government. The Prefect, unlike other civil servants, is expected to be an advocate as well as an executor of current government policies. He is expected to defend the interests of the current government against the attacks of its rivals and competitors.

There are various ways by which the ministers in Rome attempt to maximize prefectoral responsiveness to their needs and desires. The nature of the prefectoral service induces compliance with ministerial expectations. A Prefect enjoys no security of tenure: he may be removed from government service at the pleasure of the Cabinet. He may be transferred from a more prominent to a less prominent post at a moment's notice, with the stigma attaching to such an informal demotion. He may be reprimanded by his minister, although this is seldom, if ever, done publicly. He may be removed from the service and forced to suffer a significant loss in living standards. Conversely, he may be rewarded with increasingly prominent posts, eventually working up to the prefectures of Rome, Milan, Turin, or other of the major cities, or to the post of director general in the ministry. He may, after long and satisfactory service, be appointed to the Council of State or to the Court of Accounts or Government Commissioner in one of the special regions.

But perhaps equally, if not more, effective is the conditioning process that candidates for prefectoral appointment undergo on the way up the career ladder. One of the most notable differences between the French and Italian Prefects is the extent to which the Italian prefectoral service, unlike the French, tends to resemble the other state administrative career services.[49] There is no prefectoral corps as in France but only the Civil Administration career service, resembling many others in the Directive Class (the equivalent of an administrative class or a senior civil service), except for the insecurity of tenure, the informal qualifications for advancement, and the extraordinarily large number of high-ranking positions at the top of the pyramid.

Although the Cabinet has retained almost complete discretion in prefectoral appointments, it has made only a handful of such appointments from outside of the career service since the removal of the Resistance Prefects in 1946.

49. Cf. Brian Chapman, *The Prefects and Provincial France* (London, 1955), p. 156.

TABLE 12 The Prefectoral Career Ladder since 1957

Rank and number of posts on the rolls	Prerequisites and methods of appointment
PREFECT (131)	Appointed by decree of the President of the Republic, based on the decision of the Council of Ministers, on the advice of the Minister of the Interior. May be appointed from the Civil Administration career service of the Interior, from other career services, or from outside of the state administration. Three-fifths of the prefectoral posts must be filled by members of the Civil Administration career service.
VICE-PREFECT (170)	Selected on a competitive basis by the Council of Administration of the Ministry (composed of the Minister or Undersecretary, all directors general of the Ministry, and two representatives of the personnel of the Ministry co-opted by the other members of the Council) from among Vice-Prefect Inspectors with at least three years in that title.
VICE-PREFECT INSPECTOR (175)	Selected from among Section Directors with from one to three years in that title on the basis of competitive written or oral examinations, by the Council of Administration.
SECTION DIRECTOR (440)	Selected by the Council of Administration from among Councillors First Class with from nine to eleven years of service in the career on the basis of competitive written and oral examinations.
COUNCILLORS FIRST CLASS	Selected by the Council of Administration from Second-Class Councillors with at least three years in that title on the basis of a competitive examination.
COUNCILLORS SECOND CLASS (580)	Semi-automatic promotion by the Council of Administration from among Third-Class Councillors with at least two years of service in that title.
COUNCILLORS THIRD CLASS	Selected in a public competitive examination open to those with a university degree and the general requirements for state employment, and also to experienced members of the Executive Career of the Interior with a secondary school diploma.

Source: Decrees of the President of the Republic of January 11, 1956, No. 16; January 10, 1957, No. 3 and No. 362.

The few exceptions have been generals appointed as Prefects in particularly tense periods; police inspectors, given appointments shortly before retirement in reward for meritorious service; a couple of CLN Prefects who agreed to enter the career service; and one Christian Democratic politician—the president of Zone A (Trieste) in the Free Territory of Trieste—who was appointed Prefect of Trieste to symbolize Italian claims to that city and who has been given other prefectoral assignments since then.[50]

The relative paucity of outside appointments may be accounted for by the fact that career officials have what is considered better preparation and training than outside appointees; and also by the lack of pressure from the outside for prefectoral appointments, given the loss of prestige, the controversiality, the precarious existence of the institution, and its relatively poor economic standing among alternative careers in the postwar period. Preference for career officials may also be dictated by a desire to bolster the morale of the Civil Administration service, aiding the recruitment of new members and maximizing promotional opportunities. Such opportunities have been limited in the postwar period, given the large number of relatively junior officials appointed Prefects to replace those purged from the service in 1944–46. The relative youthfulness of the prefectoral service, as compared to the diplomatic service, can be seen in Table 13.

Postwar cabinets have tended to appoint career officials for two other reasons. They have done so first of all because the career officials have tended to share the same moderately conservative orientation of the postwar governing coali-

50. On Jan. 1, 1957, there were only two members of the prefectoral rolls (out of 129) who had not entered the career service before or under Fascism. See Ministero dell'Interno, *Ruoli di anzianità del personale delle amministrazioni dipendenti: Situazione al 1° gennaio 1957.*

TABLE 13 Age and Years of Service of Vice-Prefects, Prefects, and Ambassadors (1954)

Age group	Vice-prefects*	Prefects†	Ambassadors
40–44	8	2	2
45–49	66	42	8
50–54	48	27	36
55–59	48	30	41
60–64	82	28	10
65 and over	17	3	2
Years of service			
0–4	—	1	2
5–9	—	1	3
10–14	—	—	1
15–19	3	—	—
20–24	94	52	5
25–29	33	15	43
30–34	62	42	39
35–40	46	12	3
over 40	31	9	3

*The figures for vice-prefects may include the *Questori* (Provincial Police Chiefs) and all others of former Grade V in the Ministry of the Interior in 1954.

†In the figures for Prefects may be included one or two Chief Inspectors General of Public Security as they also enjoyed the former Grade IV.

Source: Istituto Centrale di Statistica, *Dipendenti delle amministrazioni statali al 30 novembre 1954* (Rome, Istituto Poligrafico dello Stato, 1956), pp. 92–98.

tions. Although almost all of the Prefects entered and rose in the career service under Fascism, they made the transfer of allegiance to the post-Fascist regime with ease. Most of them come from southern middle-class families of modest means and retain the conservatism of that milieu.[51] The prefectoral career service has traditionally attracted the most capable applicants for government employment and set the most difficult examinations for entry. Its only rivals in prestige among the state services have been the foreign service and the judiciary, both administrative and regular. It has remained relatively immune from the corruption that became endemic in the state bureaucracy under Fascism.[52]

The Prefects are among the highest officials in rank and salary of the Italian bureaucracy. They are outranked only by the First President of the Court of Cassation, the presidents of the Council of State and of the Court of Accounts, and a small group of ambassadors. First-class Prefects are on a par with lieutenant generals, the Director General of the State Railways, the Comptroller General (*Ragioniere Generale dello Stato*), special envoys, ministers plenipotentiary first class, and full professors in the state universities. Second-class Prefects enjoy the same rank as ministerial directors general, major generals, Purveyors of Public Works, and associate professors in the state universities.[53]

51. There are no statistics available on the regional and social origins of the Prefects as such. My statement is based on the unanimous opinion of the large number of officials I have interviewed in the Ministry of the Interior and the prefectures. The statement is also supported by the data available for the career Prefects in 1937. Of the twenty-two career Prefects whose regional origins can be ascertained from Savino's *La Nazione operante* (cited above on p. 183, note 33), fifteen were from the South. An unofficial survey (the results of which are reported in *L'Amministrazione Civile, 4* [Sept. 1960], v–vii) reveals the following data on the social origins of the state bureaucracy as a whole:

Father's occupation	Per cent
civil servant	53.0
professional and independent businessman	18.7
worker or artisan	17.4
landowner or farmer	10.9

52. Arturo Carlo Jemolo and G. N. Trapani, "Un Dialogo sui prefetti," *Il Mondo, 5*, No. 13 (March 30, 1954), pp. 5–6.

53. Decree of the President of the Republic, Jan. 10, 1957, No. 3.

First-class Prefects receive about $4,700 per year; second-class Prefects, about $4,350. In addition, if serving in a province, they receive a representation allowance which varies according to the social importance of the post, as well as an apartment in the prefecture, maintained by the province and furnished by the state.[54] Promotion from the second class to the first class lies at the discretion of the Cabinet but it is apparently based only on seniority. There is no necessary connection between the class of the Prefect and the importance of the provincial post that he occupies. The provinces are not, as they are in France, officially ranked according to their importance.

Of the approximately 130 Prefects, only eighty-eight can be assigned to head provinces, for three of the provinces, those in Aosta Valley and Trentino Regions, no longer have Prefects.[55] Seven others are usually assigned to head the bureaus of the Ministry of the Interior as directors general and one to act as *Capo di Gabinetto* of the minister, that is, chief of the minister's office. Five others serve as representatives of the government attached to the special regions. Others may serve as *Capo di Gabinetto* of the President of the Republic, the Prime Minister or other ministers; as head of a parastate agency; or as prefectoral commissioner to manage the affairs of important cities, the regular administrations of which have been dissolved.

54. Decree of the President of the Republic, Jan. 11, 1956, No. 19.

55. The prefectures were abolished in the Aosta Valley and the Trentino-Alto Adige Regions. In the Aosta Valley Region, the Prefect's powers were transferred to the President of the Region. In the Trentino Region, part of the Prefects' police powers were given to the Provincial Presidents, part to the state-appointed *Questori* in these provinces, and the rest to the resident Government Commissioner attached to the Region. The prefectures were legally abolished by the Statute of the Sicilian Region, but the central government has so far been successful in preventing implementation of these provisions. In Sicily as in Sardinia, the Prefects have lost most of their powers (except in public security) to the Region, including most supervisory authority over local governments.

About a dozen others may serve as inspectors on behalf of the Minister of the Interior.[56]

Almost all new Prefects, then, are appointed from the career service. Each year about a dozen new appointments are made from among the most senior vice-prefects, after about twenty or twenty-five years of satisfactory performance. Each year a new "class" is reached of those who entered the service at the same time. Those vice-prefects who are passed over or who are more senior than those already appointed Prefects have slim prospects for eventual promotion, although to prevent complete demoralization at least one appointment is made each year from among those passed over when their class was up for promotion.

Of the dozen or so new appointments, about half are made from among vice-prefects serving in the ministry, confirming the current (and worldwide) impression that centrally located personnel enjoy a considerable advantage over field personnel in securing promotion. At the ministry, apparently, one is less likely to fall victim to the kind of incidents that mar the record of a candidate for prefectoral appointment.[57]

56. Camera dei Deputati, *Annuario parlamentare, 1957–1958* (Rome, 1957), pp. 439–43.

57. Quite a few members of the career service receive prefectoral appointments without having served at all in the provinces. This has some disadvantages, of course, in that the new Prefect often finds himself without the experience necessary to cope with the immediate and pressing problems thrown up daily in a provincial post, where the effects of decisions are often immediately apparent. Service in the ministry does not provide this challenge of immediacy nor does it often permit the official to prepare himself in a wide range of problems. Those without previous field experience, however, claim that their service in the ministry provides them with considerable insight into ministerial procedures and attitudes; it also gives them connections with influential ministerial officials. In these ways, they may serve their province more effectively than Prefects with only field experience. Recently, in any event, the ministry has decided to require service in the field as a prerequisite to promotion to the upper ranks of the career.

Since the prefectoral ranks are top-heavy with relatively young functionaries appointed during the wartime and postwar purges, the number of posts available has been rather limited. Prospects for promotion above the rank of vice-prefect since the war have been poor. There has been enormous competition for the few posts at the apex of the career pyramid.

The few who succeed each year are appointed by the entire Council of Ministers, on the advice of the Minister of the Interior. The Minister reportedly bases his recommendations on his own impressions of the candidates, the suggestions of his director general of personnel, and the reports and solicitations of ministers, deputies, provincial and national party secretaries, and the clergy.

The Cabinet also passes upon the annual movement of Prefects, as well as upon those of the other high-ranking career officials—civil, military, and judicial. In theory, a strictly personal ranking system, as opposed to one like the French in which rank is tied to the status of the provincial post, should permit the Prefect to enjoy a longer tour of duty in a given province. There would be no need to transfer him to another province in order to give him promotion in rank. But in spite of this, Italian Prefects, in practice, seem to have much shorter tours of duty than their counterparts in France. There are several reasons for this.

There is an informal system of ranking posts based on obvious criteria such as the population of the province or of its capital city, and there is a regular progression in prefectoral careers from smaller to larger and more prominent cities. A Prefect will normally move from a rural, out-of-the-way provincial capital to a medium-sized capital city with greater amenities. From this latter kind of province, a Prefect may eventually end up in one of the largest cities, such as Rome, Milan, Turin, Venice, Naples, or Genoa; or as a director general in the ministry; or as Government Commissioner in one of the existing regions.

His tour of duty in any one province is apt to be rather short: the normal expectation seems to be about three or four years at the most, although it may be rather longer or suddenly much shorter.

Prefects are constantly rotated to allow for a regular development of experience in handling the problems of progressively more difficult provinces; to permit the filling of gaps left by retirements and dismissals; and to prevent them from establishing such strong alliances with local interests that they can resist directions from Rome that displease them. They are never posted to a province in which they have close family connections. A Prefect often asks for transfer out of a province in which he has become so closely identified with particular interests that he has lost all freedom of maneuver. He may also request transfer when a shift in government policy requires him to perform an awkward about-face in tactics or alliances—an about-face that might not only embarrass him but also render him ineffective because of his identification with the previous line. Transfer may also be welcome to a Prefect who has lost, or appears to have lost, the desired degree of impartiality; who has accumulated a certain amount of hostility; or who desires a change in the type of province he has been heading. He may desire a rest from a particularly grueling assignment in a province with severe social tensions where the opposition is apt to be strong and violent.

Widespread movements, affecting many prefectures, are also the rule following major political crises, such as after the wave of local Communist insurrections in 1948. In such cases, Prefects who have performed badly in the view of the government are dismissed or demoted to a province of lesser importance and those who have stood up well under fire are rewarded with a more prominent post. Clamorous cases of dismissal in the postwar period have been rare. For the most part, governments have preferred to deal with unsatisfactory prefectoral performance by placing the Prefects involved "at disposition," that is, temporarily out of public sight and attached to the ministry, or by transferring them to a less favorable post. The Prefect is somewhat compensated for his precarious tenure of office by a particularly favorable pension scheme whereby if he has served in the state service for at least ten years (instead of the usual twenty) and is involuntarily retired, he becomes entitled to his pension.[58]

A final mark of the Prefect's special status among state officials is the so-called "administrative guarantee," by virtue of which a Prefect cannot be "called to render account for the exercise of his functions, except by his ministerial superiors; nor subjected to legal proceedings for any act of his office without authorization of the Government, after consulting the Council of State, except for the case of alleged electoral crimes." This freedom from criminal prosecution and civil suit was copied by the Piedmontese from a provision in the French Constitution of the Year VIII and, although abolished by the French in 1870, has continued in Italy to the present day.[59]

The Prefect's relations with the field service directors may be summarized as follows. He provides them with the minimum conditions of public order and safety to permit them to operate. He supports their program efforts with his public safety powers, with his powers of coercion and persuasion. He provides them with political guidance. He relies upon them to help solve problems of public order. He

58. Lentini, *L'Amministrazione locale,* pp. 30–36.
59. Ibid., pp. 35–36. The provision is taken from Article 22 of the 1934 Provincial and Communal Act.

mediates and controls their relations with those institutions under his tutelary authority: communes, the Province, reclamation consortia, public charities, etc. He revises and sometimes drafts their recommendations to their ministries on the allocation of grants-in-aid to the various localities and institutions. He receives and transmits to them complaints and informal appeals against their decisions, as well as claims for special favors and patronage. He may assist them in executing their programs through the use of his special powers, such as in condemnation proceedings. He supports their requests to their ministries for action and grants—in competition with the field directors, Prefects, and politicians of other provinces. He coordinates their operations in cases of emergency and natural disaster. He provides a center for the unified overview of their respective activities.

The various ministries and agencies tend to resist attempts to reduce their complete and direct control over their field services. They are, after all, responsible for the formulation and implementation of nationwide policies and programs within their particular sector and understandably insist upon a clear line of responsibility from the minister down to the lowest echelon of the field service. They protect themselves from outside intervention by concentrating authority in the ministry and in this way retain the last word over decisions in their particular spheres of jurisdiction.

They tend, however, to view the Prefect as a useful institution and turn to him voluntarily for several kinds of assistance. They often seek his advice on political matters, usually involving the adjudication of rival claims on ministerial patronage, and consider his advice impartial and well founded. They expect and appreciate occasional prefectoral reports on political problems involving their field operations; his recommendations on the allocation of grants; his occasional reports on the impact of their programs on his province and suggestions for change and future action. They are thus not averse to requiring their field officers to consult the Prefect before submitting action proposals for central approval. For they are completely free to disregard the Prefect's recommendations.

The result is that field directors at the provincial level are generally amenable to prefectoral influence. They tend to recognize the Prefect's right to determine "nontechnical" or "political" matters, such as which locality is to receive a grant-in-aid, who is to be given a job, and whose claims are to receive prior attention by their ministry. The Prefect's claim to make such judgments is almost always respected due to his status as the representative of the government and toleration of this "political" coordination by the respective ministries, which retain the ultimate authority to overrule prefectoral determinations. Field directors, then, have only to gain from compliance with prefectoral suggestions.[60] Thus they regularly submit to the Prefect their lists for state grants in the province and allow him to modify them in accordance with his views on the relative urgency of various claims.[61] The proposed priority lists that the field directors submit to him are not formally subject

60. The Prefects do not make out the efficiency reports for any field directors other than those belonging to the Ministry of the Interior, such as the *Questore* or provincial police chief. They can and do sometimes send in complaints regarding other field directors to the Ministry of the Interior for it to take up with the field directors' own ministerial superiors. Under Fascism, prefectoral complaints could be sent directly to the technical ministry involved.

61. Field directors do not, apparently, submit *all* lists for state grants to the Prefect. The Provincial Agrarian Inspector, for example, does not submit to the Prefect his list of recommended private recipients of state aid for farm improvements.

to his determination, but his backing is necessary if the province is to compete successfully with the other provinces for the limited grants available. In France, such programs are presumably determined by the Prefect and are *his* programs, drafted with the aid of the technical specialists. In Italy, the programs and priorities are determined in the central ministries, based upon the joint recommendations of the Prefect and the technical specialists.

The actual relations between the Prefect and the technical field directors vary somewhat from province to province. Some Prefects, especially the more junior ones, have a broader conception of the Prefect's power and responsibility than their more senior colleagues. They tend to consider themselves responsible for all state action in the province and hence intervene whenever they can in those affairs of technical services that appear to affect provincial opinion about the government. Many younger Prefects also tend to be more dynamic, to be, in the Italian phrase, *garibaldini,* that is, energetic and bold: they often wish to expedite long-pending decisions in the technical ministries, to overcome the traditional lethargy and red tape of Italian administration. Other Prefects (and not always the more senior ones) take a more restricted view of their duties; they would rather avoid difficulties with the technical ministries; they tend to disclaim any right to interfere with the normal operations of the technical services.

Some field directors, on the other hand, are more independent-minded than others; more quick to resent what they consider outside interference; more apt to view the prefecture as an anachronism; or more desirous of building up their own reputations and political connections. Most specialists do not, however, appear to challenge the Prefect's right to intervene in their affairs and do not resist such intervention.

Some programs or administrative sectors impinge more directly upon matters of institutional concern to the Prefect, such as public order, politics, and local government, or are more controversial than others. The Prefect follows closely the affairs of agencies whose activities are fiercely opposed by groups in the province and likely to require the intervention of the police. He often acts to prevent opposition groups from sabotaging or discrediting a particular program. Active prefectoral support was necessary, for example, to establish the state monopoly of employment exchanges over the fierce and often violent protests of the left-wing trade unions, and to carry out the more delicate operations involved in the land reform program.

The Prefect will also tend to have closer relations with those offices of particular importance in his province as, for instance, the land reform agency in a province affected by the reform program; the mining engineer, in a province with a large extractive industry; and the port captain, in a province with a large port.

The Prefect is apt to maintain closer relations with the other state services in provinces that are relatively small in population. In such provinces, it is easier for the Prefect to follow what they are doing and almost inevitable that he do so. In larger provinces there are many distracting social duties for the Prefect to perform; he is apt to be absorbed in his own particular concerns; and the activities of the various services tend to be less prominent in the general bustle of provincial affairs.

Finally, relations between the Prefect and the state services tend to be closer in provinces dominated by the opposition parties. There is apt to be greater solidarity among state agencies in hostile territory, where the activities of all of them are closely scrutinized and sharply criticized, than in provinces supporting the government.

The Prefect tends to have most contacts, of course, with his immediate subordinates. He receives reports in person daily from the provincial chief of police (the *Questore*) and the officer commanding the Carabinieri. Among those state officials who are not his subordinates, he has most frequent contacts with the Director of the Provincial Labor Office, the Chief Engineer of the *Genio Civile* (Corps of Civil Engineers), the Intendant of Finance, the Provincial Agrarian Inspector, the District Forest Inspector, the Director of the Provincial Office for Industry and Commerce, and the Purveyor of Studies. He has relatively few contacts with the heads of the provincial branches of parastate agencies, the state railways, the postal administration, the Treasury, the military, and the judiciary. His relations with most regional officials, with the prominent exception of the Purveyors of Public Works, also tend to be remote.[62]

It is only when relations between the Prefect and a field director are close that the possibility of conflict between the two arises. Such conflicts are not so frequent as they might be if decision-making authority was not largely reserved to the central ministries in matters of any importance. Clashes sometimes occur when a field director refuses to accept a prefectoral demand that a given decision be made on political, rather than technical, grounds. A Civil Engineer may, for example, prefer to give priority to some projects that have little electoral appeal; a Labor Inspector may refuse to interpret factory legislation in a partisan manner; a Provincial Medical Officer may wish to approve the decision by a Communist communal council to distribute free polio vaccine. The Prefect may be able to make use of his personal and institutional ascendancy; he may have

62. The Purveyors of Public Works were re-established by Decree Laws of Jan. 18, 1945, No. 16, and June 27, 1946, No. 37, throughout the entire country.

to threaten to have the official transferred to Calabria (a standard threat). The official, still resistant, may appeal for help to his regional superiors, if any. Regional officials occasionally have to intervene to protect their provincial subordinates from pressures of this sort. Efforts are usually made to settle the conflict in the field, but if these are unsuccessful, the matter will be referred to the Interior and to the ministerial superiors of the resistant field director. The question will then be decided by the two ministers involved, with or without the intervention of the Prime Minister or the Cabinet as a whole. In cases of serious conflict, the outcome will involve the transfer of one of the two officials involved and perhaps the issuance of a circular to the Prefects on the matter. Such cases are apparently rare.

Generally speaking, the relations between the Prefect and other state services are neither public nor systematic. In one province, however, an experiment has been carried out in both public and systematic prefectoral coordination. This is the province of Vicenza in the foothills of the Tyrolean Alps, northwest of Venice—a province with about 600,000 people. The experiment was carried out under unusual circumstances. First of all, the Prefect who began the experiment in 1953 was one of the very few noncareer Prefects appointed since 1946. He had been a manager in the Trieste branch of the largest Italian insurance company and also a Christian Democratic party leader. Between 1946 and 1953, he served as vice-president, then president of Zone A (the city of Trieste) in the Free Territory, exercising the functions of a Prefect, except for public safety functions reserved to the Allied Military Government. He was appointed Prefect of Trieste in 1950 to demonstrate Italian claims of sovereignty over the zone. After clashes with the AMG commander, General Winterton, occasioned by

AMG repression of pro-Italian demonstrations in 1952, he
was reluctantly removed from Trieste and rewarded with
the prefecture of Vicenza. He served there from 1953 until
1958 when he was appointed director of public relations
for the Ministry of the Interior. The Vicenza experiment
owed its origin in part to the fact that the Prefect had come
into the service from private management and had the political outlook of the socially progressive wing of the Christian Democratic party. He was therefore less disposed than
most career Prefects to tolerate bureaucratic rigidities and
routine patterns of prefectoral behavior.

The experiment was also related to the fact that the province of Vicenza was overwhelmingly Christian Democratic
in politics. Of its 122 communes, 121 had Christian Democratic mayors. The basic political problem for the Prefect
of such a province is, as we have said, to keep all factions
and local notables of the dominant party contented. It is
only natural that the Prefect should attempt to "objectify"
and publicize the decisions that his colleagues in other types
of provinces preferred to make more haphazardly and dis-
creetly. The system of coordination that the Prefect evolved
was thus designed, in part, to cope with the problem of
factional diplomacy.

The system involved the creation in the Prefect's Cabinet
of an Office for the Coordination of Social Activity
(UCAS) to collect data and statistics, investigate socioeconomic problems, draft and revise priority lists for state
grants, expedite decisions in state and local offices, staff
the various conferences called by the Prefect, and follow
up on the decisions arrived at in those conferences. The
province was divided into three areas (plains, hills, and
mountains), each area into zones, and each zone into sectors; within each of these areas, the Prefect convened the
mayors and other local government officials periodically to

discuss local problems and needs. The Prefect established strict periodic reporting requirements on public works, new business enterprises, and works projects from the local government authorities; on unemployment, from the Provincial Labor Office; on relief rolls, from the ECAs (communal relief agencies); on housing conditions, from the communal health officers; and on school construction needs, from the Purveyor of Studies. He and his staff worked out objective criteria for the determination of comparative need for state grants as among the various localities, based upon such indices as the level of unemployment, the number of people on relief, and housing and school construction requirements. He convened periodic meetings of the principal state and parastate field directors in the province, usually after the series of conferences with the local government authorities, at which he informed the various directors of the problems raised by the local government authorities, worked out solutions, and sought binding commitments to action; these meetings, of which there were three or four each year, were also used to permit the clarification of jurisdictions and functions among the several agencies, as the basis for cooperative action. The Prefect also had both periodic and occasional conferences with particular state field directors for the joint preparation of recommended priority lists for state grants. A bulletin was published by the prefecture containing not only the usual ministerial and prefectoral circulars, but also the recommendations for grants, the data upon which they were based, and the final ministerial actions on those recommendations.

The system was designed, the Prefect declared, to remedy the lack of interservice contacts at the provincial level. "The horizontal aspect [in Italian field administration] is very attenuated and of purely ideal value as compared to the clear and distinct prevalence of the vertical organization." Efforts at social justice are "often endangered by this vertical organization and by mutual interferences. Therefore only clear understandings among the heads of state field offices can guarantee the proper priority listing of needs and the program of works to be executed."[63]

In the postwar period there has been a proliferation of programs of state aid in all provinces involving various and overlapping benefits and agency jurisdictions. The Prefect of Vicenza attempted to ensure that full advantage was taken of every program and that the over-all allocation of grants corresponded to the relative need of the various localities. The Prefect himself controlled the allocation of only a small portion of the state grants, the funds available under the Winter Aid program. All of the other programs were prepared and financed by the agents of other ministries: Public Works, Agriculture and Forestry, Labor, Finance, and Public Instruction. The Prefect attempted to coordinate the preparation of the several programs of these various agencies.

In attempting to determine the various priority lists of the different field services in the direction of greater objectivity, the Prefect encountered several difficulties.

The various field directors had to be handled with great tact. The Prefect frequently had to publish in his bulletin such statements as the following: "It is hardly necessary to state that the Prefect's coordinating action detracts in no way and wishes to detract in no way from the particular authority (*competenza*) of the various offices."[64]

63. Bollettino della Prefettura di Vicenza, Ufficio di Coordinamento per l'Attività Sociale, No. 19 (Oct. 1–15, 1957), *Relazione del Prefetto dott. Gino Palutan al 1° Convegno Nazionale degli Studi sulle Relazioni Pubbliche in Italia: Roma 17–18–19 1957*, pp. 7–8.

64. Prefettura di Vicenza. Ufficio di Coordinamento per l'Attività Sociale. Servizio Relazioni Organizzate. *Resoconto della IVª riunione dei capi degli uffici pubblici del 27 novembre 1956* (Vicenza, 1956), p. 11.

Field offices tended to be somewhat lax in keeping track of prefectoral publications and to forget their commitments. It was difficult for the Prefect to make cooperative action a matter of routine, to convince the directors of the utility of interagency cooperation, to break with the long tradition of mutual indifference and ignorance.

Coordination, moreover, required considerable negotiating ability on the part of the Prefect in order to reach a generally acceptable pattern of value allocation. Political leaders often preferred a much less objective system in which the more influential among them could obtain more than objective need would justify. They tended to prefer the usual "free enterprise" system in which they could exploit several different channels of access, mostly behind the scenes, as opposed to the objective allocation of state aid in a rigid and public procedure, with access unified through the Prefect. In practice, objectification meant an attempt to distribute greater aid to the numerous small communes in the rural areas which have greater difficulty than urban areas in mobilizing their political strength. The Prefect threw his weight behind these smaller communes and stimulated them to take advantage of the aid programs and to band together against the larger, more aggressive communities. His initial attempts at objectification incurred the hostility of the representatives of the larger localities, who demanded his transfer. He was able to continue his pro-rural policies only with the backing of the Minister of the Interior and the major Christian Democratic politicians of the province.

The representatives of the larger communes, such as the provincial capital, Vicenza, would have preferred to exploit their own direct access to the ministerial offices in Rome, which have the last say on the allocation of aid. The larger communes used their access to disrupt the priority lists established by the Prefect, going over his head to the central offices where they were often successful in securing changes in the Prefect's program. The Prefect attempted to combat this by publishing the programs as submitted to Rome and the programs as finally approved in Rome, calling attention to cases in which localities had obtained more than their pre-ordained share.

In part the Prefect's bias in favor of the rural mountain communes reflected a desire to strengthen their claims on the basis of objectively greater need. But it also reflected a national Christian Democratic policy in favor of the rural areas, which contribute the great bulk of its votes. The rural mountain areas are largely depressed areas, which have been bested in the past by the urban areas in the competition for state aid, due to their lesser political organization, dynamism, and wealth. The Christian Democratic party has attempted to bolster these strongholds of political catholicism by checking the mass exodus to the leftist urban areas.

There was also some resistance to the Prefect's action by politicians, especially members of Parliament, who wanted to get credit for obtaining state aid as a means of building political support. The politicians wanted to be the allocators of aid; *they* wanted to demonstrate their influence with the ministries in Rome; *they* wanted to secure favors for mayors and local party leaders in return for electoral support; *they* wanted to maximize their electoral chances rather than promote distributive justice. The Prefect was threatening to steal the limelight.

The Prefect had also to overcome the resistance of the various field directors, their tendencies toward formalism and routine, their fears of displeasing the politicians by listening to the Prefect rather than to mayors and deputies, and their desires to win credit for state grants in their own right. Field directors feared transfer or lack of promotion if they did not accede to the demands of the urban politicians. They also desired to demonstrate their own good works on behalf of the province. Collective decision-making under the aegis of the Prefect shielded them somewhat from political pressures, but also deprived them of individual credit.

Field directors sometimes differed with the Prefect on methods and criteria of allocation. To some extent, these differences mirrored differences in agency outlook and clientele. The Prefect, as we have said, tended to operate on behalf of the mountainous areas. Such an official as the Provincial Labor Director tended to favor the urban areas with large concentrations of industrial workers.

The Prefect encountered resistance, as well, from within his own prefecture. Many of the career officials were skeptical about the new coordination system and the social policies of the Prefect, preferring the traditional operating methods and routines of the prefectures.

Despite these obstacles, the experiment was deemed successful. The Prefect was brought to Rome in 1958 to work out plans for its extension to the other prefectures of the country. Other Prefects have begun to imitate the scheme although as yet on a minor scale. The ministry has called for the eventual establishment of coordination offices in all the prefectures.

The Vicenza experiment has demonstrated the possible gains of more active prefectoral coordination. The usefulness of such coordination has developed only with the enormous expansion of state programs and agencies designed to raise the standard of living of the Italian people. This expansion has brought with it the need for new methods and equipment, for new kinds of technical training, and for unwonted urgency. But the growth in the burdens of

Italian administration and the raising of standards of performance in the postwar period have come upon an administrative service gravely disrupted and weakened by the war; by the massive wartime influx of "temporary" employees without competitive examination; by the serious exodus of talented administrators to private employment; and by the obsolescence of legislation, regulations, procedures, and mentalities.[65] The expansion in responsibilities has greatly overburdened the traditional technical services and has led to the creation of new agencies and new field services designed to operate outside of the traditional framework of the state administration. Services and programs have multiplied. More frequently than ever before, the activities of one service in the field may negate, duplicate, require, supplement, or reinforce the activities of other state or parastate services and those of the minor units of government.

The Vicenza "pilot-prefecture" has shown the potential usefulness of the prefecture in attempting to mesh the proliferating activities of government within the area of the province; to spur the various services to modernize their methods, accelerate their pace, and cooperate with other services and with local governments in matters of common concern; and to prevent the haphazard application of effort and distribution of aid by the preparation of common criteria for action and the provision of a common clearing-house for information. Such attempts to rationalize field administration are especially warranted in countries like Italy in which relative poverty of resources is accompanied

---

65. Taylor Cole, "The Reform of the Italian Bureaucracy," *Public Administration Review, 13* (1953), 247–56. See also Presidenza del Consiglio dei Ministri, *Stato dei lavori per la riforma della pubblica amministrazione (1948–1953)* (3 vols. Rome, 1953); and Carlo Petrocchi, *Il Problema della burocrazia* (Rome, 1944).

by a tendency to disperse those resources in a multitude of separate, ad hoc efforts.

Basic responsibility for interagency coordination lies, of course, with Parliament which sets the tasks, provides the means, and fixes the jurisdiction of the several agencies. It lies also with the central ministries and agencies; with the instrumentalities for central coordination, such as the Council of Ministers, the Prime Minister's office, and cabinet and interdepartmental committees; with agencies, such as the Fund for the South (*Cassa del Mezzogiorno*), consciously designed to coordinate several kinds of state action within a large, but specific area of the country.

Various devices have also been developed to promote the coherent execution of policies in the provinces. These include standing interagency committees, clearance requirements, and field agencies, such as the land reform agencies, with authority to act in several administrative sectors, supplanting the normal field services within specific geographic areas of the country. The prefecture is not the only potential device for the coordination of policy execution in the field. But prefectoral coordination, if developed along the lines of the Vicenza scheme, would provide a useful supplement to the other forms of coordination—a supplement with its own particular merits. The indefinite growth of new multipurpose field agencies, such as the land reform agencies and the Po Valley Authority *(Magistrato del Po)*,[66]

66. The Po Valley Authority (*Magistrato del Po*), patterned after the Venetian Water Authority (*Magistrato alle acque*) created in 1907, was established by the Law of July 12, 1956, No. 735, with responsibility for flood control in the Po River basin. It has been given power to replace, direct, or coordinate the work of regional and provincial offices (about eighty in number) whose activities in flood and erosion control, reclamation, and internal navigation affect the hydraulic regulation of the Po drainage basin.

Eight theoretically temporary agencies were created by various laws in

threatens to fragment still further an already overcomplex administrative system and to serve as a means to avoid the reform of the services of the traditional ministries. Clearance requirements, crystallized in the form of laws and regulations, all too readily degenerate into the empty motions of formalistic, time-consuming routine. Standing interagency committees, without the constant prodding and inspiration of an impartial chairman highly sensitive to the social pressures of the area concerned, may lack a sense of urgency. Prefectoral coordination, on the other hand, can be highly flexible and applicable only when and where needed. It can also be personally inspired and take profit from the generalist outlook and political sensitivity to which the Prefects are conditioned.

Should the Vicenza scheme be extended to all the provinces, it would mark the first major readjustment of the Italian prefectoral system as such to the requirements of the democratic welfare state. It would transform the prefectures from symbols and agents of conservative control into instruments of social and economic innovation. A prerequisite to such a development is most likely the formation of that Christian Democratic-Socialist alliance which is a prerequisite also to the establishment of the regions. Such an alliance would certainly be required for the extension not only of the coordination machinery but also of the policies of objectification for which that machinery was originally designed. Without such an alliance, it is difficult to conceive of the extension of the objectivity principle to areas of leftist domination or to the southern provinces,

---

1950–51 to carry out a massive program of agrarian reform in eight special areas of the country, six of which are in the South and Islands. See, e.g., Ente Maremma, *La Riforma fondiaria in Maremma: 1951–1954* (Rome, 1955).

where the discriminatory allocation of government aid has constituted a major weapon in the political struggle.

But even with such an alliance, it is doubtful whether the prefectoral system itself will be abolished, so rooted is that system in the political mores of a country secularly riven by civil discord.

Chapter Six

GENERAL CONCLUSIONS

FROM THE PRECEDING historical study, it is possible to draw various conclusions, some bearing upon the Italian case study itself, some on broader problems of comparative administration. The first part of this chapter will deal with some general propositions concerning Italian administration; the second, with those propositions of a cross-cultural nature which the study suggests.

I

A retrospective analysis of the history of the Italian prefectoral system reveals *inter alia* that that system, as it exists today, is the product of a long, basically uninterrupted evolution, rather than the deliberate creation of a particular time. It is the continuity of the system, rather than the changes within it, that is impressive. The system has been maintained essentially intact throughout modern Italian history, organized in much the same way to serve much the same purposes.

The over-all pattern of the system since unification has been marked by four major traits:

1. a high degree of centralization, of resistance to pressures for local autonomy and power;
2. a high degree of concentration, of resistance to pressures for greater local autonomy and power within the state bureaucracy;
3. a predominantly political, rather than administrative, Prefect;
4. the substantial administrative independence from the Prefect of a growing number of technical state field services.

These constants, in turn, are closely related to the basic continuity in the purposes and origins of the ruling groups in Italy since unification. The prefectoral system was designed for and has continued to serve the purposes of social conservatism and national unity in a society with perhaps no other nationally integrative institution apart from the state bureaucracy itself. The fragmentation of the Italian political culture underlies the continuing strength of the centralizing impulses of the ruling groups. For decentralization would imply the strengthening of dissident ideological or social groups—a result which is seen to be at once immoral and dangerous.

There have been, to be sure, other factors accounting for the persistently high level of centralization: the financial straits of the national government and its inability to devolve a greater share of national resources to minor units of government in order to support greater services; the widespread preference for state, rather than local, administration, as being less partial or "factious"; the differential socioeconomic development of the various regions of the country, with concomitant differences in social skills, standards of public behavior, and economic resources. Poverty of resources, differential social development, and local factiousness are, however, only different facets of the same problem: the lack of a national political community.

The second element in this enduring pattern—the high level of concentration within the state administration itself—rests upon the same oligarchical tendencies supporting centralization. It reflects a traditional lack of responsiveness to the public at large and to pressures upon the bureaucracy for impartial, swift decision-making at a publicly convenient level. Concentration is part of a general cultural pattern of authoritarian decision-making, as, for example, is to be found in the management of private organizations, such as political parties, religious organizations, business corporations, and trade unions.[1] It is also, perhaps, a reflection of a fear of anarchical elements in the national character and of the resulting general expectation that devolved or dispersed power will be abused.

The "political" Prefect has fitted neatly into this pattern of centralization and concentration. The Prefect has existed primarily as policeman and supervisor of local government, exercising and symbolizing central government control over local groups and institutions. Administrative power in the central government agencies has remained concentrated in the capital and this concentration has avoided the pivotal problem of *integrated* prefectoral systems: how to apportion deconcentrated authority between the Prefect and the functional services of the newer agencies in the field.[2] If the various technical ministries had wished or been forced to deconcentrate large amounts of authority to the

1. See, e.g., F. H. Harbison and E. W. Burgess, "Modern Management in Europe," *American Journal of Sociology,* 55 (1954), 15–23.

2. For the specific meaning that we have attached to the term "integrated," see below, pp. 306–10. On this problem, see Alfred Diamant, "The

field, this spiny question could scarcely have been avoided.

The substantial administrative independence of the various state field services from the Prefect was established in the early years of the unified nation under the influence of the liberal ideology of the founding fathers, hesitant to create what would have seemed an oriental or Napoleonic despot in each of the provinces of the new realm. The dispersion of ministerial power among the heads of the several central departments encouraged the drive of these departments toward self-sufficiency in the field as well as in the national capital. The Prefect's major responsibilities were essentially political and nontechnical, involving the mobilization of support for the new regime and the repression of dissent. These factors and others that I have outlined in the concluding section of Chapter 2 continued to operate in the years following unification.

Under the liberal constitutional regime, the administrative independence of the technical services became firmly rooted in the custom and practices of Italian administration and in the formal laws and regulations that governed them. The few services that were placed under the directive authority of the Prefect succeeded in liberating themselves either through ministerial decree or parliamentary statute. Attempts in the 1890s to expand prefectoral control were bound to founder on the numerous shoals of vested ministerial interests; the drive for functional autonomy and freedom from political interference; ministerial resistance to deconcentration; prefectoral identification with one ministry, the Interior, and its electoral and police functions; and the political difficulties involved in redrawing the geographical areas of prefectoral jurisdiction so as to reduce

---

Department, the Prefect, and Dual Supervision in French Administration: A Comparative Study," *Journal of Politics, 16* (1954), 472–90.

the number of Prefects and to permit prefectoral coordination of regional services.

Fascism does not appear to have made any basic innovation in the prefectoral system, betraying thus its links to traditional statist conservatism. It is curious in an allegedly totalitarian dictatorship for members of the Party to deny that by permitting "political" coordination of the field services by the Prefect, they were transforming him into a Viceroy or Governor; and for a minister to deny that such coordination would in any way interfere with the "technical-administrative" decisions of the functional specialists: presumably in a totalitarian dictatorship, the ruling party would not bother to profess such scruples. In such statements and in the fact that the Prefect was never subordinated to the Party Secretary one might find grounds to doubt whether the Fascist regime merits entire inclusion in the category of *totalitarian* dictatorships.

However this may be, the reaction to the centralized dictatorship after 1943 found one of its chief targets in the Prefect, who had become a symbol of Fascist oppression, identified with the regime whose policies he had often so zealously promoted. The anti-Fascist coalition that emerged to govern the country was united on this point at least and, being hostile to the prefectoral institution in general, could hardly have been expected to favor a strengthening of prefectoral control over the rest of the state administration in the province. Given the general postwar antipathy toward the prefectoral institution, it is not surprising that the conservative governments since 1947 should have contented themselves with the mere maintenance of the institution about as it was before Fascism, rather than have attempted to strengthen the ties among the various field services in the province and thus enlarge the scope of prefectoral power.

II

The preceding study also suggests some propositions concerning prefectoral systems in general. In the introduction I have posed some of the major questions about prefectoral systems that remain to be investigated:

A. What are the major traits of a prefectoral system?

B. What are the major differences between prefectoral and functional systems with regard to (1) structure, (2) origins, and (3) functions?

C. What are the major types of prefectoral systems and how do the types differ in origins, structure, and functions?

D. What are the major challenges to the stability and survival of prefectoral systems?

E. Is there any necessary relationship between prefectoral systems and stable democracy?

Naturally, this study does not permit us to answer these questions with any degree of completeness, but it does permit us to make more informed hypotheses to be tested in subsequent research.

THE MAJOR TRAITS OF PREFECTORAL SYSTEMS

Prefectoral systems have certain common characteristics.

1. The national territory is divided into areas variously called "provinces," "departments," "governments," "prefectures," etc.

2. In each of these areas there is appointed a high functionary representative of and responsible to the central government (and in particular to a Minister of the Interior, or Justice, or Government) to carry out the following kinds of functions:

    a. political and social representation of the central government;

    b. maintenance of law and order;

    c. supervision of central government officials operating in the area;

    d. supervision of minor units of government in the area.

3. This official is a civil functionary operating independently of the military and the judiciary.

4. He does not enjoy the security of tenure enjoyed by other officials and may be dismissed or transferred at the pleasure of the central government.

5. He is not a resident or native of the area which he governs.

6. He may be either a career functionary or a "political" appointee from outside of the career service.

7. And he is usually supervised by a specialized central department—a Ministry of the Interior—which is nationally responsible for such matters as public safety and local government.

THE DIFFERENCES BETWEEN
PREFECTORAL AND FUNCTIONAL SYSTEMS

Structure

The structural differences between prefectoral and functional systems may be summarized in the following chart:

PREFECTORAL	FUNCTIONAL
1. The national territory is divided into areas of general government and in each of these is placed a general representative of the central government (Prefect).	1. There is no general representative of the central government in the various regions of the national territory.
2. Each of the central ministries issues commands to its functional counterparts in the field via the Prefect.	2. Lines of command run directly from the central ministries to their field units.

PREFECTORAL	FUNCTIONAL
3. Most state services use the areas of general government presided over by the Prefect.	3. State services use varying sets of administrative areas in accordance with their particular requirements.
4. The Prefect's area of general administration also constitutes an area of local self-government.	4. There is no necessary identity between field administrative and local government areas.
5. Central government control over minor units of government tends to be (a) more penetrating than in functional systems; (b) administrative rather than legislative; and (c) unified under the Prefect.	5. Central government control tends to be (a) less penetrating; (b) legislative rather than administrative; (c) and dispersed among several central and field institutions.

Origins

It is much more difficult to ascertain and generalize about the factors that account for the establishment and maintenance of a prefectoral, rather than a functional, system of field administration. Such a broad question has yet to be studied and certainly cannot be answered on the basis of the foregoing historical study of a single prefectoral system.* The basic factors involved would seem to be the nature of the political system; its prevailing ideologies; its relative degree of consensus, internal security, and national cohesion. Functional systems, with their greater diffusion of administrative power, are more apt to develop within liberal political systems, in states with a high degree of con-

---

*On this question, see James W. Fesler, "The Political Role of Field Administration," in Ferrel Heady and Sybil L. Stokes, eds., *Papers in Comparative Public Administration* (Ann Arbor, Institute of Public Administration, 1962), pp. 117–43.

sensus, security, and cohesion. The various areas of such states tend to be regarded as units deserving of some degree of autonomous decentralized power, rather than as dependencies and "wards" of the central government. Prefectoral systems are rarely to be found where there are strong and *generally accepted* centrifugal or decentralizing tendencies.

Conversely, more authoritarian systems and those with greater political fragmentation, dissension, and insecurity tend to develop prefectoral systems—primarily as instruments of centralization. The dominant political groups tend in such systems to view decentralization as potentially destructive of the political unity of the state. They are not averse to the concentration of administrative power in a single official within each area. They consider regional interests as dependencies requiring on-the-spot tutelage by the central government. Prefectoral systems will rarely, if ever, be found within genuine federal unions or highly decentralized unitary states. It would seem (although this remains to be tested) that the choice of a prefectoral, rather than a functional, system depends less on considerations of how the central government bureaucracy is to be organized than on what is to be the distribution of power as between the central and minor units of government. In other words, the choice hinges less on the desired pattern of *deconcentration* within the state administration as between central and field officials than on the desired pattern of *decentralization* as between central government and local government officials.

Prefectoral systems seem to suit best the purposes of absolutist governments and the traditions of those emerging from a period of absolutist, especially colonial, government. In Western Europe, prefectoral systems evolved from the institutions devised by absolute monarchs in order to centralize power and control of economic resources within their kingdoms at the expense of the nobility and medieval communes. They constituted a basic arm of monarchy in conflict with domestic feudalities and foreign dynasts. They were the major element in the royal administrative machinery designed to deprive feudal lords and communes of their privileges and functions, to transform feudal serfs into royal subjects, and to elaborate and implement the economic policies of mercantilism. Mercantilist policies had, in turn, been devised to promote national unification and national power. They called for active state intervention in social and economic life: they required and made possible the development of the royal bureaucracy.

In an age of growing overarching allegiance to the Crown and of primitive bureaucratic specialization, the prefectoral system provided for the unified symbolic representation of the Crown in the provinces of the realm; for the reliable enforcement of royal commands; and for the reproduction in each province of the unified and theoretically absolute authority of the monarch. The same purposes were served in the Napoleonic model, which rationalized and modernized the prefectoral institutions of the old regimes, abolishing venality and inheritance of office. The Napoleonic system clarified the division of functions as between civil, military, and judicial officials. It strengthened prefectoral control over minor units of government, now uniform in structure and functions and subject to nationally uniform rules. It exalted the Prefect to clear supremacy over other government officials in his province. And it emphasized monocratic as opposed to collegial forms of administrative power and responsibility.

Prefectoral systems were part of the heritage of the old autocratic regimes, together with institutions such as the monarchy, which were accepted by and adapted to the purposes of the liberal constitutional regimes established in Scandinavia, the Low Countries, and Italy during the nineteenth century, withstanding the liberal attack upon both centralization and mercantilism. Retention of the prefectoral system—as of the monarchy—may indeed have been one of the prices paid by the liberal movement to secure the acceptance of the new regime by the older ruling elements.

TYPES OF PREFECTORAL SYSTEMS

One of the major conclusions of this study is that there are at least two polar types of prefectoral systems: the integrated, exemplified by the classical French system of the nineteenth and early twentieth centuries; and the unintegrated, exemplified by the contemporary Italian system. The difference between the two systems lies in their structure, origins, and functions.

Structure

Structural differences between the integrated and unintegrated systems can be seen in the following chart.

INTEGRATED	UNINTEGRATED
a. *locus of authority*	
Authority is exclusively or largely deconcentrated from the central ministeries to the Prefects, who become a link in all or most chains of command. The Prefect is the hierarchical superior of the technical field directors in his province.	Authority is largely reserved to the specialist functional officials in several purely functional chains of command.

INTEGRATED   UNINTEGRATED

b. *communications*

The Prefect is the sole channel of communication between the functional departments in the capital and those in the field.

The Prefect is neither the normal nor the exclusive channel of communication between central and field functional units.

c. *auxiliary services*

The prefecture houses all or most of the state field offices and provides them with the administrative services needed to accomplish their technical programs.

The technical services in the province do not depend upon the prefecture for accounting, supplies, secretariat, or space, which are instead provided by the central ministries or by the technical field units themselves.

d. *areas*

Most state services use the prefecture's area of operations.

The functional services, organized independently of the prefecture, use varying sets of areas.

e. *echelons*

Regional offices, standing between the prefecture and the central ministries and/or using interprovincial areas, are exceptional.

Regional offices, with direct operational responsibilities and/or supervisory authority over provincial offices, are common.

f. *local government*

The Prefect is chief executive of the provincial self-government unit, the staff of which is organized within the prefecture.

The provincial self-government unit includes a directly or indirectly elected executive authority, with control of separately organized provincial staff.

Origins

Given these types of prefectoral systems, why is one type adopted rather than another? The reasons for the adoption of the unintegrated scheme in Italy were set forth in Chapter 2, pages 116–17. In the case of the best known *integrated* prefectoral system, that of the French, the reasons for making the Prefect the undisputed hierarchical superior of the various state services in the department probably include the clear supremacy of the chief of government, the King and later Napoleon, over his ministers; a desire by the ruler to reproduce this clear supremacy in his direct representative, the Intendant and the Prefect; the absolutist conceptions of the ruler which legitimized monocratic administrative forms; and Napoleon's military conception of responsibility, authority, and efficiency as requiring one-man direction.

Functions

One type of prefectoral system is maintained presumably because of its relative advantages over the other type, because of its functions or consequences, because of the costs of changing over to the other type. The Italian system remained unintegrated after unification for many reasons, including the continuance of several of the factors initially responsible for the adoption of such a system. Once going, the unintegrated system acquired the force of customary behavior. Ministries enjoyed and defended the almost complete control that the unintegrated system afforded them over their particular field services. Separate technical offices were established in a growing number of sectors and each of these offices was vested with an interest in self-preservation as an autonomous entity responsible only to its technical superiors in Rome.

The relative *advantages* of the unintegrated Italian prefectoral system, as opposed to the integrated system, seem to be the following:

    1. Theoretically, at least, the authority of the Prefect can

be adjusted to allow him to control or coordinate some programs or activities where the case for such coordination is particularly strong, rather than a general desideratum. It may, however, prove difficult to insert prefectoral control in the traditionally strong vertical hierarchies, given the absence of a countering tradition of prefectoral control such as has long existed in France.

2. The unintegrated system gives free rein to all the functional services which may carry out their nationwide responsibilities in accordance with their particular, technically informed judgment, allowing for the necessary geographical adaptation within their respective services.

3. The system does provide for a natural coordinator within each of the major areas of the country, a natural chairman of interagency committees, a neutral arbiter for the adjustment of interservice difficulties. It may, however, be difficult for the Prefect to coordinate the activities of services using various areas, enjoying varying amounts of deconcentrated authority, such as the unintegrated system tends to produce. The Prefect's area, moreover, may not be the appropriate level for interagency coordination in some or most matters.

4. The unintegrated system avoids the serious problem of dual supervision, of defining satisfactorily the respective spheres of authority of the central ministries, Prefects, and technical specialists in the field—or it does so long as the Prefect's authority over the technical specialists is restricted to the submission of recommendations and excludes final decision-making. Thus avoidance of the problem of dual supervision hinges upon the maintenance of a high degree of concentration in matters to be coordinated by the Prefects. Actually, the problem is not avoided but merely shifted to each of the separate field services, in some of which it may become highly acute.

The relative *disadvantages* of the unintegrated system would seem to be the following:

1. It is relatively uneconomical since, unlike the integrated system, it does not provide for common housekeeping services. The administrative overhead expenses involved in running several distinct offices is greater presumably than in running joint services in the prefecture.

2. It tends to place administrative burdens on technical field directors which distract them from their specialized tasks. They are forced to be generalist office managers and to attend to matters for which they have little aptitude, liking, or training.

3. It requires a greater over-all number of talented administrators capable of directing independent offices.

4. It tends to de-emphasize the interrelations of various technical programs within particular areas and communities.

5. It fosters a tendency toward undue concentration of administrative authority, since there are no strong generalist Prefects pressing for and defending larger amounts of authority.

6. It requires constant negotiations among the services with no hierarchical arbitrator short of the Prime Minister or Council of Ministers.

CHALLENGES TO PREFECTORAL SYSTEMS

What are the major challenges to the survival or stability of prefectoral systems?

The political challenge

The prefectoral system may become identified with a regime or with the policies of a regime and accordingly share its fortunes. If the regime falls, as Fascism fell, there is apt to be a drive to abolish the prefectoral system as an accomplice in the regime's activities.

The prefectoral system may also become identified with some of the policies of a regime or rather, with one element of the system, such as centralization, and if a drive develops to change those policies or to change one element of the prefectoral system, the whole system may be placed in jeopardy. The prefectoral system in Italy has become identified with centralization. Hence, the drive for greater local self-government has brought in its train a demand for the abolition of the prefectoral system—despite the fact that a prefectoral system is not necessarily tied to any particular level of centralization.

A political challenge of another sort may develop in a revolutionary situation in which not so much the *legitimacy* as the *effectiveness* of the system is challenged. The loyalties of the Prefects may be subjected to severe strains in a situation, such as existed in 1919–22, where the Prefects are required to act against groups to which they are socially allied and politically sympathetic. Rapid renovation of the prefectoral cadres may not prevent the undermining of prefectoral discipline.

The technical challenge

Prefectoral systems may also be undermined by processes of social and technological change, leading to the expansion of state functions into new and highly technical fields of activity. Separate central units are established to take care of the expanding functions of central administration and each of these is apt to press for an autonomous field service under its complete control. The newer technical departments in the capital, based on changed social expectations and new technological possibilities, project their drive for autonomy in the central administration into field administration as well. They will also press for the organization of their field service along lines suited to their particular function.

The prefectures are apt to be bypassed in this process of administrative growth and ramification for three reasons: (1) they will tend to lack the necessary expertise or the appropriate geographical jurisdiction to perform the new functions; (2) they cannot be as uniformly responsive as can distinct field services to the needs and desires of the newer technical central agencies; and (3) they may be the victims of a long-standing process of institutional decline, involving the routinization of duties, the flagging of esprit de corps, the petrifaction of customary ways of thinking and acting.

PREFECTORAL SYSTEMS AND POLITICAL SYSTEMS

The question of the relationships, if any, between prefectoral systems and stable democracy is as interesting as it is difficult to answer. There appears to be no simple or necessary relationship between the two. Some stable democracies have no prefectoral systems; some stable democracies do.[3] Prefectoral systems, moreover, vary considerably among themselves in at least three ways: (1) the level of centralization they sustain, (2) the degree of integration in the state field administration they permit, and (3) the policies administered through them and with which they may become identified. Of these three variables, only the first (the level

3. Seymour M. Lipset in *Political Man* (New York, Doubleday, 1960) lists thirteen European and English-speaking countries as stable democracies (p. 49). Of these thirteen, six have prefectoral systems: Belgium, Denmark, the Netherlands, Norway, Sweden, and even Luxemburg.

of centralization) and the last (the policies administered) seem relevant to the stability of the political system.

Yet just how relevant centralization is to the stability of democracy has still to be demonstrated. It is frequently asserted that stable democracy requires a considerable degree of decentralization, of local self-government. It may be, however, that there are stable democracies that are highly centralized. If there *are* no stable democracies that are highly centralized, if all stable democracies are highly decentralized, then it will follow that those stable democracies with prefectoral systems must all permit considerable local government power and autonomy. This has yet to be tested.

Possibly there is a necessary relationship between the level of centralization and stable democracy. It seems reasonable to expect that political cultures that tolerate the dispersion of power involved in decentralization may more readily support the other forms of dispersed social and constitutional power that constitute pluralistic democracy. It is often asserted, however, that centralization leads to *incivisme* and "widespread public disaffection from governmental authority."[4] One might, on the basis of this study, invert the terms and assert that it is *incivisme* and widespread disaffection that lead to centralization.

Does a prefectoral system facilitate the establishment of dictatorship, provoke the downfall of a democratic regime, or facilitate the conquest of power by undemocratic forces? It may just as easily be maintained that a prefectoral system may be used to defend a democratic regime, to bolster democratic forces, to provide a sense of security and order, and to dissolve or alleviate the tensions that might undermine a democracy. A prefectoral system is basically a neutral

4. Nicholas Wahl, "The French Political System," in Samuel Beer et al., *Patterns of Government: The Major Political Systems of Europe* (New York, Random House, 1958), p. 331.

device which can be made to serve a wide range of purposes. Like other formal structures of government, its function in the political system may be derivative and of marginal importance.[5] It is rather the social and ideological forces that work through and upon political and administrative structures that are the autonomous and decisive factors in determining the fate of a democracy.

5. This institutional skepticism seems to be shared by Lipset in *Political Man*, pp. 90–92; see also Robert A. Dahl, *A Preface to Democratic Theory* (Chicago, University of Chicago Press, 1956), pp. 134–37.

APPENDIX: ITALIAN MINISTRIES, 1963

Foreign Affairs
Interior
Justice
Budget
Finance
Treasury
Defense
Education
Public Works
Agriculture and Forestry
Transport and Civil Aviation
Post and Telecommunications
Industry and Commerce
Labor and Social Security
Foreign Commerce
Merchant Marine
State Investments
Health
Tourism and Entertainment

BIBLIOGRAPHY

PUBLIC DOCUMENTS

Atti Parlamentari (1848–present).
Camera dei Deputati. Legislatura XXVII. *La Legislazione fascista, 1922–1928.* 2 vols.
————. *Annuario parlamentare.*
————. *Bollettino parlamentare.*
Istituto Centrale di Statistica. *Compendio statistico italiano.*
————. *Dipendenti delle amministrazioni statali al 30 novembre 1954.* Rome, 1956.
Istituto Nazionale di Previdenza Sociale. *Mezzo secolo di attività assicurativa e assistenziale (1898–1948).* Rome, n.d.
Ministero dell'Interno. *Calendario generale del regno* (1824–1922).
————. *Bollettino Ufficiale* (1892–1959).
————. *Elenco dei prefetti, consiglieri delegati, sotto prefetti, consiglieri, commissari distrettuali, medici provinciali, questori, e commissari dirigenti gli uffici provinciali di pubblica sicurezza in servizio* (1897–1916).
————. *Notizie raccolte per cura della commissione istituita per proporre un progetto di legge pel concentramento nelle prefetture di servizi pubblici dipendenti dei vari ministeri.* 2 vols. Florence, 1866–68.

————. *Ruoli di anzianità del personale dipendenti dal Ministero dell'Interno* (1905–59).

————. *Statistica degli impiegati della amministrazione centrale e provinciale e degli ufficiali di pubblica sicurezza.* Rome, 1875.

————. Direzione Generale degli Affari Generali e del Personale. Divisione Affari Generali. Biblioteca. *Raccolta delle disposizioni attinenti ai servizi del Ministero dell'Interno.* Rome, 1958–(in course of publication).

Ministero per la Costituente. Commissione per Studi Attinenti alla Riorganizzazione dello Stato. *Relazione all'Assemblea Costituente.* 3 vols. Rome, 1946.

Presidenza del Consiglio dei Ministri. *Stato dei lavori per la riforma della pubblica amministrazione.* 3 vols. Rome, 1953.

———— Information Office. Documentation Centre. *Ten Years of Italian Democracy: 1946–1956.* Rome, 1956.

Raccolta ufficiale delle leggi e dei decreti del Regno di Sardegna (del Regno d'Italia, della Repubblica Italiana) (1848–1959).

Deputazione Provinciale di Milano. *L'Attuazione del decentramento regionale.* Milan, 1950.

Bollettino della Prefettura di Vicenza (1957–59).

BOOKS

Andreotti, G. *De Gasperi e il suo tempo: Trento-Vienna-Roma.* Milan, Mondadori, 1956.

Astuti, G., et al. *La Monarchia piemontese nei secoli XVI– XVIII.* Rome, La Famija Piemonteisa di Roma, 1951.

Avezou, R. *Histoire de la Savoie.* Paris, Presses Universitaires, 1949.

Badoglio, P. *L'Italia nella seconda guerra mondiale: memorie e documenti.* Milan, Mondadori, 1946.

Battaglia, A., et al. *Dieci Anni dopo: 1945–55: Saggi sulla vita democratica italiana.* Bari, Laterza, 1955.

Bellono, E. *Commentario delle leggi.* Turin, Favale, 1851–71.

Bergadani, R. *Vittorio Amedeo III (1726–1796).* Turin, Paravia, 1939.

Bianchi, N. *Storia della monarchia piemontese dal 1773 al 1861.* 4 vols. 2d ed. Turin, Fratelli Bocca, 1877–89.

Bodo, P. *Le Consuetudini, la legislazione, le istituzioni del vecchio Piemonte.* Turin, Giappichelli, 1950.

Borelli, G. B. *Editti, antichi, e nuovi de' sovrani prencipi della Real Casa di Savoia, delle loro tutrici, e de' magistrati di quà da' monti.* Turin, 1681.

Braibant, E. *L'Organisation provinciale de la Belgique.* Verviers, Le Travail, 1946.

Brancati, V. *I Fascisti invecchiano.* Rome-Milan, Longanesi, 1946.

Calamandrei, P., ed. *Commentario sistematico alla costituzione italiana.* 2 vols. Florence, Barbèra, 1950.

Caracciolo, A. *Stato e società civile: problemi dell'unificazione italiana.* Turin, Einaudi, 1960.

Carlyle, M. *Modern Italy.* London, Hutchinson, 1957.

Carocci, G. P. *Agostino Depretis e la politica interna italiana dal 1876 al 1887.* Turin, Einaudi, 1887.

Carutti, D. *Storia del regno di Vittorio Amedeo II.* Turin, Paravia, 1859.

Chabod, F. *L'Italie contemporaine.* Paris, Domat-Montchrestien, 1950.

Chapman, B. *The Prefects and Provincial France.* London, Allen and Unwin, 1955.

Chiaudano, M. *Il Bilancio sabaudo nel secolo XII.* Turin, Fratelli Bocca, 1927.

Cibrario, L. *Origini e progressi delle istituzioni della monarchia di Savoia sino alla costituzione del Regno d'Italia.* 2d ed. Florence, Cellini, 1869.

Croce, B. *A History of Italy, 1871–1915.* Translated by C. M. Ady. Oxford, Clarendon Press, 1929.

De Maria, G. *Lo Stato sociale moderno.* Milan, Ambrosiana, 1946.

De Rosa, G. *Storia del Partito Popolare.* Bari, Laterza, 1958.

Des Ambrois de Nevache, L. *Notes et souvenirs inédits du chevalier Louis des Ambrois de Nevache.* Bologna, Zanichelli, 1901.

Il Digesto Italiano.

Dolfin, E. *Con Mussolini nella tragedia.* Milan, Garzanti, 1949.

Doueil, P. *L'Administration locale à l'épreuve de la guerre, 1939–1949.* Paris, Recueil Sirey, 1950.

Duboin, F. A. *Raccolta per ordine di materia delle leggi, editti, manifesti, ecc. pubblicati sino agli 8 dicembre 1798 sotto il felicissimo dominio della Real Casa di Savoia.* 21 vols. Turin, Eredi Bianco, 1818–68.

Einaudi, L. *Il Buongoverno: Saggi di economia e politica.* Bari, Laterza, 1954.

Einaudi, M., and François Goguel. *Christian Democracy in France and Italy.* Notre Dame, University of Notre Dame Press, 1952.

Einaudi, M., J.-M. Domenach, and A. Garosci. *Communism in Western Europe.* Ithaca, Cornell University Press, 1951.

Enciclopedia Giuridica Italiana.

Ferrari, F. L. *Le Régime fasciste italien,* Paris, Editions Spes, 1928.

Ferraris, C. F. *L'Amministrazione locale in Italia.* 2 vols. Padua, La litotipo Ed. Universit., 1920.

Fesler, J. W. *Area and Administration.* University, Alabama, University of Alabama Press, 1949.

Finer, H. *Mussolini's Italy,* London, Gollancz, 1935.

Finer, S. E. *A Primer of Public Administration.* London, F. Muller, 1950.

Franchetti, L., and S. Sonnino. *La Sicilia nel 1876.* 2 vols. Florence, Barbèra, 1877.

Garosci, A., et al. *Il Secondo Risorgimento: nel decennale della resistenza e del ritorno alla democrazia, 1945–1955.* Rome, Istituto Poligrafico dello Stato, 1955.

Germino, D. L. *The Italian Fascist Party in Power: A Study in Totalitarian Rule.* Minneapolis, University of Minnesota Press, 1959.

Giannini, M. S. *Lezioni di diritto amministrativo.* Milan, Giuffrè, 1950.

Giovenco, L. *L'Ordinamento comunale.* Milan, Giuffrè, 1958.

Grindrod, M. *The Rebuilding of Italy*. London, Royal Institute of International Affairs, 1955.

Guarneri, F. *Battaglie economiche*. 2 vols. Milan, Garzanti, 1953.

Hughes, H. S. *The United States and Italy*. Cambridge, Mass., Harvard University Press, 1953.

Kaufman, H. *The Forest Ranger*. Baltimore, Johns Hopkins Press, 1960.

King, B. *A History of Italian Unity*, 2 vols. London, Nisbet, 1897.

King B., and T. Okey. *Italy Today*. New York, Scribners, 1913.

Kogan, N. *The Government of Italy*. New York, Crowell, 1962.

La Torre, Michele. *Governo e impiegati*. Florence, Publitex, 1955.

Lentini, A. *L'Amministrazione locale*. 2d ed. Como, Nani, 1953.

Leonetti, A. *Mouvements ouvriers et socialistes: (Chronologie et bibliographie): L'Italie (Des origines à 1922)*. Paris, Editions Ouvrières, 1952.

Leto, G. *OVRA: Fascismo-antifascismo*. 2d ed. Bologna, Cappelli, 1952.

Levi, C. *L'Orologio*. Turin, Einaudi, 1950.

Lorenzoni, A. *Istituzioni del diritto pubblico interno pel Regno Lombardo–Veneto*. 2 vols. Padua, Sicca, 1835.

Lowell, A. L. *Governments and Parties in Continental Europe*. 2 vols. Boston, Houghton Mifflin, 1896.

Lucifredi, R., and G. Coletti. *Decentramento amministrativo: Commento della legge di delega 11 marzo 1953, no. 150*. Turin, UTET, 1956.

Luzzatto, L. *Elezioni politiche e leggi elettorali in Italia*. Rome, Editori Riuniti, 1958.

Maranini, G., et al. *Aspetti di vita italiana contemporanea*. Bologna, Cappelli, 1957.

Marchetti, R. *La formazione del Regno d'Italia ed il decentramento*. Rome, Camera dei Deputati, 1893.

Marongiù, A. *Storia del diritto pubblico: principi e istituti di governo in Italia dalla metà del IX secolo alla metà del XIX secolo*. Milan, Cisalpino, 1956.

Monaco, M. *La Regione: sintesi storica dell'autonomia regionale in Italia*. Rome, Edizioni Cinque Lune, n.d.

Morandi, C. *La Sinistra al potere*. Florence, G. Barbèra, 1944.

Morstein Marx, F. *Elements of Public Administration*. 1st ed. New York, Prentice-Hall, 1946.

Mosca, G. *Teorica dei governi e governo parlamentare: studi storici e sociali*. 2d ed. Milan, Istituto Editoriale Scientifico, 1925.

Nasalli Rocca, A. *Memorie di un prefetto*. Rome, Mediterraneo, 1946.

Natale, G. *Giolitti e gli italiani*. Milan, Garzanti, 1949.

Nicolai, R. *Il Sindaco e la città*. Rome, Editori Riuniti, 1956.

Il Nuovo Digesto Italiano. (1937–40).

Omodeo, A. *L'Età del risorgimento italiano*. Naples, Edizioni Scientifiche Italiane, 1946.

Orlando, V. E., ed. *Primo Trattato completo di diritto amministrativo italiano*. 18 vols. Milan, Società Editrice Libraria, 1897–1935.

Petrocchi, C. *La Politica dei lavori pubblici*. Rome, Rivista Acque e Trasporti, 1926.

———. *Il Problema della burocrazia*. Rome, Migliaresi, 1944.

Pryce, R. *The Italian Local Elections 1956*. London, Chatto and Windus, 1957.

Quazza, G. *Le Riforme in Piemonte nella prima metà del settecento*. 2 vols. Modena, Società Tipografica Editrice Modenese, 1957.

Quazza, R. *Preponderanze straniere*. Milan, Vallardi, 1938.

Ragionieri, E. *Un Comune socialista: Sesto Fiorentino*. Rome, Edizioni Rinascita, 1953.

Reale Accademia Nazionale dei Lincei. *Cinquanta Anni di storia italiana*. 3 vols. Milan, 1911.

Romita, G. *Dalla monarchia alla Repubblica*. Pisa, Nistri-Lischi, 1959.

Roselli, E. *Cento Anni di legislazione sociale*. 2 vols. Milan, Bernabò, 1951.

Rossi, E. *Il Malgoverno*. Bari, Laterza, 1954.

———. *I Padroni del vapore*. Bari, Laterza, 1955.

———. *Lo Stato industriale*. Bari, Laterza, 1953.

Salomone, A. W. *Italian Democracy in the Making: The Political Scene in the Giolittian Era, 1900–1914*. Philadelphia, University of Pennsylvania Press, 1945.

Salvadori, M. *Storia della resistenza italiana*. Venice, N. Pozza, 1955.

Salvatorelli, L., and G. Mira. *Storia d'Italia nel periodo fascista*. 2d ed. Turin, Einaudi, 1957.

Sandonà, A. *Il Regno Lombardo–Veneto, 1814–1859: La costituzione, e l'amministrazione*. Milan, Cogliati, 1912.

Sandulli, A. *Manuale di diritto amministrativo*. 4th ed. Naples, Jiovene, 1957.

Savino, E. *La Nazione operante*. 3d ed. Novara, Istituto Geografico De Agostini, 1937.

Schmidt, C. *The Corporate State in Action*. New York, Oxford University Press, 1939.

Senise, C. *Quando ero Capo della Polizia, 1940–1943*. 2d ed. Rome, Ruffolo, 1947.

Smith, D. M. *Italy: A Modern History*. Ann Arbor, University of Michigan Press, 1959.

Tamaro, A. *Venti Anni di storia, 1922–1943*. 3 vols. Rome, Tiber, 1954.

Turchi, F. *Prefetto con Mussolini*. Rome, Latinità, 1950.

Ufficio Centrale Formazione della D. C. *Il Comune nello stato democratico*. Rome, 1956.

Valiani, L. *L'Avvento di De Gasperi: Tre anni di politica italiana*. Turin, De Silva, 1949.

Valsecchi, F. *Storia del risorgimento*. Turin, Edizioni Radio Italiana, 1958.

Vaussard, M. *Historie de l'Italie contemporaine, 1870–1946*. Paris, Hachette, 1950.

Ventrone, A. *L'Amministrazione dello Stato Pontificio: dal 1814 al 1870*. Rome, Edizioni Universitarie, 1942.

Vigna, S., and V. Aliberti. *Dizionario di diritto amministrativo*. 5 vols. Turin, Favale, 1840–52.

Volpe, G. *Italia moderna, 1815–1915*. 3 vols. Florence, Sansoni, 1943–53.

Zanobini, G. *L'Amministrazione locale in Italia.* Padua, Milani, 1930.

——.*Corso di diritto amministrativo.* 5 vols. Milan, Giuffrè, 1957–58.

Zuccarini, O. *Un Impegno costituzionale: autonomie locali-regione-decentramento.* Milan, Feltrinelli, 1957.

ARTICLES, REVIEWS, AND NEWSPAPERS

Acquarone, A. "La Politica legislativa della restaurazione nel Regno di Sardegna," *Bollettino Storico-Bibliografico Subalpino, 57* (1959).

Adams, J. C., and P. Barile. "The Implementation of the Italian Constitution," *American Political Science Review, 47* (1953), 61–83.

L'Amministrazione Civile (1957–present).

L'Amministrazione Italiana (1946–58).

Antonucci, A. "Le Funzioni del prefetto nel quadro della autonomia regionale," *Il Corriere Amministrativo, 7* (1951), 424–40.

Avanti! (Rome, 1946–47; 1958).

Benini, R. "La Burocrazia di stato in Italia dal 1859–1891," *La Riforma Sociale, 2* (1895), 241–60, 330–48.

Casini, B. "L'Amministrazione locale del granducato di Toscana dalla Restaurazione all'annessione (1814–1860)," *Bollettino Storico Pisano, 22–23* (1953–54), 163–88.

Ciccia, A. "Prefetti e prefetture," *Il Corriere Amministrativo, 3* (1947), 960–61.

Cirmeni, A. "Il Problema dei prefetti," *Il Corriere Amministrativo, 1* (1945), 9–14.

Cole, T. "Italy's Fascist Bureaucracy," *American Political Science Review, 33* (1938), 1143–58.

——. "The Reform of the Italian Bureaucracy," *Public Administration Review, 13* (1953), 247–56.

Il Corriere Amministrativo (1945–58).

Corriere della Sera (1922–23; 1958).

Cuneensis, G. "Antiseparatismo," *Il Corriere Amministrativo, 3* (1947), 955–57.

Diamant, A. "The Department, the Prefect, and Dual Supervision in French Administration: A Comparative Study," *Journal of Politics, 16* (1954), 472–90.

Ducceschi, P. "Prefetti e prefetture," *Nuova Rassegna de Legislazione, dottrina, e giurisprudenza, 4* (1948), 618–19.

Einaudi, M. "The Constitution of the Italian Republic," *American Political Science Review, 42* (1948), 661–76.

L'Espresso (1957–present).

Garrone, C. "Vita, morte e miracoli di un prefetto politico," *Il Ponte, 2* (1946), 861–76.

La Gazzetta del Mezzogiorno (1958).

Ghisalberti, C. "L'Unificazione amministrativa d'Italia," *Il Veltro, 3,* No. 8–9 (August–September 1959), 73–81.

Il Giornale del Mezzogiorno (1950–59).

Grieco, R. "Il Prefetto," *Rinascita, 8* (1951), Supplement, pp. 1–4.

Jemolo, A. C., "I Prefetti," *Il Mondo, 5,* No. 10 (March 9, 1954), 1–2.

Jemolo, A. C., and G. N. Trapani, "Un Dialogo sui prefetti," *Il Mondo, 5,* No. 13 (March 30, 1954), 5–6.

La Torre, M. "Prefetti e prefetture," *L'Amministrazione Italiana, 3* (1948), 311–17.

———. "Garanzie pei prefetti," *L'Amministrazione Italiana, 3* (1948), 156–57.

———. "Opinioni sui prefetti," *Nuova Rassegna di Legislazione, dottrina, e giurisprudenza, 3* (1947), 402 ff.

———. "Le Prefetture guarentigie di libertà," *L'Amministrazione Italiana, 3* (1948), 773 ff.

———. "Ancora sulle prefetture," *L'Amministrazione Italiana, 5* (1950), 124 ff.

Lentini, A. "Prefetti e prefetture," *Nuova Rassegna di Legislazione, dottrina, e giurisprudenza, 3* (1947), 387 ff.

———. "Prefetti e prefetture," *Il Corriere Amministrativo, 4* (1948), 113–17, 1017–22.

————. "Burocrazia, prefetto, e prefetture," *Il Corriere Amministrativo,* 2 (1946), 985–87.

————. "La Questione dei prefetti in Sicilia," *Il Corriere Amministrativo,* 7 (1951), 980 ff.

Il Mondo (1950–present).

Nitti, F. S. "La Burocrazia di stato in Italia," *La Riforma Sociale,* 7 (1900), 458–75.

Nuova Rassegna di Legislazione, dottrina, e giurisprudenza (1946–59).

Il Ponte (1945–present).

Ragionieri, E. "Politica e amministrazione nello stato unitario," *Studi Storici, 1* (1960), 472–512.

————. "Il Problema delle regioni cento anni fa," *Rinascita, 17* (1960), 269–79.

Rassegna di Diritto Pubblico (1946–58).

Rivista Amministrativa della Repubblica Italiana (1851–60; 1946–59).

Rivista di Diritto Pubblico (1946–58).

Rivista Trimestrale di Diritto Pubblico (1950–58).

Saladino, A. "Note per una storia delle amministrazioni civili e finanziarie del Regno delle Due Sicilie: Contributo allo studio delle fonti," *Notizie degli Archivi di Stato, 14,* No. 3 (September–December 1954), 89–94.

Soprano, D. "Prefetture," *Il Corriere Amministrativo, 14* (1958), 480–81.

La Stampa (1953–60).

L'Unione Sarda (1958–60).

L'Unità (Rome; 1950; 1953–54).

La Voce Adriatica (1958).

PERSONAL INTERVIEWS (*JANUARY 1958–JUNE 1959*)

A. Ministries: Interior, Finance, Treasury, Public Works, Agriculture and Forests, Labor and Social Security.

B. Other central agencies: Presidency of the Council (Office of Administrative Reform); Cassa del Mezzogiorno (Fund for the South); Istituto Nazionale di Previdenza Sociale (social security); Istituto Nazionale Assicurazioni Malattie (health insurance); Istituto Nazionale Assicurazioni Infortuni del Lavoro (workmen's compensation).

C. Other national organization headquarters: Christian Democratic party (local authorities section); Italian Socialist party (local authorities section); Union of Italian Provinces.

D. Regional field offices and officials: Regional Forest Inspectorates; Regional Agrarian Inspectorates; Regional Labor Offices; Regional Inspectorates of Direct Taxes; Regional Inspectorates of Indirect Taxes; Purveyors of Public Works.

E. Provincial field offices and officials: Prefectures; Provincial Police Headquarters (Questure); Istituto Nazionale Assicurazioni Malattie; District Forest Inspectorates; Provincial Agrarian Inspectorates; Civil Engineers; Purveyors of Studies; Intendancies of Finance; Chambers of Commerce.

F. Special field agencies: Magistrato del Po (Po Valley Authority, Parma); Ente Delta Padano (Po Delta land reform agency, Bologna); Ente Maremma (Maremma land reform agency, Rome).

INDEX

Page numbers in italics refer to tables and figures

YALE STUDIES IN POLITICAL SCIENCE